TRIBAL WATER MANAGEMENT HANDBOOK

TRIBAL WATER MANAGEMENT HANDBOOK

Published by the AMERICAN INDIAN RESOURCES INSTITUTE (AIRI)

In recognition of the challenge to Indian tribes to develop the expertise to wisely use, manage, and control tribal natural resources, AILTP established in 1985 the American Indian Resources Institute (AIRI). Succinctly stated, AIRI's principal goal is to assist Indian tribes develop and refine the contours of their resource management systems by: sponsoring national and regional forums on topical natural resources policy, law, and management issues which impact the use and control of tribally owned natural resources; providing training for tribal decision-makers and resource managers in the areas of natural resources law, policy, and management techniques; generating, collecting, and publishing topical information on tribal natural resources law, policy, and current developments; and establishing a network with organizations and educational institutions active in the fields of resource management, research, and conflict resolution.

ISBN 0-939890-08-9

CONTENTS

PART III: MAKING THE DIFFICULT CHOICES

PART IV: IMPLEMENTING AND ENFORCING TRIBAL WATER POLICIES AND PROGRAMS

TABLE OF FIGURES

Page

TABLE OF TABLES

PREFACE

There has been a lot said about the sacredness of our land which is our body, and the values of our culture which is our soul. But water is the blood of our tribes, and if its life-giving flow is stopped, or it is polluted, all else will die and the many thousands of years of our communal existence will come to an end.

FRANK TENORIO
Governor, San Felipe Pueblo
1978

As Indian tribes move from an era of establishing their legal and proprietary rights to water under the *Winters* doctrine to an era of managing and controlling tribal water resources, it is imperative that tribal decision-makers shift their focus from courtroom battles to practical efforts to develop and implement comprehensive watershed management plans. The transition to actual use and control will not come easily. Potential new users crowd the water market demanding a share of already overappropriated supplies. At the same time, many existing users return a polluted resource back into the watersheds. Daily, forces such as these chip away at the benefits tribes can hope to realize from their hard-won water entitlements.

In recognition of the need for Indian tribes to develop and implement effective water management strategies, the American Indian Lawyer Training Program, Inc. (AILTP) established in 1985 its American Indian Resources Institute (AIRI). Succinctly stated, AIRI's principal goal is to assist tribal governments develop or refine the contours of their resource management systems. AIRI hopes to achieve its goal by providing training and information on topics that will influence water management strategies in Indian Country. The *Tribal Water Management Handbook* is designed to promote a better understanding of the complexities involved in using, managing and regulating reservation water resources. The varied perspectives offered on the dynamics of water law and policy, science, planning, watershed management and resource economics provide an excellent framework to facilitate a comprehensive examination of the role of water resources in the future of Indian tribes as sovereign governments and to encourage further study of a constantly changing field. It is our hope that this sourcebook becomes an invaluable tool for those who must develop and implement tribal water policies.

Richard Trudell
Executive Director

ACKNOWLEDGMENTS

The American Indian Resources Institute (AIRI) wishes to acknowledge the assistance provided by those who contributed to the development and preparation of the *Tribal Water Management Handbook*. In addition, AIRI would like to express its sincere appreciation to the Ford Foundation for its support of our program activities in the field of water resources.

CONTRIBUTING AUTHORS

Ann E. Amundson

F. Lee Brown

Lloyd Burton

Shaul Ben-David

Allen V. Kneese

Douglas R. Nash

Steven J. Shupe

Catherine Vandemoer

Gary D. Weatherford

Charles F. Wilkinson

HANDBOOK PRODUCTION STAFF

Christine L. Miklas, *Managing Editor*

Charles Sheketoff, *Editor*

Deanna Martinez, *Copy Editor*

Cecilia Dennis, *Production Assistant*

Barry L. Norton, *Proofreader*

ARTWORK

The Laser Edge

Naomi Schiff Illustration & Design

FOREWORD

The history of Indian water law has been steeped in conflict, deprivation of water to reservations, and powerful but unrealized declarations of extensive Indian rights. Resolution of many long-standing conflicts by quantification of Indian entitlements to water, however, means that future issues will center on how the tribes' rights can be exercised to achieve the fullest benefits for Indian people. This calls for a new emphasis on tribal water policy, planning, and management, and demands greater technical, legal, and decision-making capabilities. This *Handbook* is designed to aid the transition to an era of Indian water management.

Indians and non-Indians have bent their past attention on determination of Indian reserved water rights through legal action—a slow, expensive process. Scores of cases have been commenced in, or are headed for, state courts, following two decades of disputes over whether a state or a federal forum is appropriate. The costs of litigation can be tens of millions of dollars for each side and can perpetuate bitterness with non-Indian communities. Thus, parties to many of these Indian water rights conflicts are opting for the negotiating table, as they grow acutely aware of the immense financial burdens and lost opportunities caused by lengthy litigation. Negotiated solutions also have the capacity to deal with practical problems of using and developing common water resources to the advantage of both Indians and non-Indians.

The results of Indian reserved water rights quantification litigation and negotiation are beginning to convert theoretical rights into tangible assets. The Assiniboine and Sioux Tribes of the Fort Peck Indian Reservation concluded a compact with the state of Montana allowing for productive use of water by both the tribes and their non-Indian neighbors. The Ak-Chin Indian Community and the San Xavier Band of the Papago Tribe have had their negotiated settlements with non-Indian interests in Arizona embodied in federal legislation. The Southern Ute and Ute Mountain Ute Indian tribes in Colorado have worked out their differences with state and local governments and are pressing legislation in Congress to implement the settlement by constructing a large water project to serve both Indians and non-Indians. After twenty years of litigation, Mission Indian bands in southern California have settled their competing claims to the San Luis Rey River with cities and water districts, enabling an expansion of water uses once the agreement is approved by Congress. The Arapahoe and Shoshone Tribes of the Wind River Indian Reservation in Wyoming won a substantial quantification of their water rights in the first Indian water rights quantification adjudication to be completed since *Arizona v. California* in 1963.

Indian tribes are now confronting the question of how to put their water rights to use. Plainly, tribes are moving from the realm of legal theory and advocacy into the practicalities of making policy choices on what to do with their valuable assets.

At the same time as Indian water rights are becoming usable assets, tribes find themselves on the cutting edge of a number of trends in western water policy. The movement toward wiser and more efficient use of scarce water resources may be either a means of stretching limited resources or of curbing expansion of Indian use. The shift away from pursuing structural solutions to water problems, such as the construction of large dams, comes as many tribes are just beginning to develop their water but after most non-Indian development has taken place. Sales of water to users in another state could provide new economic opportunities for both buyer and seller, but also risks impairing the viability of some Indian homelands. Federal water quality regulation offers tribes the prerogatives of states, along with onerous responsibilities for program management. Thus, modern water policy debates tend to be amplified in the Indian context. Tribes must understand these developments and must be prepared to draw on them to improve their own water management rather than react to others' interpretations and applications of the trends.

The *Tribal Water Management Handbook* is designed to provide tribal decision-makers and water managers with a background in the diverse expertise they need to carry out their daily missions. Questions of law and policy permeate water management. Thus, in Part I, the *Handbook* provides the reader with an historical backdrop and a discussion of current trends in these areas. The science of watershed management is explored in Part II in understandable chapters on basic hydrology and water quality problems. The emphasis of the *Handbook* is, as it must be for successful Indian tribal stewardship of water resources, on integrating technically competent management with sound long-range policy directions. Those directions must be the synthesis of economic and cultural objectives. They can be achieved using a variety of tools—including benefit-cost analysis, inventories of tribal resources, comprehensive planning, tribal regulation through water code development, cooperative regulatory efforts with state and federal agencies and other tribes, and financing water development. These methods are discussed in Parts III and IV of the *Handbook*.

Water can be the key to economic viability and cultural survival on Indian reservations. In the final analysis, the success of American Indian tribes as independent communities will depend heavily on how wisely they plan for and use their water resource wealth. The *Handbook* is intended to help Indian leaders meet that challenge and build upon, even surpass, the efforts of their state and federal colleagues in water management.

David H. Getches

Part I

THE DYNAMICS OF LAW AND POLICY

CHAPTER 1

Indian Water in Modern Tribal Policymaking

1-1. INTRODUCTION

Since the late 1950s Indian law and policy has centered upon tribal assertions of self-government and ownership of natural resources. This hypercharged quarter of a century has been marked by numerous major pieces of federal legislation and, perhaps even more distinctively, by more than seventy-five Indian law cases in the United States Supreme Court and by thousands of lawsuits in the lower federal and state courts. In the main, the tribes have prevailed. By any reasonable measure, the quantum of established legal rights currently possessed by Indian tribes is much greater than it was when this modern era began. It has been a time of intensive—and oftentimes successful—litigative and legislative activity to enforce tribal claims to governmental authority, natural resources and trust obligations.

The litigative and legislative activity in the upcoming decades is likely to take on an additional quality. To be sure, important legal questions of tribal sovereignty and resource entitlement remain unresolved. Realistically, many of them must be decided by combat in the courts; but since the legal framework is established reasonably well, much resolution of conflict is likely to take place outside of the courthouses as well. Tribes may find it expedient to negotiate with the states over the details of concurrent jurisdiction, or with private business entities who wish to develop projects within Indian Country. Ultimately, the future will be a time of shoring up, refining and building the infrastructure of tribal sovereignty so that Indian tribes will possess a full range of quality schools, hospitals, judicial systems, water projects, farms, wildlife programs mining operations and other beneficial programs. Through self-initiated efforts Indian tribes can achieve the ultimate promise of the nineteenth century treaties: that Indian reservations truly be homelands.

Such an effort will, of course, come gradually and it will not come easily. Capital, planning expertise, and technical support are required in amounts not now available. Further, since this new stage of tribal progress will focus on fundamentally different policy issues, tribal councils need consciously to shift gears in their decision-making processes. During the last twenty-five years, lawyers generally have dominated the formulation of tribal policy . From now on, however, it is likely that equal time will be given to water managers, land use planners, foresters, mining engineers, investment counsellors and other resource development specialists.

This initial chapter will trace the main developments in federal Indian policy. It also will attempt to place Indian water issues in context by assessing the preeminent role that tribal management of water resources will play in the future.

1-2. LAYING THE FOUNDATION: THE LAWS AND COURT OPINIONS OF THE LAST TWENTY-FIVE YEARS

Until approximately the end of the Civil War, federal Indian policy generally recognized the right of Indian tribes to remain separate. Indian treaties essentially guaranteed that tribes would possess in perpetuity sufficient land and resources to continue to be self-sustaining. Similarly, the treaties were intended to guarantee tribes that they would not be subject to incursions by the laws of the states. The treaties also recognized a duty of protection in the federal government, and court decisions upheld a broad federal power over Indian affairs. Thus, the treaties amounted to a promise of a measured separatism: tribes would not be entirely separate nations within the larger country, but they would be substantially independent governments and free to govern themselves, outside of state law, according to their own traditions. Ultimately, the treaties promised that Indian reservations would be permanent homelands.

Federal Indian policy changed during the late nineteenth century. The idea of separatism waned, and on various fronts, the government pursued the policy of assimilation. The General Allotment (or Dawes) Act of 1887[1] opened many reservations to homesteading by non-Indians. Another leading example of the assimilationist policy was the creation of Indian boarding schools. The schools were established to instruct young Indian children in the ways of non-Indians and to hasten their exodus from the reservations. The movement toward assimilation was arrested during the 1930s and 1940s when John Collier was Commissioner of Indian Affairs. The Indian Reorganization Act of 1934[2] was the most noteworthy legislation adopted during Collier's period. That Act recognized tribal self-government and encouraged tribes to establish formal tribal institutions. Such encouragement, however, was short-lived.

The so-called "termination era" of the 1950s was a bold policy shift reverting toward assimilation. Over one hundred Indian reservations were terminated—broken up and made subject to state laws. Tribal governments were disbanded and, in most cases, former tribal land was sold to non-Indians. Some reservations remained intact and the federal-tribal relationship was not dissolved, but state law was made applicable to many of these reservations in 1953 under a federal act called "Public Law 280."[3] In many ways the termination era was the most serious threat to tribal self-government in the entire history of federal-tribal relations. The appointment of Dillon S. Meyer as Commissioner of Indian Affairs was indicative of the tone of the era. Meyer was the former director of the War Relocation Authority, the detention camp system for Japanese-Americans.

The modern era of federal Indian policy and law began sometime in the late 1950s or early 1960s. Indians were encouraged in 1958 when Interior Secretary Fred Seaton publicly announced in a radio address the end of coercive termination.

Williams v. Lee[4] was the 1959 court decision that started the modern era. In *Williams* the United States Supreme Court recognized an expansive tribal sovereignty, even when non-Indians were involved. Later, the social programs of the Kennedy-Johnson years provided funding for programs to support tribal governments. By then the stage was set for the wide range of progressive actions taken by the Nixon and Ford administrations at the request of tribal leaders. Tribal governments had long been dormant, and the legislation and court decisions of this policy era allowed tribes to reactivate, to develop programs, and to become modern governments able to operate in contemporary society.

Many laws were adopted in response to tribal initiatives. The Alaska Native Claims Settlement Act of 1971[5] guaranteed to Alaska Natives approximately 44 million acres—about 2% of all land in the United States. The Menominee Restoration Act of 1973[6] reversed the termination of the Menominee Tribe of Wisconsin and was perhaps the most dramatic symbol that termination had ended as official federal policy. The Indian Self-Determination Act of 1975[7] reflected a fundamental philosophical change concerning the administration of Indian affairs: tribal programs were to be funded by the federal government, but the programs were to be planned and administered by the tribes themselves. The 1975 Act envisioned an end to federal domination of tribes and programs by the Bureau of Indian Affairs. The Indian Child Welfare Act of 1978 (ICWA)[8] addressed in an expansive manner one of the most critical problems facing Indian tribes—the control of their children's lives. The ICWA provided for tribal court jurisdiction over most adoptions and guardianships of Indian children, and set strict protective standards in those situations where state courts were allowed to continue to assume jurisdiction. The American Indian Religious Freedom Act of 1978[9] established a measure of federal protection for traditional Indian religious practices. Legislation adopted in the 1980s has allowed Indian tribes to pursue development projects by issuing tax-exempt bonds.

The last twenty-five years has been an extraordinarily active period for litigation involving Indian tribes. During this period the courts have recognized expansive Indian resource rights. In its 1963 decision in *Arizona v. California*,[10] the Supreme Court reaffirmed the *Winters* doctrine (discussed in great detail in Chapter 4), and ruled that Indian tribes have water rights sufficient to irrigate all "practicably irrigable acreage" within their reservations. In 1979, the Supreme Court upheld the right of Indian tribes in the Pacific Northwest to take 50% of all salmon and steelhead passing their traditional off-reservation fishing sites.[11] Recent Indian law cases also have recognized broad tribal power to regulate persons, including non-Indians, seeking to hunt or fish within the reservations. The Indian litigation offensive involving natural resources also has included several major eastern land claim cases in which tribes ultimately have been awarded large tracts of land, originally thought to have been transferred away by nineteenth century treaties with states.[12]

The tribes also have suffered their share of setbacks on resource issues. The most notable examples involve Supreme Court decisions in 1976[13] and 1983[14] which recognized the authority of states to adjudicate tribal reserved water rights. The perceived importance of finality in water law led the Court to rule that previously adjudicated Indian water rights normally will not be disturbed, even if the prior decisions were plainly unfair to the tribes. Nevertheless, tribal claims to natural resources just twenty-five years ago were cloudy at best. Today, Indian tribes across the country possess reasonably well-established rights to water, fish and wildlife, land and minerals.

Litigation over natural resources has been complemented by court opinions that recognize inherent tribal sovereignty. In 1978, the Supreme Court ruled that tribes possess no criminal jurisdiction over non-Indians,[15] but later decisions have held that tribes possess important aspects of regulatory jurisdiction over non-Indians who enter reservations. As a result, in many instances tribes can tax non-Indian activities, zone non-Indian land, and regulate non-Indian businesses. The taxation cases have an important additional benefit: businesses operating within Indian Country often are not subject to state taxation, a situation that provides some companies with an added incentive to locate on Indian reservations.

One of the most significant developments in recent case law is the affirmation that Indian tribes are independent governments with governmental responsibilities, such as providing roads, police protection, social programs, and other services for their citizens. This development in the modern era is symbolized by the 1982 Supreme Court decision of *Merrion v. Jicarilla Apache Tribe*.[16] In *Merrion* the Court noted, with appropriate irony, that it is Indian tribal governments who are charged with providing the benefits of "civilized" society to all reservation residents, non-Indians and Indians alike:

> The power to tax is an essential attribute of Indian sovereignty because it is a necessary instrument of self-government and territorial management. This power enables a tribal government to raise revenues for its essential services. . . . The petitioners [non-Indian oil companies] avail themselves of the "substantial privilege of carrying on business" on the reservation. They benefit from the provision of police protection and other governmental services, as well as from "the advantages of a civilized society" that are assured by the existence of tribal government. Numerous other governmental entities levy a general revenue tax similar to that imposed by the Jicarilla Tribe when they provide comparable services. Under these circumstances, there is nothing exceptional in requiring petitioners to contribute through taxes to the general cost of tribal government.[17]

These recent decades of legislation and litigation have worked no magical transformation, but they have produced a steady, honest progress that has benefitted most tribes. Vine Deloria, Jr., a noted Indian scholar and author, summarized the period by stating that "in spite of the brief fling with termination of federal supervision, tribal governments emerged in the closing decades of the twentieth century in a much better position and with higher status than they had entered it." Robert L. Bennett, former Commissioner of Indian Affairs, similarly concluded that "Indian tribes are beginning to enjoy their newly found opportunities under the policy of self-determination as a means for strengthening their inherent sovereign powers. . . . Self-determination as a concept, now developed into policy, is here to stay and the Indian tribes are glad of it and will make the most of it." The victory has not been total, but

Indian tribes have used the courts, the Congress, their own institutions and their own energies to establish a legal framework that, if implemented, holds out the promise of continued and substantial cultural and economic progress.

1-3. BUILDING HOMELANDS: THE CHALLENGE OF THE YEARS TO COME

The legal framework that legitimized and strengthened tribal institutions has a profound potential for Indian tribes, but enormous obstacles still must be overcome before that potential can be realized. Health care, housing, education and employment opportunities often are deficient on reservation lands.

A consensus exists among Indian people concerning the best hope for accelerating the improvement of social conditions among reservation Indians. Careful planning will allow tribal councils, implementing their inherent tribal sovereignty, to utilize tribal natural resources and the immunities from state law to provide a measure of income to the tribe and its people and to soften the adverse effects of development so that tribal traditions and sacred areas are not infringed.

Already notable successes exist. The Confederated Tribes of the Warm Springs Indian Reservation in Oregon now own and operate a hydroelectric facility on the Deschutes River. The Jicarilla Apache Tribe of New Mexico is receiving substantial tax revenues from oil and gas development on the reservation and has a tribally owned and operated drilling operation. The Colville Tribe of Washington, Menominee Tribe of Wisconsin, and many others operate tribal logging operations and timber mills. Several tribes, including the Mescalero Apache Tribe of New Mexico, operate modern resort complexes. The White Mountain Apache Tribe of Arizona owns and operates a skiing facility. Over a hundred tribes across the country run bingo operations, which are attractive to non-Indian customers because the tribes can operate outside of state law and offer larger jackpots. Although bingo is not always a popular means to obtain operating revenue, it is an example of the way in which insulation of Indian reservations from state jurisdiction can generate funds for Indian tribes.

Tribal natural resources play a central role in the future of most tribes. Indians own 53 million acres in the lower 48 states, about 2.5% of all land in the country. Tribes own approximately 10% of the currently mineable coal reserves in the United States and possess approximately 13% of the nation's on-shore oil and gas. About 5.3 million acres of commercial timber land are included within Indian reservations. Fish and wildlife resources also are substantial on many reservations and are vital to Indian economies, food supplies, and lifestyles. And, of course, as discussed in the following section, water resources are critical to tribal homelands.

1-4. THE SPECIAL ROLE OF TRIBAL WATER RESOURCE MANAGEMENT

Water is essential for most resource development in the American West. Energy projects largely are dependent upon significant quantities of water. Further, in almost all areas of the West farmland cannot support crops with only natural precipitation; land must be irrigated with water artificially applied to it. Indian tribes possess great amounts of potentially irrigable land, but they do not have the storage projects or irrigation works to put that water on the ground. Under the *Winters* doctrine, Indian tribes also have claims to vast amounts of water: in 1984 the Western Governors' Association estimated that Indians may be entitled to as much as 44 million acre-feet of water, about three times the entire flow of the Colorado River. Accordingly, the question of water rights is of pervasive importance in Indian Country.

John Gunther has written: "Touch water in the West and you touch everything." Today, tribal leaders are keenly aware of these geographical and social imperatives and are taking steps to perfect their water rights and to put water to use. This undertaking has an immediacy, and yet tribes need to proceed deliberately so that it is done right. The tie between water and tribal economies, social needs, and traditional cultures is too compelling to proceed in uninformed haste.

The federal government's failure to provide funding for Indian water reclamation projects is well documented. In 1973, the National Water Commission commented on the government's widespread practice to provide major reclamation facilities for non-Indian farmers and failure to provide similar facilities for Indians, even though reservations often were located on the same streams. The National Water Commission concluded that "in the history of the United States Government's treatment of Indian tribes, its failure to protect Indian water rights for use on the Reservations it set aside for them is one of the sorrier chapters."[18]

No one doubts that the federal government's historical failure to provide funding for Indian water projects seriously has hamstrung Indian tribes. And no one expects much in the way of federal funds in the near future. In these budget-conscious times, Congress is reluctant to fund any new reclamation projects for Indians and non-Indians alike.

In one sense, the current lack of water facilities in Indian Country can be viewed as an opportunity. In planning future water projects, tribes can engage in comprehensive, environmentally conscious watershed planning that seldom has been employed by federal or state agencies. Thus, although Indian tribes and their water managers face a substantial funding shortage, they have the chance to ensure that future water projects are done right.

The work of tribal water managers is crucial in another respect. No definitive court decision has determined the extent of the right of Indian tribes to manage water resources within their reservations. Historically, state water agencies have had broad control over water development, and that tradition runs deep in western water law. Courts, therefore, will be forced to make choices between tribal and state management authority. Other areas of Indian law have shown that courts are sometimes reluctant to uphold tribal powers when there is a perceived inexperience or lack of expertise in tribal institutions. Thus, future court decisions on the extent of tribal authority over water may depend upon the capability and quality of tribally managed programs and of those individuals who administer them.

1-5. CONCLUSION

Recently, tribal leaders have had to deal with outside institutions, mainly the Congress and the courts, in order to solidify tribal powers and resource rights. In the years to come, tribal councils are likely to give increasing attention to internal tribal structures in order to consolidate and to build upon the achievements of the modern era.

Water management will be central to this process for most tribes. Water is simply too important to Indian Country to be lost by default. This *Handbook* is addressed to that spirit and to the emerging corps of tribal water managers.

REFERENCE NOTES

1. 25 U.S.C. §§ 331-381.
2. 25 U.S.C. §§ 461-479.
3. Act of August 15, 1953, ch. 505, 67 Stat. 588 (section 7 repealed and reenacted as amended in 1968) (codified as amended at 18 U.S.C. § 1162 (1982), 25 U.S.C. §§ 1321-1325 (1982) (28 U.S.C. § 1360 (1982)).
4. 358 U.S. 217 (1959).
5. 43 U.S.C. §§ 1601-1628.
6. 25 U.S.C. §§ 903-903f.
7. 25 U.S.C. §§ 450a-450n.
8. 25 U.S.C. §§ 1901-1963.
9. S.J. Res. 102, 95th Cong., 2d Sess., Pub. L. No. 95-341, 92 Stat. 469 (codified in part at 42 U.S.C. § 1996 & Note).
10. 373 U.S. 546 (1963), *decree entered*, 376 U.S. 340 (1964).
11. *Washington v. Washington State Commercial Passenger Fishing Vessel Ass'n*, 443 U.S. 658 (1979).
12. *See, e.g., County of Oneida v. Oneida Indian Nation*, 470 U.S. 226 (1985).
13. *Colorado River Conservation District v. United States*, 424 U.S. 800 (1976).
14. *Arizona v. San Carlos Apache Tribe of Arizona*, 463 U.S. 545 (1983).
15. *Oliphant v. Suquamish Indian Tribe*, 435 U.S. 191 (1978).
16. 455 U.S. 130 (1982).
17. *Id.* at 455 U.S. 137-38 (Citations omitted).
18. National Water Comm'n, WATER POLICIES FOR THE FUTURE—FINAL REPORT TO THE PRESIDENT AND TO THE CONGRESS OF THE UNITED STATES at 475 (1973).

SUGGESTED READINGS

For concise treatment of federal-tribal policy, *see* Angie Debo, A HISTORY OF THE INDIANS OF THE UNITED STATES (1970); Wilcomb Washburn, THE INDIAN IN AMERICA (1975); and Vine Deloria, Jr., Clifford M. Lytle, THE NATIONS WITHIN: THE PAST AND FUTURE OF AMERICAN INDIAN SOVEREIGNTY (1984). Also recommended are Francis Paul Prucha's THE GREAT FATHER: THE UNITED STATES GOVERNMENT AND THE AMERICAN INDIANS (1984) (two volumes) and Wilkinson, AMERICAN INDIANS, TIME, AND THE LAW (1987). The standard treatise on Indian law is Felix S. Cohen's HANDBOOK OF FEDERAL INDIAN LAW (1982 ed.). The two textbooks on Indian law are Getches & Wilkinson, CASES AND MATERIALS ON FEDERAL INDIAN LAW (1986), and Price and Clinton, LAW AND THE AMERICAN INDIAN (1983). A shorter treatment is Canby, AMERICAN INDIAN LAW IN A NUTSHELL (1981).

CHAPTER 2

Conflicts, Trends and Challenges Facing Today's Water Manager

2-1. THE CHANGING CONTEXT OF WATER MANAGEMENT

The ancient Greek philosopher Heraclitus wisely said "It is not possible to step twice into the same river." Water is not the only thing that is always on the move—so are the human affairs surrounding its protection, development, use and management. The context in which the water manager works is ever-changing because the relationship between water supply and water demand is dynamic. Nature varies its distribution of rain and snow, and people vary their uses and abuses of the water while it is on the surface and in the ground. Though change is a constant feature of water management, some aspects of water management change very slowly or only infrequently, so that order and stability normally prevail.

This chapter is designed to give the reader an overview of some of the forces at work today, both off-reservation and in Indian Country, that will shape tomorrow's water management situation. Of necessity, the discussion is selective and brief, but it should give a sense of how broad conflicts and trends can come to affect the day-to-day life of the water manager. Later chapters further explain the details of many of the problems discussed here and provide the necessary skills to begin to address these exciting conflicts, trends and challenges.

2-2. CONFLICTS AND TRENDS

Water Availability and Demand

Drought v. Flooding: Uncovering Climatic Change

Science is discovering more about how the climate works[1] and how human use of fossil fuels, such as the burning of coal in power plants, may be altering the weather. Many experts think a warming trend will occur because of the "greenhouse effect," resulting from the increased buildup of carbon dioxide (CO_2) in the global atmosphere. Some speculate that substantial reductions in water runoff will occur in many of our river basins if the atmosphere warms by 2 degrees centigrade (*e.g.*, approximately a 40% reduction in the upper Colorado River basin and a 56% reduction in the lower; a 64% reduction in the Missouri River basin).[2] Climate-caused decreases in water runoff would deepen the conflict that already exists over water in the arid parts of the western United States and probably would intensify the sentiment in some quarters against Indian water rights.

Whatever happens with the climate, it will remain variable and challenging to predict. Floods and droughts must continue to be anticipated. The current trend in water resource planning is to try first to identify the risks associated with climatic and other uncertainties, and then to put a price tag on the flood-control and drought-mitigation measures involved with different levels of so-called "risk avoidance." This process can be expected to continue, even though many observers think the process is more art than science.

Cities v. Crops: Patterns of Urbanization and Irrigation

The population of cities generally has been expanding dramatically in recent decades in some areas such as the Sun Belt.[3] The growth in population has increased water demand, taxing local supplies, even threatening to exhaust some imported supplies. Denver, Phoenix, Tucson, Albuquerque, Santa Fe, San Diego and many other communities, large and small alike, have sought to add to their supplies. Since irrigated farms account for 85% of the water consumption in the West,[4] it is not surprising that cities and industries have purchased irrigated farmlands to acquire water rights. Urban areas, as centers of wealth and political power, can be expected to continue to be aggressive competitors for water.

Since World War II, irrigated acreage has expanded in the West to the point where now over 40 million acres are estimated to be under irrigation in 17 western states of the conterminous United States.[5] Although irrigation has been expanding in the Southeast, the West accounts for 90% of irrigation water use in the nation. The location of much of western irrigation has shifted gradually away from the Sun Belt toward the Northern Plains. This change has occurred partially as a result of the use of the center-pivot sprinklers to apply pumped ground water in Kansas and Nebraska. Overall, the national rate of growth in irrigation has been declining and is likely to continue doing so because of the cost of energy and water.

Renewable v. Nonrenewable Supplies: Ground Water Overdraft

Ground water use has been increasing rapidly in the United States for decades. Ground water is the source of one-half of the nation's drinking water and 40% of its irrigation water and supplies about 80% of the domestic and livestock needs of rural America. California and Texas account for a disproportionately large share of the total ground water use, followed by Nebraska, Idaho, Kansas and Arizona.[6]

Most usable ground water is "riverene"—an integral part of the surface flow of streams and rivers—and is recharged by the percolation of water from the surface of the land. The recharge rate in some aquifers is so slow or minimal, however, that those aquifers contain essentially "stock" or "nonrenewable" ground water. As explained later in this *Handbook*, when ground water withdrawal exceeds the recharge, an aquifer is said to be "mined" or "overdrafted." Ground water is being overdrafted in the West at the rate of about 22 million acre-feet per year, which is roughly equivalent to one and a half times the mean annual flow of the Colorado River at Lees Ferry. Whether overdrafting increases or decreases in the future will be determined by the cost of electric power for pumping, by the profitability of irrigation farming, and, to a lesser extent, by government regulation.

Pollution v. Protection: Creeping Contamination

To be of benefit, water not only must be where it is needed, but must be of a quality that is needed. Chapter 6 discusses water quality and chemistry in greater detail. Simply put, pollution makes available water unusable or unsafe. The pollution of surface water by sewage, industrial waste and sediment from eroded land has long been recognized as a problem, and extensive government regulation has brought some aspects of that problem under control. The dangers associated with ground water pollution have been recognized only recently.[7]

Discoveries of contaminated ground water are now occurring daily and will continue for many years, since society's record of poor hazardous waste management is decades old, and the poisons may take many years to migrate through geologic formations to reach a particular ground water source. Although only a small fraction of the nation's ground water supplies are now estimated to be contaminated, the impact of that contamination on the health and economy of the local areas affected can be substantial. The cost of ground water pollution containment or development of alternative water supplies is normally great. Generally, it is impractical or impossible to clean up or rehabilitate a contaminated aquifer. Many laws and regulations are now directed at the problem of ground water contamination. Localities, such as Indian reservations, that have not monitored closely the land application or disposal of toxic chemicals will be compelled to do so in the future to protect public health and natural resources.

Water Planning, Policy, Allocation and Control

Macro v. Micro: From Nations to Special Districts

Water is so important to society that many levels of government compete to control its allocation. Where a water source crosses a political boundary, the neighboring governments—nations, states, counties, water districts, and so forth—compete for it. That competition is moderated variously by litigation, treaties, compacts and legislation.

The relative political and economic power of competing governments shifts back and forth over time. A new definition of "federalism," marked by a decline in federal subsidy for water planning and development, demonstrates the current shift in federal-state relations.[8] After having built and operated reclamation projects accounting for about 20% of the irrigation in the West, at a total construction cost of almost $8 billion, the federal Bureau of Reclamation now is faced with assuming more of a caretaker role as it completes pending projects.[9] Moreover, states must redefine their water role in light of the 1982 United States Supreme Court decision in *Sporhase v. Nebraska* holding that the states do not legally own water and cannot, except in planning for such limited conditions as serious drought, prohibit water from being exported out of the reach of their citizens.[10] Congress and the courts have given states some authority over the adjudication of Indian water rights, but the tug-

and-pull for jurisdiction over the management of water between federal, state and tribal governments is destined to be a permanent part of the western waterscape.

While federal, state and tribal governments possess great legal authority over water, much of the real political and economic control over water resides in local water entities. Irrigation districts, water districts, mutual water companies, and so forth form the "grass roots" level where the future of water management primarily is shaped.[11]

Plans v. Reactions: Meandering Opinion

Water resource development and management have been the subjects of varying degrees of forethought or "planning" in the United States. Large-scale water developments inescapably involve developmental planning, such as the selection of sites and the investigation of economic and engineering feasibility. Coordinated basin-wide planning of water resources arose during the New Deal era with the creation of the Tennessee Valley Authority (TVA) in the southeastern United States. Public support for centralized political planning of resources probably peaked in that period.

In the mid-1960s comprehensive basin-wide planning of water development and management received new interest at the federal level. This was illustrated by the creation of the United States Water Resources Council and several river basin commissions.[12] Rising concern over water pollution next led to federal requirements and funding for state water quality planning and for the delegation of water quality authority to the states. The advent of environmental planning was a parallel and broader development during this period. This planning is based on the notion that foreseeable adverse impacts from publicly sponsored or approved development ought to be identified and disclosed in advance so that alternatives and mitigation measures can be considered. Environmental impact statements (EISs), opinions and requirements became commonplace and added a new dimension to water development and management.[13] Partially unresolved is the issue of how all of the federal environmental regulations relate to, or will be administered in, Indian Country.

At the inception of the Reagan presidency, a strong reaction to federal water planning requirements occurred. Then, most river basin commissions, the United States Water Resources Council, funds for area-wide waste treatment planning, and numerous other water programs were eliminated. Pressure arose for more coordination of localized planning in the water management field. When, if ever, the pendulum will swing back toward more comprehensive basin-level planning is not known. Recent amendments to the federal Clean Water Act may mean that the pendulum has begun to swing back toward watershed planning.[14]

Privatization v. Public Trust: Fundamentals Collide

From the outset of the Union the principle was accepted that private property rights could be created in the use of water. Both the eastern riparian law and the western prior appropriation law allowed the reasonable use of water to be "privatized" through ownership. The enthusiasm for privatization was particularly strong in the nineteenth century West where new settlement and economic development was strongly encouraged. At the same time the public interest in water was asserted in such phrases as "the waters belong to the public" or in the occasional exercise of federal or state authority over navigation.

Over time concern arose over some abuses from the private use and control of water, such as pollution or the monopolized control of water sources. As a result, the public interest in water resources was redefined. The effort to rediscover and expand public rights in water is symbolized in the recent growth of the "public trust" doctrine, which holds that private water and land rights relative to navigable waters are conditioned by permanent public rights of access and preservation. Not all states have recognized the public trust doctrine, but its evolution signals an ongoing process of adjusting private water rights to accommodate changing notions of the public interest, just as private land rights have become qualified to satisfy community demands.

Historic Use v. Reallocation: Scarcity Promotes Change

Much of the surface water in the West has been appropriated; it is either being used or is covered by water right claims. This means that many new demands for surface water can be supplied only if water is "reallocated" from existing uses or claims to new ones.[15] Such reallocation can happen by the transfer of all or part of the water rights owned by an existing user or claimant. In states where water rights holders are allowed to retain rights to water saved through water conservation efforts, reallocations may be possible without retiring existing uses.

As the demand on limited water supplies increases, creating greater water scarcity, the pressure for more water conservation and reallocation will build. Water reallocation will be to the twenty-first century what initial water allocation was to the last half of the nineteenth century and to a good part of this century. As already noted, much of the reallocation is expected to be from agricultural to municipal and industrial uses.

Priority v. Shortage-Sharing: Moderating Risk

Under both the prior appropriation doctrine and the reserved rights doctrine, having an early (or "senior") priority date for a water right is important. For an appropriative right the priority date is the date on which a specified act of appropriating water takes place. For a reserved right the priority date is the date on which the reservation is created.

The holder of a water right with the latest (most recent or junior) priority date will be the one first deprived of water if a shortage occurs. Junior water rights holders assume more of the risk of shortage, then, than do senior right holders. The increased risk associated with junior water rights can discourage investment and development. As a result, senior water rights are more valuable. Cities and industries seeking dependable water supplies prefer to acquire senior rights.

The gap in risk between senior and junior water rights can be narrowed or closed by contract. The affected parties can agree to "share" a portion or all of any "shortage" that might occur in a dry period. For example, such an arrangement underlies the San Juan-Chama Diversion and the Navajo Indian Irrigation Project in New Mexico. As new users seek water in the future, the holders of senior water rights in the West, including many Indian tribes, can be expected to be approached by parties wanting to purchase some of the priority contained in those rights. New ways to moderate and to share the risk of water shortage probably will develop in response.

Politicians v. Brokers: Emerging Pricing and Marketing

For the most part, water in the West has been allocated politically for private benefit. Governments have handed out, without charge, rights to use the water. In some instances governments also have subsidized the construction and operation of dams, canals and other waterworks. As a result, water rights generally have not been bought and sold for a price that reflects either the economic value of water or the actual cost of water development.[16] In other words, a water "market" has not existed. The pressure for water marketing and full-cost pricing is building, however, as water is being reallocated. Some specialized water markets involving brokers already exist. These markets can be seen, for example, along the Front Range in Colorado.

Water's economic value rises when increased demand or decreased supply make it more scarce. To the degree that a market operates in the reallocation of water, water prices will increase as scarcity worsens. Higher water prices, in turn, will mean less waste and more water conservation.

Appropriation v. Reservation: Promises Old and New

During the settlement and development of the West, governments made different water promises to different people, and those promises have not always been kept. In the latter half of the nineteenth century, Congress essentially told the western states and their citizens that non-navigable waters in the public domain were available for the taking. Yet while the states, for the most part, promised the first water users the better rights, the federal government also recognized reservations for Indians, promising support and protection for the survival of these homelands.

Early in this century the federal government established a reclamation program, which held out the promise of subsidized irrigation development for arid lands. Shortly thereafter the United States Supreme Court recognized the reserved water right in the *Winters* case. *Winters* established the principle that all reservations of land from the public domain also reserve by implication water needed for the achievement of the purposes of the reservation. Unlike an appropriative water right, the reserved right remains valid even when it is not being used. When a senior reserved right finally is exercised, it can cut off water to the holder of a junior appropriative right who has relied on the water for years. Such displacement, and conflict, is on the horizon in Indian Country.

As large-scale reclamation projects were planned and authorized, congressional promises of future subsidies and development were made to many areas of the West, including Indian reservations. Some of those projects have been variously scaled down, delayed, restructured financially to reduce the subsidy, or canceled. Old and new promises alike will be modified or broken as competition for scarce water and public subsidy heightens and courts and legislative bodies make hard decisions.

Litigation v. Negotiation: Shifting Sands

Many water rights in the West, particularly reserved rights, have not been "quantified"; that is, the amount of water that lawfully can be used under the right has not been recognized officially. Quantification normally results from litigation, as in a stream adjudication, where a court issues a decree defining the scope, limits and priorities of the water rights of the parties in the lawsuit. Such litigation is expensive and lengthy, and often it is risky. For those reasons, efforts frequently are made to settle as much of the controversy as possible through negotiation.

Negotiation has been viewed as a method to quantify Indian water claims independent of litigation. In 1958 the Navajos reached an agreement with non-Indian water interests that led to the Navajo Indian Irrigation Project. In 1979, the state of Montana established the Reserved Water Rights Compact Commission to negotiate and settle reserved rights. Although the Fort Peck Indian Reservation and the state of Montana finalized the Fort Peck-Montana Compact in 1985, the Montana effort has been slow in its progress and is not yet completed. In 1982 the Tohono O'odham Nation (formerly called the Papago Tribe) reached a negotiated settlement in the context of an act of Congress involving federal payments and guarantees. The Ak-Chin Community was a party to settlement legislation in 1984. The Ute Mountain Utes andd Southern Utes reached settlements in 1986 with state and federal interests concerning the Animas-La Plata Project.

The status of federal funding may impact whether tribes take the settlement route. Unfortunately, the outlook for federal funding to make settlement attractive is bleak. The catalyst of capital, so necessary in the Tohono O'odham and Ak-Chin settlements, appears less likely to be forthcoming from the federal government for other tribes involved in negotiations. Whether litigation or negotiation will be favored in the future will depend on each tribe's assessment of the costs and risks inherent in its particular situation.

Old Boys v. New Voices: Information and Participation

Most water decisions affecting the West have been made by representatives of people and interests benefitted by water projects. During the early decades of water development, the public generally supported public works projects that held the promise of increased settlement and economic growth and rarely questioned how water was allocated or how water project funds were spent. As a result, a few water leaders in each region came to wield great influence.

Today, more people recognize that every water decision produces winners and losers. Overall, some people receive more water while paying less, others pay more while receiving less. The growing scarcity of both water and public subsidies makes it easier to distinguish the winners from the losers. More people, particularly those who have lost in the past, are becoming better informed on water matters and are realizing that they have a stake in water decisions. They want to participate, to be heard, and to be represented. Gradually, water management is likely to become more "democratized" as a result of those new voices.

Commodity v. Communal: Interplay of Water Values

Although the economic value of water has been recognized since the earliest days of nineteenth century settlement in the West, a feeling also has persisted that "water is different." Communities have placed a special value on water that cannot be reduced to dollars and cents and that has made it different from resources normally treated as commodities. Other natural resources, such as oil and gas, have been regarded as commodities of interstate commerce for many decades. Only recently, however, have the courts begun to regard water as a commodity, even though rights to water use began to be privatized in the last century.

The rapid rise of the commodity view of water has not overwhelmed the communal view. Many groups and individuals are resisting the mounting pressure to have water move to the highest bidder. They want their lifestyles and cultures to be protected from the reach of the dollar. The tension between the commodity values and community values can be expected to continue indefinitely in most settings, including Indian reservations.

Water Protection, Development, Use and Management

Waste v. Conservation: Toward Greater Efficiency

It has always been unlawful to waste water, yet in practice marginal but significant amounts of water have been wasted and continue to be wasted. As water demand increases and a higher value is placed on water, waste becomes less acceptable and methods of saving water increase in popularity. In the last decade or so new technologies and practices of water conservation have appeared and resulted in greater efficiency of water use in the home, factory and field. Conservation techniques include the use of low-flow toilets and showerheads, native ornamental plants, laser-leveling of fields, irrigation scheduling, gated pipes, sprinklers, soil-moisture monitoring and increasing-block water rates.

In some states water users lose some of their rights to water if they use less ("use it or lose it"). Other states provide an incentive for water conservation by allowing the person who conserves water to market the saved water. More changes in law and technology to foster water conservation can be expected as water becomes even more scarce. Water managers will continue to be required to know about the most advanced and workable ways of gaining more utility out of available water supplies.

Old v. New Technology: Marginal Operations in Peril

The trend toward water conservation and greater efficiency involves new technology.[17] Other changes in the way water is applied and consumed involves new technology as well. Many of the more advanced technologies require front-end capital investments that some water users cannot afford. Examples for some farmers include the cost of sprinkler irrigation or tail-water return systems or computerized soil-moisture monitoring systems. The result can be that some economically marginal operations can no longer compete or cannot comply with regulatory standards that are based on more advanced technology.

In the various sectors of water use—irrigation, manufacturing, electric power production, municipal supply and waste treatment—as in the other sectors of activity in our society, new technology is replacing old. The water manager must take this replacement process into account in water planning and in the adoption and implementation of management strategies.

Conjunctive Use v. Disjunctive Use: Facing Facts

For too long surface waters and ground waters were developed and managed independently, even though they commonly are physically interconnected. Ground water aquifers are underground reservoirs where water can be stored purposefully during wet periods to provide supplies for drier periods. Opportunities for such new or expanded conjunctive management exist in many settings. Taking advantage of these opportunities can be problematic. Sometimes the law is unclear as to whether the party who stores water in an aquifer covered by other water right claims can retain the right to that stored water. Conflict and competition between political entities and agencies that share a common stream and aquifer also can prevent or obstruct conjunctive management. Such obstacles are likely to be overcome increasingly, however, due to the influence of heightened water demand and cost-consciousness.

Consumption v. Instream Flows: Shifting Benefits

The prior appropriation doctrine has encouraged the diversion and consumption of water and neglected the importance of instream flow for the preservation and enhancement of fish, wildlife, recreation and water quality. Public appreciation of instream benefits has grown, however, and given rise, in some states, to policies and laws designed to protect minimum stream flows. The traditional dominance held by consumptive uses probably will diminish further as the concern for instream protection grows. The vast quantity of existing water rights favoring consumptive uses, however, will persist and constrain efforts to restore minimum flows in most stretches of developed waterways. The opportunity to protect instream flows before development takes place still exists in some parts of Indian Country.

Storage v. Shortage: Close Judgment Calls

With the development of the last amounts of unappropriated water in some areas, considerable attention is being focused on the remaining opportunities to store water in surface reservoirs. Storing water in wet seasons for use in dry seasons, and in wet years to "carry over" for dry years, has been a conventional way of avoiding or mitigating shortage. When new surface reservoirs are created, however, a price is paid as land and riparian habitat are lost due to flooding and water is lost to evaporation and seepage. In each setting the trade-offs must be considered carefully by water planners and managers before significant commitments of money and resources are made.

Nonstructural v. Structural Solutions: Savvy for Cement

Many of the major water problems, such as floods and droughts, have more than one solution. Sometimes a water manager is presented with a choice between a structural solution, such as a flood-control dam, and a nonstructural solution, such as the management of vegetation in an upper watershed. For example, the coordinated scheduling of reservoir releases and irrigation has avoided the need for new capital improvements in some settings. The rising costs of construction, operation and maintenance associated with structural answers to water problems, and a greater sensitivity to environmental impacts, have prompted a search for more nonstructural solutions. Water managers, therefore, must have the ability to weigh the advantages and disadvantages of structural and nonstructural solutions.

Rehabilitation v. Decay: Paying Now or Later

Many of the dams, canals, pipelines, sewers and waste treatment facilities built decades ago are deteriorated and in need of repair or replacement. Decaying waterworks are part of a larger public works infrastructure problem in the United States that is symbolized vividly by crumbling highways.[18] After the failure of the Teton Dam in Idaho in 1976, a nationwide review of the condition of dams was begun, causing some closings and considerable repairs. The competition for capital to rebuild the public works infrastructure is keen. New water projects now are competing with the repair of old water projects for limited capital. What makes the matter worse is that each year rehabilitation is delayed, the ultimate cost is increased. As a result of the infrastructure problem, one lesson being relearned in many water management circles is the importance of ongoing maintenance and repair.

As the public becomes more aware of the infrastructure problem and the unavoidable costs that must be shouldered to solve it, water and sewer rates and water management budgets should begin to reflect the full cost of maintenance, repair and replacement. Here, as in other areas, the water manager is going to be called upon to be articulate and persuasive in dealing with other officials, the media and the public.

2-3. CHALLENGES

Becoming Better Informed and Better Trained

Training for the Indian water manager, as with any other skilled person in society, is a lifelong process. It does not stop with an educational diploma, degree or certificate. Trends and developments in the water management field are dynamic and ever-changing, requiring the modern manager to dedicate time to keeping abreast of advances in the field. Reading, comparing experiences with fellow managers elsewhere, attending conferences and workshops, and taking more course work are among the additional activities that Indian water managers must undertake to better manage the water resource.

Redefining Conflict and Moderating Competing Values

Conflict among the water constituencies and users is one of the major problems facing many water managers. Sometimes the conflict is unnecessary and can be avoided by the discovery of mutual interests or common objectives. Sometimes an alert water manager, flexible and open to new approaches, can defuse conflict before positions harden and polarize. Mediation services and procedures also can be employed with success to resolve water-related conflict.

Designing Flexible Strategies and Systems

Since patterns of water use and demand can change unpredictably, there is wisdom in preserving management options and in developing contingency plans for the future. One example of wise, flexible design is a dam that allows water to be released at a number of elevations in the structure, depending on the water temperature desired for a downstream fishery. When faced with a management decision, the Indian water manager should ask, "If conditions change later, will the tribal decision that is about to be made leave us in a position to respond or adapt effectively?" One eye needs to be kept on the future.

Respecting Natural Limits and Processes

The history of water development shows that unnecessary damage has been done to the environment and to natural systems of plant and animal life. Irrigation projects have been developed over formations that make drainage and salt management impractical or impossible. Dams have been constructed with unworkable fish ladders. Water projects have induced land uses that cause erosion and produce sediment, which situation limits the life of reservoirs or degrades the quality of water. Ground water has been mined to the point of causing land subsidence or salt water intrusion. To avoid causing such problems, the Indian water manager needs to know how to obtain and apply information from environmental scientists.

Integrating Decisions Affecting Human and Natural Resources

Sound water decisions are not made in a vacuum, isolated from other human concerns and needs. Water protection, allocation, use and management ought to promote the well-being of people. This means that "natural resource" decisions should take account of "human resource" needs. In practice, decisions that commit human resources affect natural resources and vice versa. For instance a reservation's preschool, day-care or nutrition program may be deprived of funds if federal money is spent on a tribal water project. Water management priorities will compete with priorities in other areas. The modern water manager must be able to see and to demonstrate the importance of water decisions for the surrounding human community so that water management finds its proper place on the political agenda.

Balancing Immediate and Long-Term Goals

Much of a water manager's time is spent responding to "brush fires," matters that seem to demand immediate attention. Some of these matters are crises of sorts; most are not. In any case, they tend to crowd out what little time there is for thinking and planning for the future. Doing what is expedient to solve a pressing problem is easier than pausing to seek a solution that meets both short-term and long-term needs. Water managers, however, must face tall orders. They are expected to solve immediate problems without causing or worsening future ones.

2-4. CONCLUSION

Water in a pool or vessel can serve as a mirror. Similarly, a tribe's water management system reflects the image the tribe has of itself and the environment. Important choices of values and goals are involved in water management decision-making. Water is one of the most important community and commodity resources in Indian Country. As such, it is a lively subject for conflicts, trends and challenges, only some of which have been summarized in this chapter. The water resource field is both complex and manageable. It is up to the water manager to use insight and skill to identify and respond today to tomorrow's water conflicts, trends and challenges in Indian Country.

REFERENCE NOTES

1. National Research Council, CLIMATE, CLIMATIC CHANGE, AND WATER SUPPLY (1977).
2. Natural Academy of Science, Carbon Dioxide Assessment Committee, CHANGING CLIMATE (1983).
3. *See* Stan G. Daberkow and Herman Bluestone, PATTERN OF CHANGE IN METRO AND NON-METRO LABOR FORCE, 1976-1982 (1984).
4. For a general description, *see* U.S. Department of the Interior (and others), IRRIGATION WATER USE AND MANAGEMENT (1979).
5. *See* Kenneth D. Frederick, *The Future Role of Western Irrigation*, THE SOUTHWESTERN REVIEW, vol. 1, no. 1 at 19-33 (Spring 1981).
6. *See* Congress of the United States, Office of Technology Assessment, I PROTECTING THE NATION'S GROUNDWATER FROM CONTAMINATION (1984); *also*, Comptroller General of the United States, GROUND WATER: AN OVERVIEW (June 21, 1977) and United States Geological Survey Water Supply Paper 2250, NATIONAL WATER SUMMARY 1983—HYDROLOGIC EVENTS AND ISSUES at 36-45 (1984).
7. *Ibid.*
8. *See* Barbara T. Andrews and Marie Sansone, WHO RUNS THE RIVERS? (1983).
9. *See* Iver Peterson, *Changes Are Confronting U.S. on Water Projects*, THE NEW YORK TIMES, March 17, 1985.
10. 458 U.S. 941 (1982).
11. *See* James N. Corbridge, Jr. (ed.), SPECIAL WATER DISTRICTS: CHALLENGE FOR THE FUTURE (1983).

12. *See* National Water Comm'n, WATER POLICIES FOR THE FUTURE—FINAL REPORT TO THE PRESIDENT AND TO THE CONGRESS OF THE UNITED STATES at 397-433 (1973).
13. *See generally*, Frederick R. Anderson, Daniel R. Mandelker and A. Dan Tarlock, ENVIRONMENTAL PROTECTION: LAW AND POLICY (1984).
14. *See* Water Quality Act of 1987, § 316, 101 Stat. 52 (adding section 319 to the Clean Water Act).
15. *See* Gary D. Weatherford (ed.), WATER AND AGRICULTURE IN THE WESTERN U.S.: CONSERVATION, REALLOCATION AND MARKETS (1982).
16. *See* Terry L. Anderson, WATER CRISES: ENDING THE POLICY DROUGHT (1983).
17. For applications of water conservation technology, *see* California Dept. of Water Resources Bulletin 198-84, WATER CONSERVATION IN CALIFORNIA (July 1984).
18. *See generally*, Pat Choate and Susan Water, AMERICA IN RUINS (1981).

SUGGESTED READINGS

Numerous newsletters, magazines and journals report or comment on current developments and issues in water policy and management. Among them are: U.S. WATER NEWS (Halstead, Kansas), WESTERN STATES WATER (Salt Lake City, Utah: Western States Water Council), WATER RESOURCES BULLETIN (Bethesda, Maryland: American Water Resources Association), WESTERN WATER (Sacramento, California: Western Water Education Foundation), ENVIRONMENT REPORTER, CURRENT DEVELOPMENTS (Washington, D.C.: Bureau of National Affairs), and WATER MARKET UPDATE (Santa Fe, New Mexico: Western Network). Books which survey a range of timely topics include: AMERICA'S WATER, CURRENT TRENDS AND EMERGING ISSUES (1984), and Ernest Engelbert (ed.), WATER SCARCITY, IMPACTS ON WESTERN AGRICULTURE (1984).

CHAPTER 3

Western State Water Law

3-1. THE ROOTS OF THE PRIOR APPROPRIATION SYSTEM

Mr. Irwin and Mr. Phillips were frustrated. They had not made the difficult journey to California in order to spend their time in court. They had come to strike it rich, to hit the Mother Lode amidst the Sierra Nevada foothills. Nor did they wish to pay out their hard-earned gold into the pockets of lawyers arguing before the California Supreme Court. But that is what they found themselves doing in 1855; because in order to flush the gold from the hillsides and to wash it from the streambeds, these two miners needed water. And there was not enough of this precious resource for both of them.

Irwin arrived in the Gold Country first and proceeded to set up a claim that he named "Irwin's Diggings." In the spring of 1851, he began diverting water through a lengthy canal from the south fork of Poor Man's Creek to rinse the gold from his diggings. In order to provide additional water to his operation, as well as to other miners in the area, Irwin next constructed a dam in the creek. By 1852, Irwin had established a lucrative operation, not only from the gold that was washed from the distant hillsides by his waterworks, but also through his marketing of the excess canal water to other miners. All was proceeding well until one morning Irwin awoke to find that someone had ripped out part of his dam. Phillips and his seven partners recently had staked a claim along the banks of Poor Man's Creek—and they needed the stream flow blocked by Irwin's dam.

The Riparian Argument

Phillips believed that he had a right to interfere with Irwin's canal and dam in order to protect the flow of the stream through his downstream claim. This argument reflected the riparian doctrine of water rights that recently had evolved in the eastern states. "Riparian" means relating to the banks of water bodies, such as riparian land and riparian vegetation. Under the riparian doctrine, landowners adjacent to a natural stream have a right to use the flow, but only to the extent that such use does not interfere with the concurrent right of downstream riparian landowners to use the water also. This concept followed from the notion that if persons obtain land next to a stream, they have a right to expect the stream to continue flowing and a right to use its water to a reasonable extent. The riparian doctrine, however, precludes large-scale consumption of water from the stream, since downstream landowners may object to significant depletions of the natural flow. In addition, the doctrine prevents diversion and consumption of the stream water except by those who actually control the riparian land.

These constraints on water use did not pose any significant problems for nineteenth century easterners who had plentiful rainfall and runoff. Diversions for municipal and industrial purposes were not highly consumptive and rarely depleted the flow of eastern streams to a significant degree. Also, in the humid climate of the East, water withdrawn from the streams generally was not needed elsewhere to irrigate crops.

So Phillips looked to this riparian heritage of water law and argued that he should have the right to enjoy the use of the stream flow running through his mining claim. Irwin, however, strongly disagreed.

The Power of Custom

Irwin pointed out the ways in which the riparian doctrine was unsuited to the California region and how it had been rejected by local custom. The custom that had grown up in the rugged foothills reflected the fact that significant diversions of flow from the streambed were needed for successful mining operations. The custom also involved the notion that the first person to utilize the stream flow had a right to depend on continued use of it. If someone else tried to divert the stream in order to work a gold stake, the prior user had a generally recognized right to enforce his earlier claim to the water. Enforcement took a variety of forms in this region—and seldom relied upon the slow process of the courts.

After trying self-help and then requesting arbitration from the local mining committee, Irwin and Phillips eventually selected adjudication as the means for settling their dispute. The subsequent jury verdict in favor of Irwin was appealed; thus in 1855, the California Supreme Court handed down its decision in the matter. (*Irwin v. Phillips.*[1]) The court rejected Phillips's riparian-type argument, recognizing that "[c]ourts are bound to take notice of the political and social condition of the country, which they judicially rule."[2] Noting that some local customs are subject to dispute and fluctuation, the court went on to point out that there are other customs

> which a universal sense of necessity and propriety have so firmly fixed that they come to be looked upon as having the force and effect of *res judicata* [established law]. Among these the most important are the rights . . . of those who, by prior appropriation, have taken the waters from their natural beds, and by costly artificial works have conducted them for miles over mountains and ravines, to supply the necessities of gold diggers, and without which the most important interests of the mineral region would remain without development.[3]

Priority of Appropriation

In resolving the dispute between Irwin and Phillips, the California Supreme Court concluded with the Latin phrase of equity, translated simply as "first in time, first in right."[4] This concept formed the basis of the prior appropriation doctrine that reflected the needs of the miners in the California foothills. Unlike the riparian doctrine, the prior appropriation system allowed for intensive diversion and use of limited stream flows. A miner who arrived at the stream first could command the entire flow, if needed, without having to leave any water for the use and enjoyment of downstream riparian landowners. Also, the new system did not restrict use simply to the lands that lay next to the watercourse, it also allowed gold to be washed from distant and scattered hillsides. Perhaps most importantly, the concept of priority of appropriation provided a degree of certainty to those who wished to invest in waterworks to further their goals. Such investments were safeguarded by the prior appropriation doctrine, since future water users could not lawfully interfere with the earlier miner's right to continue to divert the stream.

This doctrine that allowed for maximum certainty and exploitation was consistent not only with the needs of the miners in California, but also with those of newcomers in other parts of the West. For instance, an early Colorado case, *Coffin v. Left Hand Ditch Co.* (1882), demonstrated that similar water shortages and emotions existed there:

> In 1879 there was not a sufficient quantity of water in the St. Vrain to supply the ditch of appellee and also irrigate the said lands of appellant. A portion of appellee's dam was torn out, and its diversion of water thereby seriously interfered with by appellants.[5]

The fight over irrigation water spilled from the banks of the St. Vrain River into the Colorado Supreme Court, giving that state's highest judges the opportunity to confirm the growing strength of the prior appropriation doctrine in the West. In ruling that the riparian doctrine was inapplicable to the needs of the region's water users, the court noted that:

> The climate is dry, and the soil, when moistened only by the usual rainfall, is arid and unproductive; except in a few favored sections, artificial irrigation for agriculture is an absolute necessity. Water in the various streams thus acquires a value unknown in moister climates. Instead of being a mere incident to the soil, it rises, when appropriated, to the dignity of a distinct usufructuary estate, or right of property. . . .
>
> The right of water in this country, by priority of appropriation thereof, we think it is, and has always been, the duty of the national and state governments to protect. . . . And we hold that, in the absence of express statutes to the contrary, the first appropriator of water from a natural stream [has] a prior right thereto, to the extent of such appropriation.[6]

By the early 1900s, the concept of prior appropriation had come to dominate the allocation of water rights throughout the western states. Although each state had different specific aspects to its water law, three basic requirements generally were needed to establish a water right under the prior appropriation doctrine. First, the water had to be applied to some recognized beneficial use. Second, the water had to have been structurally diverted from the streambed prior to use. And third, the right could not be created until the user actually manifested an intent to appropriate the water. These elements of the prior appropriation system and their evolution over the past decades are discussed in the following sections.

3-2. THE CONCEPT OF BENEFICIAL USE

Although the prior appropriation doctrine was born amidst an ethic of resource exploitation, it was not completely devoid of safeguards against the wasting of water. In each of the western states, a water right could be established only to the extent that the water was being applied to some beneficial use. The concept of beneficial use created two limitations upon water utilization. First, lawful appropriations could be established only for specified purposes that were considered to be beneficial applications of water. Second, since the appropriation was limited to the amount of water that was being applied to beneficial use, blatant waste of water was unlawful and nonuse of an established appropriation could result in a loss of the right.

Specified Beneficial Uses

The first limitation embodied within the beneficial use concept reflected the desire of state lawmakers that water be applied to promote economically productive purposes. Early statutes typically limited beneficial uses to domestic, agricultural, stockraising, mining, and manufacturing purposes. Although these purposes were read broadly to allow varied applications of water, such lists also were invoked to prohibit specific uses that were considered inappropriate in light of limited water supplies. Value judgments were made to rank the uses. For example, one court had to decide whether a proposed hydropower project should be deprived of water in order to maintain a waterfall "rare in beauty" that formed the chief attraction of an existing resort complex. A federal circuit court concluded that the falls did not constitute a protectable beneficial use and that the resort "is not entitled to a continuance of the falls solely for their scenic beauty."[7] Other examples of value judgments appear in court records, such as where the drowning of gophers and the winter wetting of fields were deemed nonbeneficial uses when other people wanted to apply the water for more traditional purposes.[8]

The relative importance of the various beneficial uses was addressed in provisions of western statutory and constitutional law. For instance:

> [W]hen the waters of any natural stream are not sufficient for the service of all those desiring the use of the same, those using the water for domestic purposes shall have the preference over those claiming for any other purpose, and those using the water for agricultural purposes shall have preference over those using the same for manufacturing purposes.[9]

Such provisions, however, often have a limited impact. Under the prior appropriation system, senior rights are protected from newcomers, even if the new uses are superior in the law's beneficial use hierarchy. The practical effect of the hierarchy is that municipalities may lay claim to irrigation waters and other senior rights, but only upon the payment of just compensation to the holders of the rights.

With certain modifications, the concept of beneficial use remains strong today. As technology has developed and societal values have changed, the definition of beneficial use has evolved under the law as well. Of particular importance is the recognition of water's non-economic value. The current statute that defines beneficial use in the state of Washington reflects this trend:

> Uses of water for domestic, stock watering, industrial, commercial, agricultural, irrigation, hydroelectric power production, mining, fish and wildlife maintenance and enhancement, recreational, and thermal power production purposes, and preservation of environmental and aesthetic values, and all other uses compatible with the enjoyment of the public waters of the state, are declared to be beneficial uses.[10]

Not all states have legislated such a broad category of beneficial uses. Nor is it clear to what extent courts will protect the noncommodity values (*e.g.*, aesthetic, religious) of water against those which produce tangible economic benefits. But the chance for recognition and protection of noncommodity values as a beneficial use is much greater now than in past decades.

The Effect of Nonbeneficial Use

The concept of beneficial use in the prior appropriation doctrine has been invoked not only to limit water applications to certain types of use, but also to limit the quantity of the water right. It has often been said in western courts and legislatures that "beneficial use shall be the basis, the measure, and the limit of the right to the use of water." In other words, a user cannot appropriate more flow than is needed in order to derive the benefits from the water. The standard limiting water quantity was designed to prevent the wasting of water, particularly regarding the overapplication of irrigation supplies. If an irrigator used a practice that did not comport with the custom of the area and that resulted in the diversion of too much water, the court would not recognize the wasted amount as being part of the vested water right. As stated by the New Mexico Supreme Court in disallowing an inefficient practice:

> [N]o matter how early a person's priority of appropriations may be, he is not entitled to receive more water than is necessary for his actual use. An excessive diversion of water, through waste, cannot be regarded as a diversion to beneficial use. . . . Water in this state is too scarce, and consequently too precious, to admit waste.[11]

As scarcity problems increase and the need for conservation of water grows, the notion of limiting the amount of the water right strictly to the beneficial use may be implemented increasingly. Many existing water rights were established based upon the customary practices of a previous century, and much room for improved efficiency exists. Unfortunately, state courts and legislatures have thus far been reluctant to invoke the concept of beneficial use in order to disallow wasteful practices that prevail in the West. Without such a move by the courts and the legislatures, the prior appropriation doctrine will continue to protect inefficient uses. Only when a water right has fallen into complete disuse has the requirement of beneficial use commonly been invoked by the courts to extinguish the right.

Forfeiture and Abandonment Through Nonuse

When a water right ceases to be applied to a beneficial use, its holder risks losing the right through either forfeiture or abandonment. In the early days of the prior appropriation doctrine, abandonment was the sole means for extinguishing a lapsed water right. A concept developed by the courts (*i.e.*, "common law") the abandonment principle required two criteria to be proved before the water right was extinguished: (1) the water had to have ceased being used, and (2) the water rights holder had to have actually intended to abandon the water. The showing of an intent to abandon was a difficult hurdle to overcome in the courtroom, thus water rights rarely were extinguished through this procedure.

The concept of water forfeiture was created by western state legislatures in order to minimize the difficulties posed by common law abandonment claims. As with abandonment, forfeiture requires nonuse of the water, but unlike abandonment, forfeiture dispenses with the requirement of intent. A typical forfeiture statute declares that a water right has been abandoned simply through nonuse for a specified period of years:

> Whenever the owner of a perfected and developed water right ceases or fails to use the water appropriated for a period of five successive years, the right to use shall cease, and the failure to use shall be conclusively presumed to be an abandonment of water right. Thereafter the water which was the subject of use under such water right shall revert to the public and become again the subject of appropriation in the manner provided by law, subject to existing priorities.[12]

Continuous beneficial use is an essential element in establishing and maintaining a water right under the prior appropriation doctrine. Beneficial use alone, however, is not sufficient for obtaining a vested water right. Other prerequisites must be met before water users can feel secure in their right to appropriate water under western state law.

3-3. ADAPTATIONS OF THE DIVERSION AND INTENT REQUIREMENTS

In order for a water right to be deemed valid, the prior appropriation doctrine traditionally required that water be diverted from a stream and that the appropriator use a physical structure to divert the water, with the intent to apply it to some beneficial use. The requirement of a diversion structure has led to much case law in various states, with little consistency in results. For instance, does the farmer who obtains irrigation water from the natural overflow of high runoff also obtain a protectable water right? Utah and Nevada courts have said no, while Oregon and Colorado courts have indicated the opposite. Similar contradictions arise regarding whether a water right is created in the owner of cattle that drink directly from a stream. Although controversy continues, modern courts have tended to be somewhat less stringent about requiring a diversion structure. This is particularly true regarding instream flow uses of water.

Recognizing Instream Flow Uses

The 1913 case cited in the previous section involving Cascade Town's scenic falls and the hydropower project demonstrated the judicial reluctance to recognize protectable water rights in nondiversionary instream flows. As public awareness regarding the values of free-flowing water grew, however, state legislatures began taking actions to protect such values. For instance, in 1973 the Colorado Legislature provided for appropriations by the state of "such waters of natural streams and lakes as may be required to preserve the natural environment to a reasonable degree."[13] This statute was attacked by water users who asserted that a lawful appropriation required a diversion, and that the instream flow rights would impair the state's constitutional mandate that "[t]he right to divert the unappropriated waters of any natural stream to beneficial uses shall never be denied."[14]

The Colorado Supreme Court, in *Colorado River Water Conservation District v. Colorado Water Conservation Board* (1979), subsequently upheld the validity of the statute and the right of the state to protect instream flows.[15] It cited an earlier decision by the Idaho Supreme Court in finding that an actual physical diversion of water was not required to validate the statutorily created minimum stream flow program. Other states also have legislation protecting nondiversionary instream uses.

The courts may be reluctant to recognize a protectable water right in nondiversionary instream flows, but that does not mean they always will allow the destruction of instream flows to be a necessary cost of the prior appropriation system. In one of the most significant natural resource decisions of the last few decades, the California Supreme Court, in the Mono Lake case, held that the public trust doctrine modified the diversions by the Los Angeles Metropolitan Water District from the streams feeding Mono Lake.[16] Even though the diversions had been claimed earlier in the century, with great care taken to comply with both prior appropriation and riparian law, the court found that public trust rights in Mono Lake always existed, had never been extinguished and must be accommodated when consumptive water rights are granted. Just as it had done a century and a quarter earlier in *Irwin v. Phillips*, the California Supreme Court looked to current societal values, finding that "the public trust has evolved in tandem with the changing public perception of the values and uses of waterways." The court concluded that environmental factors, as well as appropriative rights, must be taken into account: "Mono Lake has long been treasured as a unique scenic, recreational and scientific resource, but continued diversions threaten to turn it into a desert wasteland. . . ."[17]

The court found that:

> The state has an affirmative duty to take the public trust into account in the planning and allocation of water resources, and to protect the public trust uses whenever feasible. Just as the history of [California] shows that appropriation may be necessary for efficient use of water despite unavoidable harm to public trust values, it demonstrates that an appropriative water rights system administered without consideration of the public trust may cause unnecessary and unjustified harm to trust interests.[18]

The court also held that "the state is not confined by past allocation decisions which may be incorrect in light of current knowledge or inconsistent with current needs."[19]

The Mono Lake decision provides the single strongest statement that historic uses must accommodate modern needs. Water law throughout the West in the years to come probably will be directly and indirectly impacted by the decision.

No state, however, recognizes the right of private individuals to appropriate such instream flows. This restrictive vestige of the diversion requirement leads to the anomalous situation where a private party may divert water into a pond to grow fish, but that person cannot obtain a protectable water right in the streambed in order to achieve the same result. Further case law will be developed on the subject as Indian tribes, fishing organizations, rafters and other groups attempt to protect the many values of free-flowing waters.

Filing Procedures

A main reason that the diversion requirement was incorporated into the prior appropriation doctrine was to provide notice to other people along the stream that a lawful appropriation had been made. The notice promoted certainty of priority and allowed potential users to determine whether unappropriated flows were still available for future development. Current statutes and regulations throughout the West, however, make the notice rationale largely irrelevant.

Essentially all western states currently require that an application be filed for any new diversion to take its lawful place in the priority system. The filing is a public record and serves notice that the appropriation has been initiated. In many instances, a list of the filings is published in local newspapers in order to facilitate the notice process. Upon completion of the procedures, a state agency generally issues a permit for the requested use, and the appropriation takes its place in the priority system. In Colorado, however, the filing is made to a water court rather than to an administrative agency.

Conditional Rights

Under the appropriation procedures, protectable rights to water may be obtained prior to the water actually being put to a use. Such a "conditional" water right becomes "absolute" at the time at which the water is actually put to beneficial use. It is at this point where the third requirement—intent—comes into the picture.

As soon as a potential user formulates an intent to apply unappropriated water to a beneficial use and manifests that intent through an overt physical act (*e.g.*, on-site surveys, filing of permit applications), the user is said to have initiated an appropriation. The user is then able to claim that date of initiation as the priority date for the water even though no beneficial use has yet taken place. The user obtains a conditional water right based on that date, and upon perfection into an absolute right, maintains the original priority as against other users.

This system of conditional rights, based upon intent, provides safeguards to those who intend to build large structures to appropriate water. For instance, a municipality may take a decade or more to identify the source of needed water, plan the new facilities, construct the necessary dam, and lay the distribution network. All this effort would be wasted if the city were not protected from other potential appropriators who might begin diverting during the construction period. Under current procedures, a city simply may apply for a conditional right to the water that it intends to develop, thereby obtaining a senior priority relative to any subsequent water use along the stream.

To prevent abuse of the system and to avoid mere speculation in water, a holder of a conditional right must demonstrate "due diligence" in completing the project and in applying the water to beneficial use. If the conditional water right is not developed and made absolute in a timely manner, the holder risks losing the original priority date.

This ability to lose a priority date, and the forfeiture and abandonment principles discussed earlier, highlight the fact that a vested water right is not a traditional property interest in the sense of ownership. As such, other important limitations are involved in its exercise and use.

3-4. LIMITATIONS ON CHANGES OF USE

Many water users in the West believe that they own the water that flows through their diversion headgates. But courts have made clear that the state systems of prior appropriation do not give users ownership interests in the water. Rather, the protectable property interest in a water right is the right simply to use the water, not to own it. Moreover, states are empowered fully to regulate water use, such as by mandating forfeiture of a right when it has not been applied beneficially for a period of years. Also, since water rights holders do not own the water, they are restricted under the prior appropriation doctrine in their ability to transfer the use of the water to another purpose or to change the point of diversion.

The Appurtenancy Rule

A few courts highly restrict any change in use or diversion, and follow the "appurtenancy rule." They are of the view that

> a water right is attached to the land on which it is beneficially used and becomes appurtenant thereto, and that the right is not in any individual or

> owner of the land. It is in a sense a floating right, nor can the right, once having attached to a particular piece of land, be made to do duty on any other land. . . .[20]

Most states, however, do not follow this restrictive appurtenancy view. Generally, water rights may be transferred for use on another plot of land so long as certain conditions are met. These conditions arise from one basic premise of the prior appropriation doctrine—that all users who have made appropriations have a right to rely on the continuation of the stream flow situation that existed at the time of their original appropriation. No changes can be made by other diverters along the stream (even by those with senior priority dates) that may interfere with the ability of existing users to withdraw their appropriations. Such a situation is demonstrated by the simple example beginning with Figure 3-1.

Changes in Points of Diversion

In Figure 3-1, User A made an appropriation in 1875 of the entire 20 cubic feet per second (cfs) flow of Western Creek for irrigation of the family farm. Eight cfs of the diversion were consumed by the crops, while the remaining 12 cfs returned to the creek. In 1950, User B built a fish hatchery upstream of A and appropriated the entire 20 cfs to run through the hatchery's raceways and rearing ponds. No water was consumed in the hatchery, so the 20 cfs returned to the creek and were available to satisfy User A's senior right. Each user received the proper permits and took their respective places in the state's priority system.

The problem began in 1985 when the current User A (who inherited the water right) decided to change the diversion to point C upriver from User B (above User B's headgate) in order to irrigate different land (Figure 3-2). As a consequence, User A currently removes the entire stream flow at point C, with the 12 cfs of flow returning. This change resulted in User B now having only 12 cfs rather than 20 cfs available for the hatchery. User B filed suit, asserting that a senior right could not be changed in a manner that is detrimental to other users on the stream. User B had invested much money in the hatchery in reliance upon having 20 cfs available to divert, and User A could not change the stream condition to defeat User B's use. Under the precepts of the prior appropriation system, the court would agree with this argument and rule against the change in User A's point of diversion.

Transfers to Different Uses

Similar protections are afforded water users along a stream when a senior water rights holder attempts to transfer the right to a different type of use. For example, after being thwarted in the attempt to change the point of diversion, User A decided to transfer the water right across the creek to a power company for industrial purposes (Figure 3-3). The power company planned to divert User A's 20 cfs and use the water in cooling towers where it would be consumed completely. Unfortunately for User A and the power company, User D farmed land downstream from the power facilities and had relied upon diverting the 12 cfs that had historically

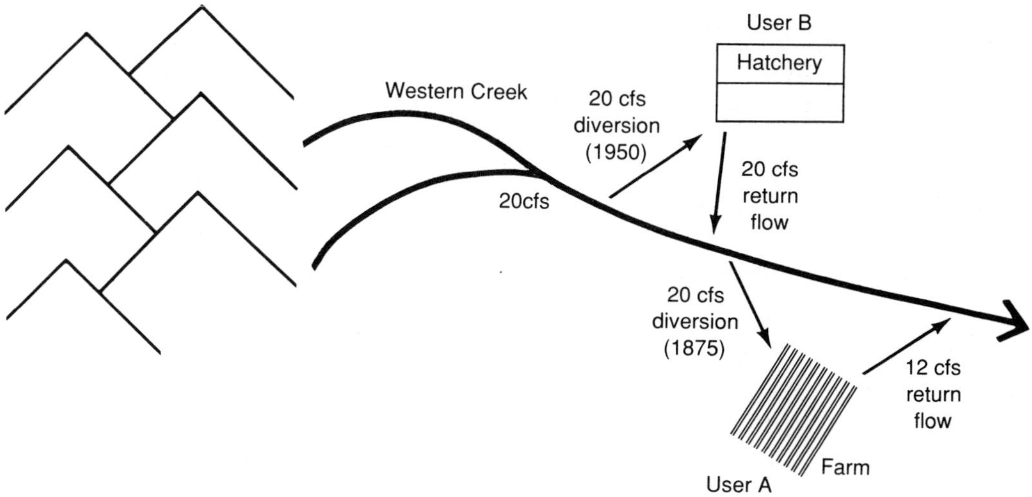

Figure 3-1. Initial Compatible Uses.

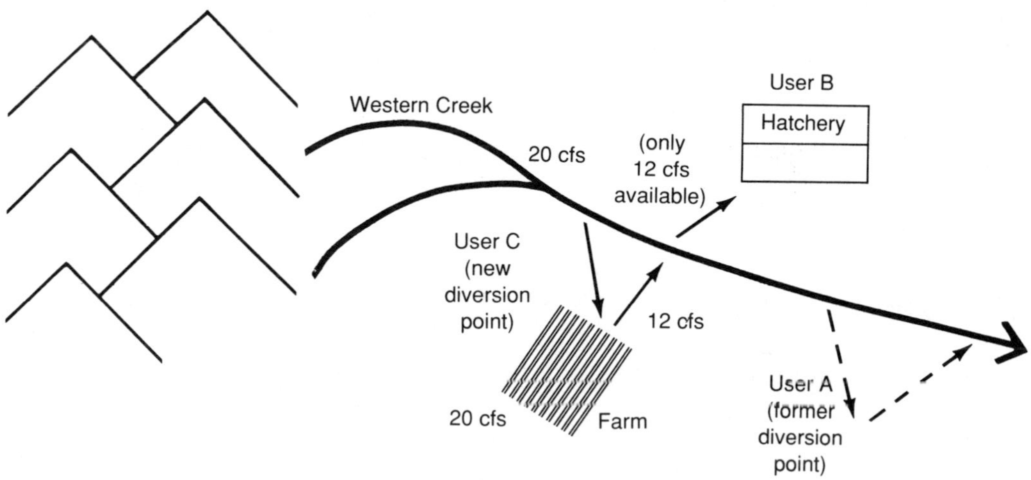

Figure 3-2. Change in Point of Diversion.

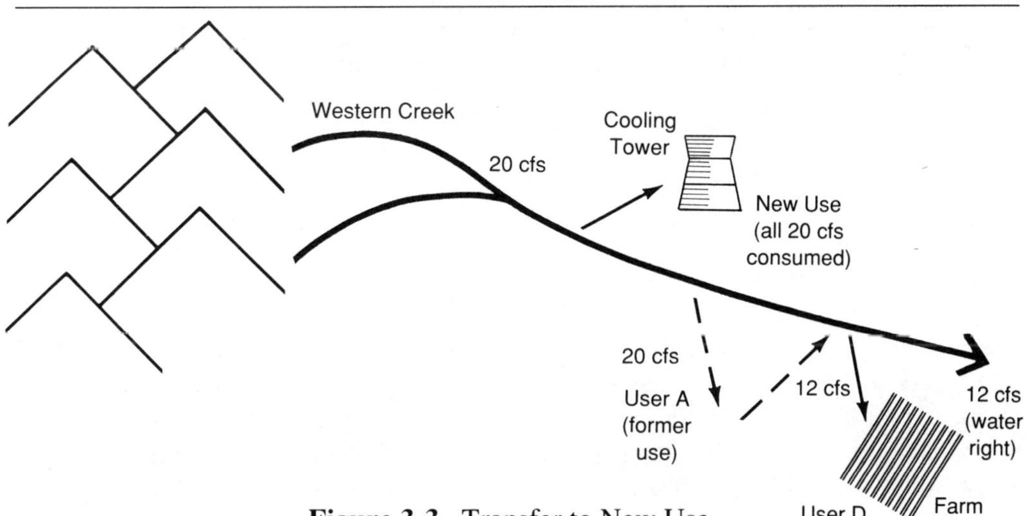

Figure 3-3. Transfer to New Use.

returned to the creek from User A's farm. Consequently, any transfer of User A's water right to a different use would be limited by the requirement that 12 cfs of historic return flow remain in the stream in order to satisfy User D's right. This would limit the power company to consuming only 8 cfs of User A's water right in the cooling tower, and it would have to find an additional source for its remaining water needs.

Historic Consumptive Use

Throughout the West, junior users receive a large portion of their water supply from the return flows of senior water users. When a change of use for a senior water right is proposed, therefore, courts and water administrators generally look to the historic consumptive use associated with the right rather than its decreed rate of withdrawal. In many instances only this consumptive use component can be transferred for other purposes, since junior users along the stream already have a right to use the return flows that historically have resulted from the senior diversion. When a court assesses a proposed change of a senior irrigation right, the court must determine such things as historic cropping patterns, the amount of land formerly irrigated, and the meteorological patterns of the area. This information helps the court establish how much of the senior water right historically was consumed through irrigation. This amount then becomes the measure of the transferable right that may be consumed for other purposes.

3-5. ADMINISTRATION

It quickly becomes apparent in reviewing the elements of state water law that river basins throughout the West are filled with a complex brew of transferred uses, abandoned waters, conditional rights, senior withdrawals, changed diversion points, junior users and forfeited rights. Riparian rights recognized in some western states and many senior rights established prior to the statutes requiring permit applications further complicate western state water law. Moreover, title to water may become hazy as deaths, sales and transfers of land and water occur over the decades.

Prioritizing the Rights

State water officials have wrestled with alternatives to sort through the various rights. "General stream adjudications" have been a popular and relatively effective means through which to establish respective rights in a particular basin. The process generally involves joining all parties with a legal interest in the basin's waters into a single proceeding and prioritizing their rights after a thorough analysis of all the claims. Requiring permits for any new rights and changes of use is another popular mechanism implemented by states to aid in the prioritization process. The permitting procedure can be taken a step further by making senior water rights holders apply for retroactive permits in order to maintain their lawful appropriations. A further alternative is to require all users to file individual applications with the appropriate court. This method also has proven an effective, although somewhat cumbersome, way of prioritizing water uses and changes.

Making the Call

Such prioritization of water rights is only the first step in the complex task of administering water use. The real work takes place out along the stream banks where often thousands of headgates must be operated to insure that a limited stream flow goes to the lawfully entitled users. The basic system for controlling the headgates is similar in most western states. The state agency responsible for water administration generally employs a number of individuals who are each charged with the duty of controlling diversions within a specific region of the state. These individuals (called water masters, ditch riders, water commissioners, and other assorted names) usually are residents of the area and are thoroughly familiar with the local water situation. When they receive a call from a senior user who is not receiving sufficient water, they must determine whose diversion is to be curtailed, and then act accordingly. Sometimes such action merely involves a telephone call to the appropriate junior users, telling them to close their headgates so that the seniors receive their rightful supply. In many instances, however, the junior users are not particularly cooperative in shutting off the water important to their livelihoods, and the water masters must themselves do the physical act of curtailing the out-of-priority diversions. It is not an easy job, nor one of the safest positions in state government.

Although practical difficulties exist, once the priorities are established and the water master develops a routine for a locale, the prior appropriation system provides a straightforward means of allocating limited stream flows. When a shortage occurs, the most junior users are curtailed in sequence until the "call" comes off the river. Junior users bear the entire burden during times of shortfalls. The water master must keep track of all the lawful uses and changes to ensure that the limited stream flows are being distributed correctly.

Throughout the West, junior water rights holders became tired of having their headgates closed off from thirsty fields in the latter part of the irrigation season as streams cycled into their low flow regime. Many of these farmers solved the dilemma by drilling wells to supplement their late season supply. Other farmers also tapped into ground water in order to open up new land in areas where the stream flows were appropriated fully. These developments have resulted in undermining the growing optimism of state water officials who had begun to hope that finally they were getting the administration of water rights under control. Ground water indeed complicates the picture.

3-6. GROUND WATER REGULATION

Thousands of large capacity wells were drilled into aquifers after World War II to provide irrigation water to millions of acres. It was not until the 1960s, however, that the impact of ground water development became a major concern. The impacts of ground water withdrawals fell into two categories. First, the decline of the ground water level in some ancient aquifers made states aware of the need to regulate withdrawals from this nonrenewable resource. Second, scientists and water officials began to understand the hydraulic connection between shallow ground water and surface streams. This led to the realization that, in many regions of the West, ground water pumping was robbing senior water users of their surface rights.

The responses of the states to these dilemmas have been varied. In order to extend the life of finite aquifers and to protect existing wells from interference, many western states have enacted statutes and regulations limiting new withdrawals. The more difficult task, however, has been attempting to regulate ground water withdrawals that impact surface streams. As explained in the following section, effective regulation of wells in order to protect surface rights is inhibited by limited scientific knowledge and by economic realities.

Protecting Surface Rights From Well Withdrawals

The English common law that was carried to North America gave landowners absolute control over ground water beneath their acreage. American courts slightly modified the unbridled right to pump water, requiring simply that the use be "reasonable." Under this reasonableness standard, the thousands of wells that were drilled in the mid-twentieth century in the West were allowed to operate so long as they did not waste the ground water blatantly.

It soon became apparent, however, that such a standard was not appropriate in the West. As stated in the 1973 National Water Commission Report to the President and the Congress:

> In several Western States, notably Arizona, Colorado, and New Mexico, heavy use of ground water caused reduced flows in rivers that form the source of supply for surface water appropriators with much earlier priorities. Serious difficulties arise in attempting to identify particular pumpers who are responsible and to determine the amounts by which each is depleting the surface stream. It may be equally difficult to identify the surface rights that have been injured, since the stream may have been losing water to ground water diversions over extended periods of time.[21]

Awareness of the problem led western legislatures and water officials to modify ground water law in an attempt to have it address modern needs. The task has been neither easy nor totally successful. The main problem stems from the lag time associated with a well's operation. Once a well starts pumping, it may take days or even decades before its impact is felt on surface streams. The pumping gradually lowers the ground water table which eventually causes stream flow to seep into the ground. (*See* Chapter 6 for a more detailed discussion of ground and surface water interrelatedness.) Conversely, the depletions to the stream caused by the lowered water table may continue for days or decades after the pumping is terminated. Wells, therefore, cannot be administered like surface headgates when they are called out-of-priority. In most cases, shutting off a well during the late summer shortage would not make water available to the senior user until long after the irrigation season has ended.

The simple administrative solution to such a problem is to prohibit all pumping from junior wells in overappropriated basins of the West. From a political and economic standpoint, however, such an option is not feasible: too many farmers, ranchers and municipalities are dependent upon out-of-priority well withdrawals. As a consequence, state officials have made attempts to integrate ground water into the prior appropriation system in some fashion that allows for continued use of wells while protecting surface rights.

A common first step in this process has been for states to exempt certain small capacity wells from administration. This provides for unrestricted pumping for uses such as domestic and livestock, based upon the assumption that the effect of such withdrawals on surface rights is minimal. Limits may be put on the size of the installed pump or on the total amount of water that may be withdrawn annually.

Many different approaches have been pursued to mitigate the impacts large capacity wells have on surface waters. For instance, attempts were made in the South Platte Basin to allow for unrestricted early season pumping, followed by curtailment of wells on certain dates during the summer in accordance with their distance from the river. A simpler approach has been taken in the upper Arkansas River area. There, existing wells are allowed to pump for only three days each week, while approval for proposed wells is predicated on the owner finding a means for augmenting the stream flow that will be depleted by the pumping. Means for augmentation may include buying out and retiring senior surface rights, providing for reservoir storage, or importing water from a basin that is not overappropriated. Provisions for well augmentation are becoming popular in western basins for allowing out-of-priority wells to operate while still protecting senior surface rights.

The Tributary/Nontributary Distinction

If a well is a great distance from any natural stream, a state may consider that the ground water that it pumps is "nontributary." In such an instance, the state will not regulate pumping of the well in order to protect senior surface rights. The question that each state faces in this approach is a determination of where the tributary/nontributary distinction is drawn. Should a ground water user have to go to the expense of augmenting today's well pumping when the depletive effect on the stream will not occur for hundreds of years? Most state officials would agree that such a requirement would be a waste of current resources in order to protect surface water users of future centuries. But what if the impact of current ground water pumping would rob surface users in 50 years? Or in 5 years?

State courts have faced such an issue on a number of occasions. An early Colorado case held that a well 13 miles from any river and with a pumping impact that would not be felt for 40 years by surface users was nonetheless tributary and must be regulated within the prior appropriation system.[22] In a later case, however, the Colorado Supreme Court chose to deem ground water pumping "nontributary" when impacts would not be felt by surface users for more than a century. In deciding not to protect surface rights from the delayed effects of such ground water pumping, the court offered the following justification:

> By the time the rivers are affected by the pumping from this basin [100 years], we have little doubt but what scientific progress will have solved many of the problems caused by the failure of this water to then reach the stream.[23]

Although other state regulatory schemes may handle conjunctive management of tributary ground water and surface streams somewhat differently than Colorado, each regulatory strategy reflects the need for improved technology—as well as a bit of wishful thinking.

Nontributary Pumping Restriction

If a particular well is deemed nontributary, it is not automatically free from regulation. True, the well is not administered within the prior appropriation system in order to protect surface rights; but it still faces pumping restrictions designed to prolong the life of nontributary aquifers. As states became aware of declining water tables in major aquifers (*e.g.*, the Ogallala Formation), many took actions to protect the economies based upon the limited ground water supply.

Typical regulatory schemes attempt to limit nontributary well diversions in order to maintain the water table level within economic pumping costs for a reasonable period of time. For instance, in one region of the West, new ground water appropriations will be denied if, in addition to existing wells, the proposed withdrawals will deplete the ground water within a three-mile radius more than 40% in 25 years. The 40% drop in the ground water level was selected to reflect a limit at which pumping costs would become prohibitive, while the 25-year parameter represents the average period needed for paying off irrigation wells and equipment.[24]

Another regulatory scheme prohibits new appropriations if annual declines in the nontributary water table exceed 2.5 feet;[25] while a third limits declines to 1% per year of the total nontributary ground water underlying the well owner's land.[26] This latter scheme was attacked by landowners as unlawfully infringing upon their rights of ownership to the underground waters. The Colorado Supreme Court, however, struck down their argument by pointing out that

> given the state's plenary control over development of water law, the traditional property concept of fee ownership is of limited usefulness as applied to nontributary ground water and serves to mislead rather than to advance understanding in considering public and private rights to utilization of this unique resource.[27]

3-7. ROLE OF ENVIRONMENTAL REGULATION

A discussion of state water law would be incomplete if it failed to mention environmental regulation. Water quantity and quality are controlled by numerous federal statutes, such as the Clean Water Act and the Safe Drinking Water Act.

Some of the federal statutes establish federal permitting and regulatory procedures. Others establish minimum federal environmental requirements and allow states (and, in some statutes, tribes) to implement and enforce the federal standards. Typically, before a state can gain federal approval to implement and enforce the federal environmental law, the state must adopt its own laws and regulatory program to establish the power and framework to implement the federal standards.

The prior appropriation doctrine remains the centerpiece of western state water law. Yet, federal and state environmental laws that impact water quantity and quality now play a significant role and have new implications for ground and surface water management. Today's tribal water manager must be familiar with these new and sometimes complex requirements. A coordinated approach to water management recognizes the complexities of environmental regulatory programs. Chapter 11 provides details on the regulatory implications of water use options.

3-8. CONCLUSION

The Colorado Supreme Court referred to "the state's plenary [absolute] control over development of water law." Although the states' ability to mold the development of the prior appropriation doctrine is unquestioned, the Colorado justices exaggerated their power regarding the course of water law in the West. With the advent of the twentieth century—and the *Winters* decision—the states were shown clearly that they did not have control over the development of law regarding tribal waters or over federal rights.

REFERENCE NOTES

1. 5 Cal. 140 (1855).
2. *Id.* at 146.
3. *Id.* at 146.
4. *Id.* at 147 ["*qui prior est in tempore potior est injure*"].
5. 6 Colo. 443, 444 (1882).
6. *Id.* at 446-47.
7. *Empire Water & Power Co. v. Cascade Town Co.*, 205 F. 123, 129 (8th Cir. 1913).
8. *See, e.g., Hennings v. Water Resources Dept.*, 662 P.2d 333 (Or. App. 1981).
9. Colo. Const. art. XVI, § 6.
10. Wash. Rev. Code Ann. § 90.54.020(1).
11. *State v. McLean*, 308 P.2d 983, 987 (N.M. 1957).
12. Or. Rev. Stat. § 540.610(1).
13. Colo. Rev. Stat. § 37-92-102(3).
14. Colo. Const. art. XVI, § 6.
15. 594 P.2d 570 (Colo. 1979).
16. *National Audubon Society v. Superior Court of Alpine County*, 33 Cal. 3d 419 (1983), *cert. denied*, 464 U.S. 977 (1983). *See also United States v. State Water Resources Control Board*, 182 Cal. App. 3d 82 (1986).
17. *Id.* at 33 Cal. 3d 431.

18. *Id.* at 33 Cal. 3d 446.
19. *Id.* at 33 Cal. 3d 447.
20. *Salt River Valley Users' Ass'n v. Kovacovich*, 411 P.2d 201 (Ariz. Ct. App. 1966).
21. National Water Comm'n, WATER POLICIES FOR THE FUTURE—FINAL REPORT TO THE PRESIDENT AND TO THE CONGRESS OF THE UNITED STATES at 234 (1973).
22. *Hall v. Kuiper*, 510 P.2d 329 (Colo. 1973).
23. *Kuiper v. Lundvall*, 529 P.2d 1328, 1331 (1975).
24. *See Fundingsland v. Colorado Ground Water Commission*, 468 P.2d 838 (Colo. 1970).
25. Rules promulgated pursuant to N.M. Stat. Ann. § 72-12-12.
26. Colo. Rev. Stat. § 37-90-137(4).
27. *Colorado v. Southwestern Colorado Water Conservation District*, 671 P.2d 1294, 1316 (Colo. 1983).

SUGGESTED READINGS

For a good overview of water law concepts, *see* David H. Getches, WATER LAW IN A NUTSHELL (1984). For those with interest in more detail, R.E. Clarke's seven-volume treatise on WATERS AND WATER RIGHTS (1967) (with pocket parts) provides a comprehensive guide. Finally, Steven J. Shupe's article on *Waste in Western Water Law: A Blueprint for Change*, 61 OR. L. REV. 483 (1982) helps to put state water law systems in modern perspective.

Chapter 4

The Source and Scope of Indian Water Rights

4-1. CONGRESSIONAL DEFERENCE TO STATE WATER LAW

It is understandable that in the late 1800s states had come to believe that they had absolute power over the development of water law. As the prior appropriation doctrine developed, the states initially worried about the federal government's legal position on water, particularly regarding the flows that arose on federal lands. State water users commonly appropriated the water that ran through the public domain and were concerned that the United States government might choose to interfere with the custom of prior appropriation. The federal government's authority to do so was stated clearly in the Constitution under the property clause:

> The Congress shall have Power to dispose of and make all needful Rules and Regulations respecting the Territory or other Property belonging to the United States; . . . .[1]

Also, the United States could invoke the supremacy clause to override the state systems that had developed for allocating water if they intruded upon federal rights:

> This Constitution, and the Laws of the United States which shall be made in Pursuance thereof; and all Treaties made, or which shall be made, under the Authority of the United States, shall be the Supreme Law of the Land; and the Judges in every State shall be bound thereby, any Thing in the Constitution or Laws of any State to the Contrary notwithstanding.[2]

States also were concerned that the commerce clause[3] and the power it gave to the Congress over navigable waters could be invoked to control the allocation of river flows. Congress, however, soon passed legislation that allayed these fears of federal intrusion into the development of state water law. In the Act of July 26, 1866, the United States acquiesced in the way that miners and others were appropriating the water from federal lands. After declaring that the mineral lands in the public domain were open to exploration and to occupation by all citizens, Congress provided that

> [w]henever, by priority of possession, rights to the use of water for mining, agricultural, manufacturing or other purposes, have vested and accrued, and the same are recognized and acknowledged by the local customs, laws and

decisions of courts, the possessors and owners of such vested rights shall be maintained and protected in the same.[4]

Further congressional deference to state systems of water appropriation came in 1870. The Act of July 9, 1870 made clear that all federal grants of lands and homesteads to private individuals "shall be subject to any vested and accrued water rights, or right to ditches and reservoirs used in connection with such water rights."[5] Then in 1877, Congress adopted a bill that legally severed the waters from the public domain lands and gave state law the control over the distribution and use of such waters.[6] The United States Supreme Court, in looking at the Desert Land Act of 1887 a few decades later, stated that the measure's effect was to make water "subject to the plenary control of the designated states, . . . with the rights in each [state] to determine for itself to what extent the rule of appropriation or the common-law rule in respect to riparian rights should obtain."[7]

So, state officials entered the twentieth century with little doubt that they controlled the use of water. Then, in 1908 the *Winters* holding came along to demonstrate the error of such a conclusion.

4-2. THE POWER OF THE *WINTERS* DOCTRINE

In 1888, the Fort Belknap Indian Reservation was established in the territory of Montana. This reservation had been carved out of a much larger parcel of land that had been occupied by several tribes in accordance with an earlier treaty approved by Congress in 1874. The northern boundary of the new reservation extended to the middle of the channel of the Milk River, diversions from which were needed for successful farming in this arid region of Montana. An Indian water project was initiated in 1898 to withdraw 120 cfs (cubic per second) from the river for irrigation purposes.

The problem with this plan was that 120 cfs was no longer regularly available from the Milk River during the farming season. After the tribal land base had been diminished in 1888, many non-Indians settled in the area upstream of the reservation and began diverting large amounts of flow from the river. Since these farmers had started irrigating prior to the Indian project of 1898, they believed that they were entitled to the flow under the prior appropriation doctrine. The tribes disagreed. Consequently the United States, acting on behalf of the tribes, sued to stop the upstream users from interfering with the ability of the reservation Indians to divert 120 cfs. Success for the tribe, of course, meant shutting down the existing upstream diversions during times of shortages in the Milk River. It was a controversial case, and one which soon found its way to the United States Supreme Court. (*Winters v. United States* (1908).[8])

The Opinion

Although its opinion was somewhat ambiguous and inartfully written, the Supreme Court made its ultimate ruling clear: the Indians had a superior right to use the limited waters of the Milk River. This right had been reserved and the tribes' waters were not subject to use under the state system. The prior appropriation doctrine did not apply to the situation, and the earlier, upstream users had to defer to the reserved rights of the tribes.

Reservation by the Tribes

The ambiguity in the holding involved the nature of the water reservation that existed to protect tribal use. In the early portion of the opinion, the Court seemed to be building off its recent decision in *United States v. Winans* (1905),[9] where it had stated that a "treaty was not a grant of rights to the Indians, but a grant of rights from them. . . ." In other words, a tribe had historic rights to use the resources of its native lands and gave them up only to the extent that the tribe intended to grant away such rights through a treaty. As the *Winters* opinion pointed out, it cannot be presumed that the Indians in an arid region would have intended to give away rights to water in treating with the United States:

> The lands were arid and, without irrigation, were practically valueless. And yet, it is contended, the means of irrigation were deliberately given up by the Indians and deliberately accepted by the Government. . . .The Indians had command of the lands and the waters—command of all their beneficial use, whether kept for hunting, "and grazing roving herds of stock," or turned to agriculture and the arts of civilization. Did they give up all this? Did they reduce the area of their occupation and give up the waters which made it valuable or adequate? . . . If it were possible to believe affirmative answers, we might also believe that the Indians were awed by the power of the Government or deceived by its negotiators. Neither view is possible.[10]

Reservation by the United States

The *Winters* Court then shifted to a discussion of the federal government's authority to reserve waters at the time of the establishment of the land reservation:

> The power of the government to reserve the waters and exempt them from appropriation under the state laws is not denied, and could not be. [Cites omitted.] That the government did reserve them we have decided, and for a use which would be necessarily continued through the years. This was done May 1, 1888, and it would be extreme to believe that within a year [when Montana was granted statehood] Congress destroyed the reservation and took from the Indians the consideration of their grant, leaving them a barren waste. . . .[11]

Regardless of which source of authority—tribal or federal—the reserved water rights sprang from, the *Winters* case gave the Fort Belknap tribes a right superior to the non-Indians who had been using the Milk River for irrigation. The case also established a doctrine of major importance to tribes, with significant repercussions for other western water users as well. Decades passed, however, before the *Winters* doctrine again reached the Supreme Court for further refinement.

4-3. RELEVANT TENETS OF FEDERAL INDIAN LAW

Before leaping into the year 1963 for additional discussion of the *Winters* doctrine, it is useful to take a brief look at the general provisions of federal Indian law that lay behind the Court's decision in *Winters*. First, Indian tribes are independent sovereigns that possess all governmental powers except those that Congress clearly and specifically has abolished or those powers that have been impliedly lost as a result of the overriding sovereignty of the United States.[12] The powers decreed lost by implication are very limited and, to date, include only the powers to have relations with foreign nations, to dispose of tribal land without federal consent, and to exercise criminal jurisdiction over non-Indians.[13]

A second tenet of federal Indian law is that unclear provisions in treaties are to be interpreted in favor of the tribes. One reason for this rule, espoused by the Supreme Court on several occasions (including in both *Winters* and *Winans*, above), is that the language of the signed treaties was often foreign to the tribes. A third principle is that only Congress, not state government, has the power under the Constitution to "regulate Commerce with . . . the Indian Tribes."[14] Finally, a trust relationship exists between the tribes and the United States, imposing a duty upon the federal government to deal fairly with Indians.[15]

This trust responsibility presumably should have encouraged the United States to help the tribes obtain their lawful water supplies following the *Winters* decision in 1908, but such was clearly not the case. *Winters* rights received relatively little attention from the courts for decades, largely due to the fact that, in practical terms, the tribes were not serious competitors for water. In particular, federal reclamation programs provided water projects for non-Indian farmers, but not for Indians. The National Water Commission made this observation in its 1973 Final Report:

> Following *Winters*, more than 50 years elapsed before the Supreme Court again discussed significant aspects of Indian water rights. During most of this 50-year period, the United States was pursuing a policy of encouraging the settlement of the West and the creation of family-sized farms on its arid lands. In retrospect, it can be seen that this policy was pursued with little or no regard for Indian water rights and the *Winters* doctrine. With the encouragement, or at least the cooperation, of the Secretary of the Interior—the many large irrigation projects were constructed on streams that flowed through or bordered Indian Reservations, sometimes above and more often below the Reservations. With few exceptions the projects were planned and built by the Federal Government without any attempt to define, let alone protect, prior rights that Indian tribes might have had in the waters used for the projects. . . . In the history of the United States Government's treatment of Indian tribes, its failure to protect Indian water rights for use on the Reservations it set aside for them is one of the sorrier chapters.[16]

4-4. REFINEMENT UNDER *ARIZONA v. CALIFORNIA*

The case that ended the 50-year drought of Indian water decisions in the Supreme Court was *Arizona v. California* (*Arizona v. California I*, 1963).[17] This case, however, was not strictly an Indian law matter. Rather, it encompassed a broad spectrum of issues surrounding the overall allocation of Colorado River water between the various southwestern states, the tribes, and the federal government. The Supreme Court has "original jurisdiction" to hear such conflicts that involve interstate water; consequently the Justices retained a Special Master to assess the complicated facts and to make a preliminary determination of law in the matter. Of particular concern was how much of the Colorado River flow allocated to the lower basin (totaling an average of 7,500,000 acre-feet annually) belonged to the tribes. The Court summarized this aspect of the case and the Master's findings as follows:

> The Government, on behalf of five Indian Reservations in Arizona, California, and Nevada, asserted rights to water in the mainstream of the Colorado River. The Colorado River Reservation, located partly in Arizona and partly in California, is the largest. It was originally created by an Act of Congress in 1865, but its area was later increased by Executive Order. Other reservations were created by Executive Orders and amendments to them, ranging in dates from 1870 to 1907. The Master found both as a matter of fact and law that when the United States created these reservations or added to them, it reserved not only land but also the use of enough water from the Colorado to irrigate the irrigable portions of the reserved lands. The aggregate quantity of water which the Master held was reserved for all the reservations is about 1,000,000 acre-feet, to be used on around 135,000 irrigable acres of land.[18]

Rejecting Equitable Apportionment

Arizona pursued a number of arguments before the Supreme Court in an attempt to reverse the Master's findings. First, it asserted that, in the process of allocating limited waters between the competing governments, the tribes should be viewed the same as the states. When one state is fighting another state for a river supply, the Supreme Court uses the doctrine of equitable apportionment—which means simply that after considering the facts, the Court will rule what it deems as being most fair to each of the states. In holding against Arizona's argument that conflicts involving tribal waters should be judged by this standard, the Court concluded:

> An Indian Reservation is not a State. And while Congress has sometimes left Indian Reservations considerable power to manage their own affairs, we are not convinced by Arizona's argument that each reservation is so much like a State that its rights to water should be determined by the doctrine of equitable apportionment.[19]

Upholding the *Winters* Doctrine

Arizona's second argument was that a *Winters* reservation of water rights did not occur because a large portion of the reservations had been established simply by executive order of the President, not by treaty and congressional approval. The Court found this argument to be without merit, noting that land and water reserved by executive order is just as valid a reservation as those negotiated by treaty and approved by Congress. The Court next disposed of a third argument involving the protection of states' rights in navigable rivers, citing the overriding powers granted to the United States by the Constitution.

The Court moved to the more basic arguments involving the *Winters* doctrine:

> Arizona also challenges the Master's holding as to the Indian Reservations on two other grounds: first, that there is a lack of evidence showing that the United States in establishing the reservations intended to reserve water for them; second, that even if water was meant to be reserved the Master has awarded too much water. We reject both of these contentions. Most of the land in these reservations is and always has been arid. If the water necessary to sustain life is to be had, it must come from the Colorado River or its tributaries. It can be said without overstatement that when the Indians were put on these reservations they were not considered to be located in the most desirable area of the Nation. It is impossible to believe that when Congress created the great Colorado River Indian Reservation and when the Executive Department of this Nation created the other reservations they were unaware that most of the lands were of the desert kind—hot, scorching sands—and that water from the river would be essential to the life of the Indian people and to the animals they hunted and the crops they raised. . . . The Court in *Winters* concluded that the Government, when it created that Indian Reservation, intended to deal fairly with the Indians by reserving for them the waters without which their lands would have been useless. *Winters* has been followed by this Court as recently as 1939 in *United States v. Powers*, 305 U.S. 527 [holding that non-Indian successor to allotted lands may share in the reservation's waters]. We follow it now and agree that the United States did reserve the water rights for the Indians effective as of the time the Indian Reservations were created.[20]

The Source of the Water Reservation

This finding squarely confirmed the strength of the *Winters* doctrine to protect tribal waters for use on the reservation. The Court, however, focused solely on the power of the federal government to reserve the waters for the Indians, rather than looking to ancient water rights that were never relinquished by the tribes. As a consequence, the tribal water right in this case took a priority date coinciding with the establishment of the reservation, rather than extending back through history and, thereby, being senior to all non-Indian appropriative claims. Under some circumstances, such a distinction may prove important and tribes may want to assert their right dating back to "time immemorial."

Quantifying the Right

The final major Indian issue examined by the Supreme Court in its *Arizona v. California* decision involved quantifying the amount of water reserved. The Master had searched for a fair means by which to determine the amount of water that had been reserved along with the land and had come up with the concept of "practicably irrigable acreage." By identifying all the acreage within the reservations that was susceptible to irrigation and quantifying the corresponding water needs, the Master arrived at a total annual tribal water right of 1,000,000 acre-feet. This amounted to a significant portion of the overall water available in the lower Colorado River basin, thus Arizona strongly objected to the standard set forth by the Master. The Supreme Court, however, did not find the state's argument compelling:

> We also agree with the Master's conclusion as to the quantity of water intended to be reserved. He found that the water was intended to satisfy the future as well as the present needs of the Indian Reservations and ruled that enough water was reserved to irrigate all the practicably irrigable acreage on the reservations. Arizona, on the other hand, contends that the quantity of water reserved should be measured by the Indians' "reasonably foreseeable needs," which, in fact, means by the number of Indians. How many Indians there will be and what their future needs will be can only be guessed. We have concluded, as did the Master, that the only feasible and fair way by which reserved water for the reservations can be measured is irrigable acreage. The various acreages of irrigable land which the Master found to be on the different reservations we find to be reasonable.[21]

The "practicably irrigable acreage" (PIA) standard has become the major test for assessing the quantity of water reserved for tribal purposes. It involves a scientific assessment of the water and lands of a reservation in order to identify where crops feasibly can be grown under irrigation. (Chapter 10 provides a detailed description of the elements that go into a PIA determination.) Although PIA is now used widely for reservations where farming is a major activity, other standards for quantifying the amount of water needed by a reservation also may be applied. For instance, stream flow may be claimed in an amount necessary to protect religious values or to maintain viable fisheries.[22]

Quantification of tribal water rights under PIA and other standards is still in its formative stage, and new cases are expected to refine the standard as tribes increasingly assert their rights under the *Winters* doctrine.

4-5. FEDERAL RESERVED WATER RIGHTS

Many non-Indians with interests in water were dismayed by *Arizona v. California I*. They were disheartened by both the affirmation of the *Winters* doctrine and the quantity of the Indian rights established under the PIA standard. These holdings, however, were only the beginning of their troubles. Toward the end of its opinion in the *Arizona v. California I* case, the Court concluded that the principle of reserved water rights "was equally applicable to other federal establishments such as

National Recreation Areas and National Forests."[23] In other words, federal water rights were reserved, independently of state appropriation systems, at the time that the federal lands were removed from the public domain. This concept has been refined in the courts over the past two decades, with potentially significant impacts on the future of Indian *Winters* rights.

Growth of the Concept

The Court's acknowledgment in 1963 of federal reserved rights should not have come as a complete surprise to proponents of the prior appropriation doctrine. Two previous Supreme Court cases had hinted that such rights existed. In 1899, the Court had issued an opinion, in part favorable to western water interests, that recognized a state's power to override the common law riparian doctrine through establishment of the prior appropriation system.[24] In the dicta (that is, discussion not essential to the holding) of that case, however, the Court identified a limitation that foreshadowed the coming of the federal reserved rights doctrine:

> [I]n the absence of specific statutory authority from Congress a State cannot by its legislation destroy the right of the United States, as the owner of lands bordering on a stream, to the continued flow of its waters; so far at least as may be necessary for the beneficial uses of the government property.[25]

An additional glimpse of federal reserved water rights was seen in *Federal Power Commission v. Oregon*.[26] In that 1955 case the Court held that a federal reservation of a power site limited the use of waters under state law. The federal reserved water rights concept then took root in *Arizona v. California* before breaking into full bloom in the 1976 case of *Cappaert v. United States*.[27]

Cappaert v. United States

Devil's Hole National Monument was established near Death Valley, California by presidential proclamation in 1952. It was set aside in order to preserve "unusual features of scenic, scientific and educational interest," including an underground pool containing the only remaining population of an ancient pupfish. In order to spawn, these fish needed the water level of the pool to remain above a certain ledge in the underground cavern.

In 1968, the Cappaerts began pumping ground water for their 12,000-acre ranch nearly two-and-a-half miles away. This ground water was connected to the source of the Devil's Hole pool, and by 1970 the pool had dropped below the level of the spawning ledge. The National Park Service protested the pumping and asserted that it had a reserved right to the water in the pool that could not be interfered with by the Cappaert wells.

In holding in favor of the National Park Service, the Court began by reviewing the basis of the reserved rights doctrine:

> This Court has long held that when the Federal Government withdraws its land from the public domain and reserves it for a federal purpose, the

> Government, by implication, reserves appurtenant water then unappropriated to the extent needed to accomplish the purpose of the reservation. In so doing the United States acquires a reserved right in unappropriated water which vests on the date of the reservation and is superior to the rights of future appropriators. Reservation of water rights is empowered by the Commerce Clause, Art. I, § 8, which permits federal regulation of navigable streams, and the Property Clause, Art. IV, § 3, which permits federal regulation of federal lands. The doctrine applies to Indian reservations and other federal enclaves, encompassing water rights in navigable and nonnavigable streams.[28]

The Court then proceeded to refine the doctrine in two ways. First, it limited the quantity of water associated with a reserved right to "that amount of water necessary to fulfill the purpose of the reservation, no more."[29] The Court also identified intent as being key in the initial determination of whether a federal reserved right exists:

> In determining whether there is a federally reserved water right implicit in a federal reservation of public land, the issue is whether the Government intended to reserve unappropriated and thus available water. Intent is inferred if the previously unappropriated waters are necessary to accomplish the purposes for which the reservation was created.[30]

Another issue raised in the case was whether ground water was encompassed in the reserved rights doctrine. The state of Nevada argued that the doctrine was limited to surface waters. The Court did not rule directly on point since it decided that the underground pool was technically surface water. It did state clearly, however, that ground water withdrawals could be regulated to protect reserved surface rights.

United States v. New Mexico (1978)

The next major test of the federal reserved rights doctrine took place when the United States claimed waters for the Gila National Forest in New Mexico. The Forest Service wanted instream flows for the preservation of the forest environment and asserted that such flows had been reserved by Congress. In rejecting this claim in *United States v. New Mexico* (1978),[31] the Supreme Court looked to congressional intent and concluded that preservation of the forest was not a primary purpose for which Congress had reserved the lands. Consequently, no reserved water rights could be established for secondary instream flow purposes in the national forests.

The Court also reiterated the standard set forth in *Cappaert* that a reserved water right was limited to the minimal need of the federal reservation:

> While many of the contours of what has come to be called the "implied-reservation-of-water doctrine" remain unspecified, the Court has repeatedly emphasized that Congress reserved "only that amount of water necessary to fulfill the purpose of the reservation, no more." [Cites omitted.] Each time this Court has applied the "implied-reservation-of-water doctrine," it has carefully examined both the asserted water right and the specific purposes for which the land was reserved, and concluded that without the water the purposes of the reservation would be entirely defeated.[32]

Implications for Indian Rights

Theoretically, the above-discussed restrictions on federal reserved rights should have no bearing on the future of the *Winters* doctrine. *Winters* rights are based upon potentially ancient claims and a broad range of Indian law tenets (*e.g.*, treaties construed in favor of tribes, trust responsibilities). Federal rights, on the other hand, spring solely from the powers of the United States over its property and commerce provided in the Constitution. (*See Cappaert* quote, above.) Despite these differences, the trend in the Supreme Court seems to be to merge these two concepts into the same category; thus, the federal restrictions may have a bearing on the *Winters* doctrine. In *Cappaert*, the Court referred to only one reserved rights doctrine, stating that it "applies to Indian reservations and other federal enclaves. . . ."[33] In *United States v. New Mexico*, the Court likewise treated Indian reservations simply as one more type of federally reserved land: "Substantial portions of the public domain have been withdrawn and reserved by the United States for use as Indian reservations, forest reserves, national parks, and national monuments."[34]

All of the repercussions of this trend remain to be seen. In one area, however, tribes have already experienced the negative effects of their *Winters* rights getting incorporated into the law of federal reserved waters. This area involves the important issue of state court jurisdiction over federal and Indian water claims.

4-6. COURT JURISDICTION

A common feature of many legal systems is the concept that a government cannot be sued by its citizens. This concept of "sovereign immunity" prevails in the United States and, under various circumstances, has protected federal, tribal and state governments from being brought into court. A government, however, can waive its immunity and consent to being sued and joined in court actions.

The McCarran Amendment

The sovereign immunity of the federal government proved very frustrating to states that wanted to include the United States in water adjudications—the United States could not be compelled to come to state court to have its rights determined relative to other water users of the region. The federal government's sovereign immunity in such matters was waived by Congress in 1952. Primarily through the efforts of western representatives, Congress consented to the federal government's being brought into state general stream adjudications. The waiver was enacted in the so-called McCarran Amendment:

> Consent is hereby given to join the United States as a defendant in any suit (1) for the adjudication of rights to the use of water of a river system or other source, or (2) for the administration of such rights, where it appears that the United States is the owner of or is in the process of acquiring water rights by appropriation under State law, by purchase, by exchange, or otherwise, and the United States is a necessary party to such suit. The

> United States, when a party to any such suit, shall (1) be deemed to have waived any right to plead that the State laws are inapplicable or that the United States is not amenable thereto by reason of its sovereignty, and (2) shall be subject to the judgments, orders, and decrees of the court having jurisdiction, and may obtain review thereof, in the same manner and to the same extent as a private individual under like circumstances: Provided, That no judgment for costs shall be entered against the United States in any such suit.[35]

In 1971, the Supreme Court ruled that, although the language of the McCarran Amendment was limited to general stream adjudications, it applies to suits involving federal reserved rights as well.[36] Consequently, all actions involving the quantification of federal water rights now may be brought in state court. This procedural rule does not affect the rule that federal law is to be used to quantify the United States' reserved rights; but it does hand over to state judges the power to determine the intent of Congress, the minimal need of a reservation, and the other questions involved in quantifying federal reserved rights. If the federal government is dissatisfied with the state trial judge's decision, appeals will be heard by the appropriate state supreme court and eventually by the United States Supreme Court—if the Justices have the time and desire to hear the matter.

Application to Tribal Waters

Most observers agree that tribes will fare considerably better in federal, rather than state, courts. Federal courts are believed to be more sympathetic toward federally based *Winters* rights, and state judges presumably are more likely to be influenced by state laws and policies. The question of court jurisdiction over Indian reserved rights was first treated by the Supreme Court in 1976 in *Colorado River Conservation District v. United States*.[37] *Colorado River* held that the McCarran Amendment, enacted by Congress in 1952, required the removal of an Indian water rights case to a Colorado state court simultaneously conducting a comprehensive adjudication involving the same issues. *Colorado River* marked the first time an Indian water rights case was transferred to state court. The following chapter will analyze the major developments in Indian water law since *Colorado River* was decided in 1976.

REFERENCE NOTES

1. U.S. Const. art. IV, § 4.
2. *Id.* art. VI.
3. *Id.* art. I, § 8.
4. 14 Stat. 253.
5. 16 Stat. 218.
6. Act of March 3, 1877, 19 Stat. 377.
7. *California-Oregon Power Co. v. Beaver Portland Cement Co.*, 295 U.S. 142, 164 (1935).

8. 207 U.S. 564 (1908).
9. 198 U.S. 371 (1905).
10. 207 U.S. at 576.
11. *Id.* at 577.
12. *E.g., United States v. Wheeler*, 435 U.S. 313 (1978).
13. *Oliphant v. Suquamish Indian Tribe*, 435 U.S. 894 (1978).
14. U.S. Const. art. I, § 8.
15. *See* Cohen, HANDBOOK OF FEDERAL INDIAN LAW at 220-28 (1982 ed.).
16. National Water Comm'n, WATER POLICIES FOR THE FUTURE—FINAL REPORT TO THE PRESIDENT AND TO THE CONGRESS OF THE UNITED STATES at 474-75 (1973).
17. 373 U.S. 546 (1963); *decreed in final form at* 376 U.S. 340 (1964).
18. 373 U.S. at 595-96.
19. *Id.* at 597.
20. *Id* at 598-600.
21. 373 U.S. at 600-01.
22. *See United States v. Adair*, 478 F. Supp. 336, 350 (W.D. Or. 1979), 723 F.2d 1394 (9th Cir. 1983), *cert. denied*, 467 U.S. 1252 (1984); *Colville Confederated Tribes v. Walton*, 647 F.2d 42, 48 (9th Cir. 1981).
23. 373 U.S. at 601.
24. *United States v. Rio Grande Ditch & Irrigation Co.*, 174 U.S. 690 (1899).
25. *Id.* at 703.
26. 349 U.S. 435 (1955).
27. 426 U.S. 128 (1976).
28. *Id.* at 138.
29. *Id.* at 141.
30. *Id.* at 139.
31. 438 U.S. 696 (1978).
32. *Id.* at 700.
33. 426 U.S. at 138, quoted above (*see* footnote 29).
34. 696 U.S. at 699.
35. Codified at 43 U.S.C. § 666(a).
36. *United States v. District Court in and for the County of Eagle*, 401 U.S. 520 (1971).
37. 424 U.S. 800 (1976).

SUGGESTED READINGS

Felix S. Cohen's HANDBOOK OF FEDERAL INDIAN LAW (1982 ed.) provides a comprehensive treatise on Indian law concepts. For more details on tribal waters, *see* WHAT INDIAN WATER MEANS TO THE WEST by John Folk-Williams (1982) and INDIAN WATER RIGHTS IN THE WEST prepared for the Western Governors' Association by the Western States Water Council (1984). Also recommended are Miklas and Shupe, INDIAN WATER 1985: COLLECTED ESSAYS (1986) and Steven J. Shupe, *Water in Indian Country: From Paper Rights to a Managed Resource*, 57 U. COLO. L. REV. 561 (1986).

Chapter 5

Recent Judicial Decisions Involving Indian Water Rights

5-1. INTRODUCTION

Since the Supreme Court's 1976 *Colorado River* decision,[1] the dominant opinions involving Indian water rights were handed down in 1983, when the Supreme Court decided three cases that, taken together, are as significant as any in Indian law in the last several years. *Arizona v. San Carlos Apache Tribe of Arizona*,[2] as well as several recent lower court opinions, has provided continuing interpretation of the McCarran Amendment and its effect on Indian reserved water rights. *Arizona v. California* (*Arizona v. California II*)[3] and *Nevada v. United States*[4] involved the finality of judicial decrees quantifying Indian water rights. In general, these three decisions raised substantial procedural barriers for tribes but did not alter the traditional rules for determining the amount of water to which tribes are entitled under the *Winters* doctrine. Opinions by lower federal and state courts have dealt with the nature and extent of Indian water rights, regulation of water rights, and water rights on allotments. A more detailed discussion follows.

5-2. JURISDICTION AND PROCEDURE

The McCarran Amendment

State Adjudication of Water Rights: The San Carlos Decision

Arizona v. San Carlos Apache Tribe of Arizona[5] is the most recent Supreme Court opinion to deal with the jurisdictional issues raised by the McCarran Amendment, which waived the sovereign immunity of the United States in comprehensive state water adjudications. It provides a sequel to the Court's 1976 opinion in *Colorado River*. In *Colorado River* the Supreme Court had said that the McCarran Amendment evidenced a clear federal policy to allow states to adjudicate water rights, including those of the United States, to achieve "the avoidance of piecemeal adjudication of water rights in a river system." This general policy also applies to suits brought by the United States to adjudicate water rights.

The determination of when a federal court proceeding should be deferred in favor of a parallel state proceeding is to be based upon "considerations of wise judicial administration," rather than technical procedural rules of state and federal comity or abstention. Holding in *Colorado River* that the water suit at issue should be heard in state court, the Supreme Court cited several factors: the fact that the state court proceedings were fairly far along while the federal case had not progressed beyond filing; the comprehensive nature of the state proceedings; the avoidance of duplicative litigation that might yield inconsistent results; the extensive involvement of state water rights in the suit; the fact that the United States had participated in other water cases in Colorado state courts; and the convenience of the parties, many of whom were located 300 miles from the federal court in Denver.

The *Colorado River* opinion was viewed by some as an exception. Seven years later, however, the Supreme Court made clear in the *San Carlos* decision that in most cases, rather than in exceptional ones, a federal court should defer to a concurrent comprehensive state water rights adjudication, because "water rights adjudication is a virtually unique type of proceeding, and the McCarran Amendment is a virtually unique federal statute. . . ."[7]

Issues Raised in San Carlos

The two issues to be decided in *San Carlos* were: (1) whether a federal suit brought by an Indian tribe, rather than by the United States, raising only Indian claims is subject to dismissal in favor of a simultaneous state proceeding; and (2) whether the McCarran Amendment extends to "disclaimer" states. On the first issue the United States and the tribes argued that Indian rights traditionally have been left free of state interference, which may be inhospitable to Indian rights; that the McCarran Amendment expressly waived only the sovereign immunity of the United States, not of Indian tribes; that Indian rights generally are based upon federal rather than state law; and that, as a practical matter, Indian water rights do not need to be adjudicated together with state rights—they can be incorporated easily into the state decree at the conclusion of state proceedings. The Supreme Court rejected these arguments, stating:

> [C]oncurrent federal proceedings are likely to be duplicative and wasteful, generating, "additional litigation through permitting inconsistent dispositions of property." [Cite omitted.] Moreover, since a judgment by either court would ordinarily be *res judicata* [binding law] in the other, the existence of such concurrent proceedings creates the serious potential for spawning an unseemly and destructive race to see which forum can resolve the same issues first—a race contrary to the entire spirit of the McCarran Amendment and prejudicial, to say the least, to the possibility of reasoned decisionmaking by either forum. [Footnote omitted.][8]

The Court further stated that the McCarran Amendment "allows and encourages state courts to undertake the task of quantifying Indian water rights in the course of comprehensive water adjudications."[9] The Court noted, however, that federal courts do possess concurrent jurisdiction in Indian water cases, and that federal suits need not always be dismissed in favor of state proceedings if "wise judicial administration" dictates otherwise. Importantly, the Court made it clear that the

McCarran Amendment confers judicial jurisdiction only; Indian water rights continue to be determined by federal substantive law:

> We also emphasize, as we did in *Colorado River*, that our decision in no way changes the substantive law by which Indian rights in state water adjudications must be judged. State courts, as much as federal courts, have a solemn obligation to follow federal law. Moreover, any state court decision alleged to abridge Indian water rights protected by federal law can expect to receive, if brought for review before this Court, a particularized and exacting scrutiny commensurate with the powerful federal interest in safeguarding those rights from state encroachment.[10]

The Supreme Court also ruled in *San Carlos* that the McCarran Amendment applies to disclaimer states—those states admitted to the Union under federal enabling legislation that specifically reserved "absolute jurisdiction and control" over Indian lands to Congress, or whose state constitutions disclaimed state jurisdiction over Indian lands. The Court noted, however, that state courts have authority to resolve questions of state law, leaving open the possibility that a state court may interpret its constitutional disclaimer to bar McCarran Amendment jurisdiction over Indian water rights as a matter of state law.

At present, no state court has ruled that the permission conferred by the McCarran Amendment to adjudicate Indian water rights is barred by state law. Several suits have been brought by the United States, tribes and others in state courts seeking dismissal of state adjudications on jurisdictional and constitutional grounds. The Arizona Supreme Court recently ruled that neither the state's constitutional disclaimer nor due process issues raised by the participation of state agencies in state adjudicatory proceedings were constitutional impediments to state adjudication of Indian water rights.[11] And in December 1985, the Montana Supreme Court held that the disclaimer clause of Montana's Constitution does not prohibit the Montana Water Court from adjudicating Indian water rights and that, on its face, the water adjudication process provided for in the Montana Water Use Act is legally adequate to adjudicate federal and Indian reserved water rights.[12]

Deferring Federal Adjudication: Recent Decisions

Three recent federal court decisions have dealt with the issue of deferring a federal adjudication of Indian water rights in favor of a concurrent state court proceeding. Two of the district courts separated the Indian water rights issues in the cases, designating some issues for federal court determination and deferring to concurrent state proceedings on other issues.

Salt River Pima-Maricopa Indian Community v. United States (D. Ariz. 1985)[13] involved water rights claimed by the community from three sources. The court ruled that the community's *Winters* rights and its water rights obtained under a decree from a prior general adjudication should be enforced in an existing state proceeding. The Indian community's third claim was for a federal court review, under the Administrative Procedure Act, of a decision by the Secretary of the Interior to exclude Indian lands from participation in the Salt River Reclamation Project, and it involved charges of invidious discrimination. The community also asserted that the

Secretary had failed to designate a number of plots on the reservation and to provide for water rights to irrigate them in perpetuity, as required by a 1916 federal act. The Arizona district court stated, "This is more than a water rights adjudication action," because of the claims of invidious discrimination, and ruled that the determination of which Indian lands are entitled to water rights is a matter of federal agency action that should be decided by a federal court.

United States v. Adair[14] was decided by the Ninth Circuit Court of Appeals four months after *San Carlos*. In *Adair* the Ninth Circuit upheld the decision of the district court to determine the Klamath Tribe's reserved water rights in the federal proceeding; the district judge deferred actual quantification and administration of the water rights determined by the federal court to later proceedings to be conducted by the Oregon Water Resources Director. *Adair* involved a complex factual situation, since it was brought to determine whether and to what extent water rights reserved to the tribe in its 1864 Treaty survived termination of the tribe and sale of all its lands. A concurrent state adjudication involving the same issues was filed four months after *Adair*, and the state of Oregon also intervened in the federal suit as a defendant.

In ruling that the district court properly decided the federal issues in the case, the appellate court noted that the district court in the *San Carlos* case had itself decided to dismiss the action in favor of a state court adjudication. The court of appeals found that the decision to dismiss for reasons of judicial administration is to be decided on a case-by-case basis and is "largely committed to the discretion of the district court."[15]

In assessing how the interests of wise judicial administration would best be served, the court of appeals said:

> First, we note that the district court carefully tailored its exercise of jurisdiction to decide only the priority among water rights created under federal law. . . . Second, the contemporaneous state proceeding for adjudicating water rights was, and still is, nascent. Finally, the district court has taken evidence, heard extensive argument from all of the parties, and developed a multi-volumed record on which to base its decision of the water rights questions presented by this case. Both the individual defendants as well as the intervenor, State of Oregon, have been offered, and have taken, a full opportunity to participate in all aspects of this litigation. The district court's determination of water rights is more than "well enough along," it is complete. Given this factual setting, it is clear to us that neither the policies of the McCarran Amendment, nor the interest of wise judicial administration would be served by a decision from this court reversing and vacating the district court's judgment without reaching the merits. . . . Far from improperly intruding on the role of the state court, we find that in exercising federal jurisdiction in this fashion the district court coordinated its adjudication of water rights with adjudication by the state court so as to allow each forum to consider those issues most appropriate to its expertise.[16]

Other factors the court in *Adair* cited were: (1) that the case involved only rights derived from Indian reserved rights, and (2) that determination of the priority among reserved rights would require a separate proceeding in the state adjudication prior to the general quantification of water rights in the basin because reserved water rights are established by reference to the purpose of the reservation rather than by actual beneficial use of water.

Following *San Carlos*, the third case to decide questions of federal and state court jurisdiction over Indian water adjudications is *United States v. Bluewater-Toltec Irrigation District* (D.N.M. 1984).[17] In *Bluewater-Toltec* the district court rejected an attempt to "remove" a state adjudication involving Indian water rights to federal court, although a federal case to determine the same issues was already in progress when the state adjudication was initiated by defendants to the federal suit.

Much of the district court's decision was based on a narrow interpretation of technical rules of federal question removal: (1) that the state court actions were not properly removed to federal court because the plaintiffs in the state action (all private parties) did not claim a federal right as an essential element of their cases; and (2) that all defendants in the state cases had not joined with the United States in the removal petition. The court also decided to dismiss, rather than stay, a trespass claim by the United States against the defendants in the federal suit, pending the state court adjudication. The court reasoned that the federal trespass proceeding would be duplicative and that the "general adjudication will have a profound effect on the nature and extent of any claims made by the United States."[18]

The court in *Bluewater-Toltec* also ruled that the state water adjudication was comprehensive enough under the McCarran Amendment, although all the claimants were not named in the complaint. Additional water claimants are expected because New Mexico law allows them to be brought into the proceeding as they are identified.[19] The court further held that no separate waiver of sovereign immunity by the Acoma and Laguna Pueblos is necessary to include them in the state adjudication; the guardian relationship between them and the United States is sufficient to establish the United States as trustee for the pueblos for purposes of the McCarran Amendment.

Finality

During 1983 the Supreme Court handed down two major decisions concerning the finality of judicial decrees quantifying Indian water rights, *Arizona v. California II*[20] and *Nevada v. United States*.[21] Both cases indicate that quantification of Indian water rights in judicial decrees is likely to remain final.

The Importance of Certainty of Rights: Arizona v. California II

Arizona v. California II is an outgrowth of the original action in the Supreme Court brought in 1952 to determine the water rights of the states of Arizona, California, Nevada, Utah and New Mexico to the Colorado River. The United States intervened, seeking water rights for federal lands and for the Colorado River Tribes, the Fort Mojave Tribe, the Chemehuevi Tribe, the Cocopah Tribe and the Fort Yuma (Quechan) Tribe. After extensive and complex litigation the Court issued its decisions in 1963 and 1964, awarding the five Indian tribes present perfected water rights with priority dates as of the creation of their reservations, based upon the practicably irrigable acreage on the different reservations.[22] Article II(D)(5) of the decree stated that the quantities of water awarded the tribes "shall continue to be subject to appropriate adjustment by agreement or decree of this court in the event that the boundaries of the respective reservations are finally determined."

In 1977, the five Indian tribes intervened as parties in the litigation and sought to have the amounts of their water rights increased for: (1) "omitted lands" (*i.e.*, irrigable acres within the 1964 reservation boundaries but not claimed in the earlier litigation); and (2) "boundary lands" finally determined to be within the reservations.

The Court ruled against the tribes on the omitted lands issue, finding that reopening the original quantification of reserved water rights within the reservations was barred by strong *res judicata* (finality of legal decision) principles. The Court said:

> Recalculating the amount of practicably irrigable acreage runs directly counter to the strong interest in finality in this case. A major purpose of this litigation, from its inception to the present day, has been to provide the necessary assurance to states of the Southwest and to various private interests of the amount of water they can anticipate to receive from the Colorado River system.[23]

The Court went on to say that "a fundamental precept of common-law adjudication is that an issue once determined by a competent court is conclusive," and that certainty of rights is particularly important with respect to water rights in the western United States. Therefore, adjudication of water rights will not be reopened absent changed circumstances or unforeseen issues not previously litigated.

Boundary changes made in judicial decrees entered after 1964 were ruled to be "finally determined" within the meaning of the boundary provision of the 1964 decree, and the tribes' request to increase their water rights accordingly was granted. Boundary changes made by order of the Secretary of the Interior, however, were not "finally determined" under the decree, and the Court said that they should be litigated in federal district court before being incorporated into the decree.

Finally, the Court rejected the tribes' contention that they were not represented adequately by the United States in the earlier suit because of its interest in securing water rights for other federal property, stating that the United States often represents varied interests in water rights litigation, and that there was no evidence of conflict of interest in this case. The government's error in calculating the amount of irrigable acreage was found not to be, in itself, inadequate representation under ordinary standards of attorney conduct.

Interpreting Changed Circumstances and Unforeseen Issues not Previously Litigated: Nevada v. United States

Nevada v. United States was decided by the Supreme Court three months after *Arizona v. California II*, and its result confirmed that the Court narrowly will construe the circumstances in which judicial decrees quantifying water rights will be reopened.

The water rights of the Pyramid Lake Paiute Tribe, including its reserved rights under the *Winters* doctrine, were quantified in a general stream adjudication of the Truckee River in Nevada that resulted in the 1944 *Orr Ditch* Decree. In 1973, the United States and the tribe filed suit in district court seeking additional water because the Newlands Reclamation Project has diverted so much of the Truckee River that the level of Pyramid Lake, fed solely by the Truckee, has dropped substantially, threatening its aquatic life. Two kinds of fish that have been declared endangered species live in the lake. The tribe and the United States contended that the *Orr Ditch* litigation only determined the reservation's reserved water right for irrigation, and that the current claim for sufficient water to maintain tribal fisheries in the lake and river is another purpose for which the reservation was created.

The Court reversed the Ninth Circuit Court of Appeals and ruled that the United States and the tribe are barred from relitigating the tribe's reserved water rights by *res judicata* because the present suit is the same cause of action litigated in *Orr Ditch*, and because the principles of *res judicata* apply not only to claims that were litigated but also to those that might have been presented. The Court also held that the tribe and the farmers owning land in the Newlands Project were sufficiently adverse in the *Orr Ditch* litigation to be barred from relitigating the water rights allocated in the decree, although neither were parties in the first action and both were represented simultaneously by the same government attorneys. The Court noted that all parties to the *Orr Ditch* litigation had intended that it be the final determination of all water rights of the parties, that the matter was fully litigated, and that the United States had tried to get as large an amount of water allocated to the tribe as it could.

In *Nevada* the Court gave only limited weight to the fact that both the tribe and the reclamation project were represented by the same attorneys:

> [T]he Government cannot follow the fastidious standards of a private fiduciary, who would breach his duties to his single beneficiary solely by representing potentially conflicting interests without the beneficiary's consent. The Government does not "compromise" its obligation to one interest that Congress obliges it to represent by the mere fact that it simultaneously performs another task for another interest that Congress has obligated it by statute to do.[24]

5-3. QUANTIFICATION OF RESERVED RIGHTS

The extensiveness of the general stream adjudication and the technical complexity of the practicably irrigable acreage standard developed in *Arizona v. California I* have caused Indian water cases to move slowly through the courts. As a result, relatively little law has developed concerning the intricacies of the practicably irrigable acreage standard and other measures of water quantity under the *Winters* doctrine.

The general adjudication in the Big Horn River system in Wyoming[25] has progressed the furthest of the state comprehensive adjudications. In 1988, the Wyoming Supreme Court upheld a lower court decision that the Arapaho and Shoshone Tribes of the Wind River Reservation have reserved water rights only for irrigation (including livestock, municipal, domestic and commercial uses), not for minimum stream flows or for industrial or mineral development, based on its finding that the 1868 reservation was established primarily for agricultural purposes.[26] The court also held that the tribes have no reserved right to ground water.[27] All water rights on the reservation were given an 1868 priority date, with non-Indian purchasers of allotted land being required to show on remand to the lower court that their practicably irrigable acreage was irrigated by their Indian predecessors or put under irrigation within a reasonable time.[28]

United States v. Adair,[29] which involved the water rights of the Klamath Tribe of Oregon, resulted in major rulings on several points. The court ruled that the tribe's 1864 Treaty reserved water sufficient for the purposes of hunting, fishing and agriculture on the reservation. The water rights have a priority date of time immemorial because they were not created by the treaty; rather the treaty confirmed the continued existence of the tribe's aboriginal rights. Further, these rights were not affected by the Klamath Termination Act,[30] although the tribe no longer owns any reservation lands.

The court in *Adair* found that the water right to support game and fish adequate to the needs of Indian hunters and fishers is nonconsumptive: it does not involve diversion of the water but is rather the right to prevent other appropriators from depleting waters in the streams below a protected level—a water right to instream flow. The court interpreted the reserved right to be that amount of water necessary to support the hunting and fishing rights currently exercised by tribal members, not as they were exercised in 1864. The court also found applicable the "moderate living" ceiling first announced in *Washington v. Fishing Vessel Ass'n*:[31] "Indian treaty rights to a natural resource that once was thoroughly and exclusively exploited by the Indians secures so much as, but not more than, is necessary to provide the Indians with a livelihood—that is to say, a moderate living."[32]

Another recent, leading case concerning quantification of Indian water rights is *Walton III*.[33] *Walton I* was decided in the district court in 1978,[34] appealed to the Ninth Circuit Court of Appeals in 1981 (*Walton II*),[35] and *Walton III* was handed down in 1985.

Walton is a general stream adjudication of No Name Creek, which is located entirely within the boundaries of the Colville Reservation in Washington, to apportion the reservation's reserved water rights between the tribal fishery, the Indian allottees, and Walton, a non-Indian allotment purchaser. All of the former tribal land involved passed into private ownership under the General Allotment Act of 1887[36] and is presently owned by the Indian allottees and by allotment purchasers.

In *Walton II*, as in *Adair*, the court of appeals held that a reserved water right exists both for the protection of fisheries on former reservation land and for irrigation. The court also found that the reserved right encompasses sufficient water to allow the irrigation of all practicably irrigable acreage on the reservation and that a ratable share of tribal water passed to the Indian allottees and to the purchasers of allotments. The case was remanded to the district court to quantify the water rights of the users accordingly.

On appeal again, the Ninth Circuit held in *Walton III* that the No Name Creek water system yields 1000 acre-feet per year available for allocation and that the tribe is entitled to 350 acre-feet per year to maintain its tribal fishery. The court reversed the district court's allocation to the tribe of only 187.2 acre-feet which was based on the amount "available for other purposes" after water for the Indian allottees and the allotment purchasers was subtracted from 1000 acre-feet. The appellate court held that the rights of the three groups of users should be adjusted on a pro-rata basis if necessitated by a water shortage, since all have date-of-the-reservation priority dates. The court also dealt with other issues relating to allotment water rights, which are discussed in section 5-5 of this chapter.

Tribes in recent years have pursued means other than *Winters* reserved water rights to obtain water for their reservations, especially to protect fish runs. In *Kittitas Reclamation District v. Sunnyside Valley Irrigation District* (1985),[37] the Yakima Nation obtained an injunction requiring the Bureau of Reclamation to release sufficient water from a reclamation dam so that redds (salmon spawning beds) on the reservation would not run dry. In *Kittitas*, the district court was asked to interpret and administer a 1945 consent decree that set forth the rights of various contract holders in the Yakima Irrigation System. The Yakima Nation was not a party to the consent decree, and the earlier proceeding was not a general adjudication. Yet, the Yakima Nation wanted the water master appointed under the consent decree to maintain the water flow for the redds. The water master turned to the court for instructions. Without deciding the scope of fishing rights reserved to the Yakima Nation, the Ninth Circuit upheld the district court judge's opinion that both ordered the Department of the Interior to study the problem and temporarily ordered the water level maintained to preserve the redds.

In addition, the Pyramid Lake Paiute Indian Tribe has been successful in invoking the Endangered Species Act and other laws to require that federal dams be operated in such a manner as to provide adequate flows to support two endangered species, the Lahontan cutthroat trout and the cui-ui. In *Carson-Truckee Water Conservancy District v. Clark*,[38] the Ninth Circuit Court of Appeals ruled that the Secretary of the Interior is permitted to allocate all the water from the Stampede Dam and Reservoir on the Little Truckee River to Pyramid Lake in order to protect the endangered species living there. It was held that the Secretary's obligations under the Endangered Species Act[39] supersede obligations under the Washoe Project Act[40] and related federal reclamation laws. In a related case also involving Pyramid Lake, *Truckee-Carson Irrigation District v. Secretary of the Department of the Interior*,[41] the Ninth Circuit upheld the Secretary's termination of an irrigation district's contract to operate the Newlands Reclamation Project after the district admitted to intentionally diverting more water than regulations permitted, depriving Pyramid Lake of the waters.

Tribes in the Puget Sound region have taken the position, in *Washington v. Fishing Vessel Ass'n*,[42] that their judicially recognized fishing rights cannot be fulfilled unless there are sufficient flows of clean water to provide an adequate fish habitat. Early rulings in this major litigation, called *United States v. Washington (Phase II)*, have been inconclusive.[43]

5-4. TRIBAL REGULATION

As indicated in earlier sections, litigation has dealt with the issue of the quantity of water to which tribes are entitled under the *Winters* doctrine; cases have also dealt with the matter of the proper court to hear questions of water quantity. A separate issue concerns governmental authority to regulate water use. That is, under what circumstances do state or tribal governments have authority to regulate and manage water rights of Indians and non-Indians within reservation boundaries?

The right of tribes to regulate Indians within Indian Country, and the concomitant lack of state regulatory authority over Indians, appears to be well-established.[44] More difficult questions have arisen concerning the power of tribes to regulate water use by non-Indians. In *Walton II*,[45] the court found that the state has no role in regulating non-Indian water users within the No Name Creek hydrological system, located completely within reservation boundaries. The water system was held to be critical to the development of reservation resources and to the lifestyle of its residents; as a result, outside regulation would interfere with tribal sovereignty. Thus state regulation was said to be preempted by the creation of the reservation and the power to regulate rests exclusively with the tribe or the United States. The court also emphasized that the No Name Creek system has no impact on state-controlled waters off the reservation, so the state has little interest in regulation of the creek.

United States v. Anderson[46] reached the opposite result. In *Anderson* the court ruled that the state, not the tribe, had regulatory authority over the use of excess water (water available after tribal needs have been met) on lands owned by non-Indians within the reservation boundaries. The court held that regulation of the Chamokane Creek water system, which borders the reservation on one side but flows for a long distance outside of the reservation, had no "direct effect on the political integrity, the economic security, or the health or welfare of the Tribe." Thus, there is no preemption of state law by tribal regulatory authority. The court noted that the water rights belonging to the tribe are quantified and protected by the federal water master, and went on to say:

> The tribe is, of course, entitled to utilize its water for any lawful purpose. If the tribe chooses to use water reserved for irrigation in a non-consumptive manner [*e.g.*, to maintain instream flows to protect fisheries], it does not thereby relinquish any of its water rights to state permittees or subject the exercise of its rights to state regulation. The state may regulate only the use, by non-Indian fee owners, of excess water. Any permits issued by the state would be limited to excess water. If those permits represent rights that may be empty, so be it. [Citation omitted.][47]

Anderson was distinguished from *Walton II*, where the state was held to have no regulatory power within reservation boundaries, by the fact that the water system involved in *Walton II* is small, nonnavigable and encompassed entirely within the reservation boundaries. Chamokane Creek, on the other hand, lies primarily outside the reservation, so that the state's interest in developing a comprehensive water program weighed in favor of state regulation of excess water in the Chamokane basin. Further, in *Walton* the area in question had been allotted to Indians but had never been opened for settlement under the general homesteading laws, as in *Anderson*; therefore the tribal interest in *Walton* might be considered to be greater.

The Yakima Nation, as is true with an increasing number of tribes, adopted a comprehensive water code that applies to all waters within its reservation, including excess waters on land owned by non-Indians. The Washington Departments of Ecology, Game, and Natural Resources, as well as individual plaintiffs, filed suit in federal district court[48] to determine the authority of the tribe to adopt and enforce the water code, including the jurisdiction of the tribe over the individual plaintiffs. The court rendered a decision in September 1985,[49] disallowing tribal authority over non-Indian use of excess waters.

5-5. ALLOTMENTS

From the passage of the General Allotment Act of 1887[50] until enactment of the Indian Reorganization Act of 1934,[51] the United States pursued a policy on many reservations of transferring substantial amounts of tribal lands as allotments to individual tribal members. Tens of millions of acres of tribal lands were allotted, and much of that land was transferred by Indian allottees to non-Indian purchasers. The basic policy of the Allotment Act was to promote farming on these lands, which requires irrigation in most areas of the West. As a result, water rights on Indian allotments, and on former allotments, are of considerable importance across the West.

The General Allotment Act does not mention water rights except to authorize the Secretary of the Interior to make a "just and fair distribution" of water for irrigation on Indian reservations, and to provide generally that "no other appropriation or grant of water by an[y] riparian proprietor shall be authorized or permitted to the damage of any other riparian proprietor."[52] Legislative history on the Act is scant. Thus the question of the reserved water rights of Indian allottees and non-Indian purchasers of allotments is a matter of determining an unexpressed congressional intent.

The leading, recent case on these issues is *Walton II*.[53] First, the court followed *United States v. Powers*,[54] making it clear that a ratable portion of reserved *Winters* rights passed from the tribe to Indian allottees when allotments were made. The court noted that the quantification of reserved water, but not the use of it, is determined by the purposes for which the reservation was created. Thus, Congress had the power to allot reserved water rights to individual Indians, and that is consistent with the general purpose for the creation of reservations—providing homelands for the survival of Indians and their way of life.

The *Walton* court held that non-Indian purchasers of allotted lands also obtain a right to reserved waters, thus arriving at the same result as *United States ex rel. Ray v. Hibner*,[55] the only prior case squarely to rule on the water rights of successors to allottees. The *Walton* court worked from the general rule that there must be express legislation or a clear inference of Congress' intent to diminish Indian rights. Applying this principle, the court reasoned that an Indian allottee must be able to transfer his or her right to reserved water with a date-of-the-reservation priority—any later priority date would diminish the right of the Indian allottee. The court noted that the early priority date "is the principal aspect of the right that renders it more valuable than the rights of competing water users, and therefore applies to the right acquired by a non-Indian purchaser."[56]

The court also held, however, that the water rights of non-Indian successors are limited by principles of nonuse in a way that reserved rights of tribes and Indian allottees are not. The non-Indian acquires by purchase a right to reserved water, but the water must be put to use by the non-Indian with reasonable diligence after the conveyance; otherwise the water is lost by the non-Indian successor. Thus a non-Indian may obtain the full ratable share of the allottee's reserved water right, with a date-of-the-reservation priority date, but only if the water is developed reasonably promptly.

In 1985, the Ninth Circuit Court of Appeals handed down its opinion in *Walton III*,[57] which had been remanded to the district court for quantification of the water rights involved in accordance with the court's prior ruling. *Walton III* dealt with the "reasonable diligence" standard in determining the present reserved water right of the non-Indian purchaser, Walton. The court held that Walton was not entitled to a date-of-the-reservation water right for all of the acres he was currently farming, as the lower court had determined. The due diligence standard applies to the amount of water appropriated with due diligence by the *first* successor of the Indian allotment and used continuously up to the present owner. For some 37 years prior to Walton's purchase of his allotment, his predecessors had irrigated only 30 acres, and the appellate court ruled that Walton's reserved water right was limited to that amount.[58]

The court also found that the lower court had erred in applying principles of nonuse to Indian allottees, holding that Indian allotments should receive the full amount of water for all their irrigable acreage, regardless of how much acreage is actually irrigated. As noted earlier, *Walton III* also held that all date-of-the-reservation water rights—those of the tribe, of the Indian allottees and of the non-Indian successors—must be adjusted on a pro-rata basis if necessitated by water shortages.

The conclusions reached in *Walton* regarding the water rights of Indian allottees were also arrived at in *United States v. Adair*.[59] The court in *Adair* interpreted a section unique to the Klamath Termination Act,[60] which provides that Klamath water rights are subject to Oregon state law on abandonment 15 years after termination. The court narrowly construed the provision, concluding that it did not apply to unused reserved rights; rather, only "reserved waters actually appropriated" could be lost under Oregon abandonment law.[61]

United States v. Anderson[62] also is in accord with the *Walton* decisions concerning water rights of allottees and allotment purchasers. In addition, *Anderson* held that former reservation lands that were homesteaded and later reacquired by the tribe have a priority date of the reacquisition rather than of the reservation's creation, if the land's reserved water right had not been perfected or was lost under state law. This is because former reservation lands were first declared public domain before being homesteaded, and no federal water rights are acquired by the transfer of public lands into private ownership.[63] The *Anderson* Court said:

> This result is supported by the fact that *Winters* rights were only intended to assist in accomplishing the needs of the reservation; where the land has been removed from the Tribe's possession and conveyed to a homesteader, the purposes for which *Winters* rights were implied are eliminated.[64]

The *Anderson* court also ruled that homesteaded lands with perfected water rights carry the priority date they are entitled to under state law. Allotments sold to non-Indians carry a date-of-the-reservation priority for water rights continuously used, in accordance with *Walton*.

As noted above, the Wyoming Supreme Court also addressed the issue of priority dates for purchasers of allotted lands. The court applied the Ninth Circuit's *Walton* decision and required non-Indian purchasers of allotted land to show that their practicably irrigable acreage was irrigated by their Indian predecessors or put under irrigation within a reasonable time.[65] The court also held that allotted lands reacquired by Indian or tribal purchasers also are entitled to the 1868 reservation priority date.[66]

5-6. CONCLUSION

Indian water rights cases are moving through state and federal courts across the West.[67] Judicial guidelines have been set on many issues but major questions remain unresolved. Perhaps the overriding issue in current Indian water litigation is whether the Supreme Court actually will engage in "particularized and exacting scrutiny" of state court rulings, as it stated in the *San Carlos* opinion.

One important decision for individual tribes is whether they will pursue the possibility of negotiated settlements. Some tribes are adamantly opposed to any quantification of their *Winters* rights, which they believe should remain open-ended in order to meet future needs. Other tribes have willingly litigated in order to achieve a final, decreed determination of their *Winters* rights. Several other tribes have considered the strategy of negotiation in order to obtain wet water for their reservations.

Whatever result obtained in individual situations, the Indian water cases will have considerable impact, both on the tribes and on the interests that oppose them. Many of the legal doctrines are complex, even arcane, but they will decide social and economic matters of the first order of magnitude. By any standard, the struggle over Indian water has become one of the major resource battles in the American West.

REFERENCE NOTES

1. *Colorado River Conservation District v. United States*, 424 U.S. 800 (1976).
2. 463 U.S. 545 (1983).

3. 460 U.S. 605 (1983).
4. 463 U.S. 110 (1983).
5. 463 U.S. 545 (1983).
6. 43 U.S.C. § 666.
7. 463 U.S. at 571.
8. *Id.* at 567.
9. *Id.* at 569.
10. *Id.* at 571.
11. *United States v. Superior Court of Arizona*, 12 Indian L. Rep. 5024 (Ariz. Sup. Ct. 1985).
12. *Montana ex rel. Greely v. Confederated Salish & Kootenai Tribes of the Flathead Reservation, et al.*, 13 Indian L. Rep. 5003 (Mont. Sup. Ct. 1985).
13. 12 Indian L. Rep. 3009 (D. Ariz. 1985).
14. 723 F.2d 1394 (9th Cir. 1983), *cert. denied*, 467 U.S. 1252 (1984).
15. 723 F.2d at 1402-03 (quoting *Will v. Calvert Fire Insurance Co.*, 437 U.S. 655, 664 (1978)).
16. *Id.* at 1405-06.
17. 580 F. Supp. 1434 (D.N.M. 1984).
18. 580 F. Supp. at 1447.
19. Sections 72-4-17, -19, N.M. Stat. Ann. (1978).
20. 460 U.S. 605 (1983).
21. 463 U.S. 110 (1983).
22. 376 U.S. 340 (1964).
23. 460 U.S. at 620.
24. 463 U.S. at 128.
25. *In Re the General Adjudication of All Rights to Use Water in the Big Horn River System and All Other Sources, State of Wyoming*, 750 P.2d 681 (Wyo. 1988).
26. 750 P.2d at 699-705.
27. 750 P.2d at 705.
28. Without such a showing the non-Indian purchaser of allotted land would not gain the 1868 reservation priority date. 750 P.2d at 718-19.
29. 723 F.2d 1394 (9th Cir. 1983), *cert. denied*, 467 U.S. 1252 (1984).
30. 25 U.S.C. §§ 564-564w.
31. 443 U.S. 658 (1979).
32. *Id.* at 686.
33. *Colville Confederated Tribes v. Walton*, 752 F.2d 397 (1985).
34. 460 F. Supp. 1320 (1978).
35. 647 F.2d 42 (9th Cir.), *cert. denied*, 454 U.S. 1092 (1981).
36. 25 U.S.C. §§ 331-381.
37. 763 F.2d 1032 (9th Cir.), *cert. denied*, 54 U.S.L.W. 3409 (1985).
38. 741 F.2d 257 (9th Cir. 1984).
39. 16 U.S.C.A. §§ 1531(b,c), 1532(3), 1536(a)(1,2).
40. 43 U.S.C.A. §§ 614-614d.
41. 742 F.2d 527 (9th Cir. 1984).
42. 443 U.S. 658 (1979).
43. *See United States v. Washington*, 506 F. Supp. 187 (W.D. Wash. 1980), *reversed and remanded*, *United States v. Washington*, 759 F.2d 1353 (9th Cir., Apr. 29, 1985) (remanding to district court for further fact finding). *See generally* Hornstein, *Indian Fishing Rights Return to Spawn: Toward Environmental Protection of Treaty Fisheries*, 61 OR. L. REV. (Nov. 1, 1982); M. Getches,

Anadromous Fish Runs and Indian Treaty Rights: The Boldt II Saga, COASTAL LAW MEMO (Oct. 1983) (Sea Grant Program, Oregon State University).

44. *See, e.g.*, Felix S. Cohen, HANDBOOK OF FEDERAL INDIAN LAW at 604 (1982 ed.); *United States v. Adair*, 723 F.2d 1394, 1416 (9th Cir. 1983), *cert. denied*, 104 S. Ct. 3536 (1984).
45. *Colville Confederated Tribes v. Walton*, 647 F.2d 42 (9th Cir. 1981), *cert. denied*, 454 U.S. 1092 (1981).
46. 736 F.2d 1358 (9th Cir. 1984).
47. *Id.* at 1365.
48. *Holly v. Totus*, No. C-78-002 (E.D. Wash. 1978).
49. Under the name of *Holly v. Confederated Tribes and Bands of the Yakima Indian Nation*, 655 F. Supp. 557 (E.D. Wash. 1985), *aff'd sub nom. Holly v. Totus*, 812 F.2d 714 (9th Cir.), *cert. denied*, 56 U.S.L.W. 3226 (Oct. 6, 1987).
50. 25 U.S.C. §§ 331-381.
51. 25 U.S.C. §§ 461-479.
52. 25 U.S.C. § 381.
53. 647 F.2d 42 (9th Cir. 1981), *cert. denied*, 454 U.S. 1092 (1981).
54. 305 U.S. 527 (1939).
55. 27 F.2d 909 (D. Idaho 1928).
56. 647 F.2d at 51.
57. *Colville Confederated Tribes v. Walton*, 752 F.2d 397 (9th Cir. 1985).
58. The policy issues regarding allotment water rights continue to be debated. Differing views are discussed in two law review articles: Collins, *Indian Allotment Water Rights*, 20 LAND & WATER L. REV. 421 (1985); and Getches, *Water Rights on Indian Allotments*, 26 S.D.L. REV. 405 (1981).
59. 723 F.2d 1394 (9th Cir. 1983), *cert. denied*, 467 U.S. 1252 (1984).
60. 25 U.S.C. § 564m.
61. 723 F.2d at 1416.
62. 736 F.2d 1358 (9th Cir. 1984).
63. *California Oregon Power Co. v. Beaver Portland Cement Co.*, 295 U.S. 142 (1935).
64. 736 F.2d at 1363.
65. 750 P.2d at 719.
66. *Id.*
67. A range of other issues do not deal with Indian water rights per se, but bear upon *Winters* rights. Detailed treatment, however, is beyond the scope of this chapter. For example, a number of cases have dealt with the question of ownership of riverbeds and lake bottoms. The rule that the tribes reserved all lands within their reservations collides with the principle that ownership of beds of navigable watercourses passes to the states at the time of statehood. *Montana v. United States*, 450 U.S. 544 (1981), ruled that the navigable portion of the Big Horn River passed to the state of Montana because the evidence did not establish substantial aboriginal use of the river by the Crows. In other cases, tribes have been able to establish ownership of beds to navigable watercourses as against claims by the states. *See, e.g., Puyallup Indian Tribe v. Port of Tacoma*, 717 F.2d 1251 (9th Cir. 1983); *Confederated Salish and Kootenai Tribes v. Namen*, 665 F.2d 951 (9th Cir. 1982); *Yankton Sioux Tribe v. Nelson*, 521 F. Supp. 463 (D.S.D. 1981). Several pending cases deal with the licensing procedures of the Federal Energy Commission. The Supreme Court has held that FERC, in issuing licenses for hydroelectric projects, must accept without modification protective conditions set by the Secretary of the Interior with respect to reservations within which projects are located; FERC is not so bound in regard to reservations on which a project is not actually located. *Escondido Mutual Water Co. v. LaJolla, Rincon, San Pasqual, Pauma & Pala Bands of Mission Indians*, 466 U.S. 765 (1984). Recent administrative policy within the Environmental Protection Agency offers promise of greatly increased tribal responsibilities under the Clean Water Act, 42 U.S.C. §§ 1251-1376, and other environmental laws, but those initiatives are still in their infancy.

Part II

SCIENCE OF THE LIVING WATERSHED

CHAPTER 6

Hydrology and Watershed Management

6-1. INTRODUCTION

Hydrology, in its broadest sense, is the science that relates to water in the environment: its occurrence in the earth, its physical and chemical interactions with earth material, and its relation to the life of the earth. Since hydrology is the science that underlies the development and control of water resources, a basic understanding of the science and of the cycle of water through reservations is essential to the development of effective tribal water management policy (1,2).

Familiarity with the fundamental terms *hydrologic cycle* and *watershed* is necessary to begin the study of hydrology. The *hydrologic cycle* concerns how water circulates through the environment. A *watershed* is a fundamental geographic unit of water management.

An introduction to the main components of the hydrologic cycle is presented in Figure 6-1. The figure shows that energy supplied by the sun *evaporates* water from the oceans, lakes, rivers and soil surface. This water, in the form of *water vapor*, travels through the atmosphere in large air masses. When the moist air is cooled, water vapor *condenses* and falls as *precipitation* in the form of rain, snow, sleet, hail or dew. Some precipitation *infiltrates*, or sinks into, the ground surface through fractures in rocks or through stream channel bottoms to become part of the ground water resource, while other precipitation may penetrate the soil surface only partially and become part of the soil moisture storage. Some precipitation is evaporated directly by the sun or used by plants in a process known as *evapotranspiration*. Finally, some of the precipitation that falls may *run off* the land surface, making its way to streams and rivers.

A *watershed* is the area of land drained by a stream or river, or by a system of streams or rivers. The term watershed implies a system within geographic boundaries that can and should be used as the basic unit in water resources management. Within the social science context, the watershed has emerged rather recently as a logical unit of policymaking. Any land use practice within a watershed can affect water quantity and quality throughout the watershed through the hydrologic cycle. Thus, development planning must be done within the context of an entire river basin or watershed. Such comprehensive planning, over the long term, will protect the water resource.

Within the watershed unit, the water resources planner strives to seek an understanding of and the balance between water *inflow*, *storage* and *outflow* (3). A detailed accounting procedure for water resources within any particular reservation watershed is necessary to develop policies that accurately reflect the potential, distribution and reliability of water resources on Indian lands. The procedure that establishes the amount of water in a watershed is the *water balance* method, a concept that will be discussed in more detail later.

However, before examining the components of the hydrologic cycle that allow a water resources management planner to analyze the water balance in a watershed, it is useful to grasp a general understanding of ground and surface water resources—their source, distribution and utilization.

6-2. WATER RESOURCES: THE SOURCE

Approximately one percent of the total moisture drifting in the atmosphere above the United States falls to the ground as precipitation on an average day. This amounts to 4.2 trillion gallons of water descending daily in the form of rain, sleet, hail, and snow across the contiguous 48 states, or 4,200,000,000,000 gallons per day. This staggering quantity is nearly impossible to conceptualize; yet such a task is necessary in order to begin assessing the water resources of the United States.

Scientists are fond of expressing this total as 4,200 billion gallons per day (bgd), as if the concept of such a number were somehow more easily grasped when written in this form. Although it is easy to picture a single gallon of water, what do thousands of billions of these look like? Even the oft-used standard of a football field—4,200 billion gallons of water would cover such a field to a depth of over 2,000 miles—fails to bring this figure into a comprehensible dimension. Perhaps it is helpful to convert this flow into the concept of 10 Mississippi Rivers, or about 25 Columbia Rivers, constantly pouring down upon the United States. Whatever the case, it is a tremendous amount of water that brings to mind one obvious question: where does it all go?

As illustrated in Figure 6-1, about two-thirds of the total daily precipitation returns to the atmosphere through direct evaporation and transpiration of plants. Almost one-quarter becomes part of the ground water. An amount equal to approximately 30% of daily precipitation flows from ground and surface waters into the oceans. Of the 4,200 bgd of precipitation, only 100 bgd actually is diverted and consumed.

So why are there cries of water shortages when consumption is less than 3% of the amount of water available each day? Because too often it is painfully clear to water users—particularly those on the arid lands of the West—that abundant water resources are not always in the right place at the right time.

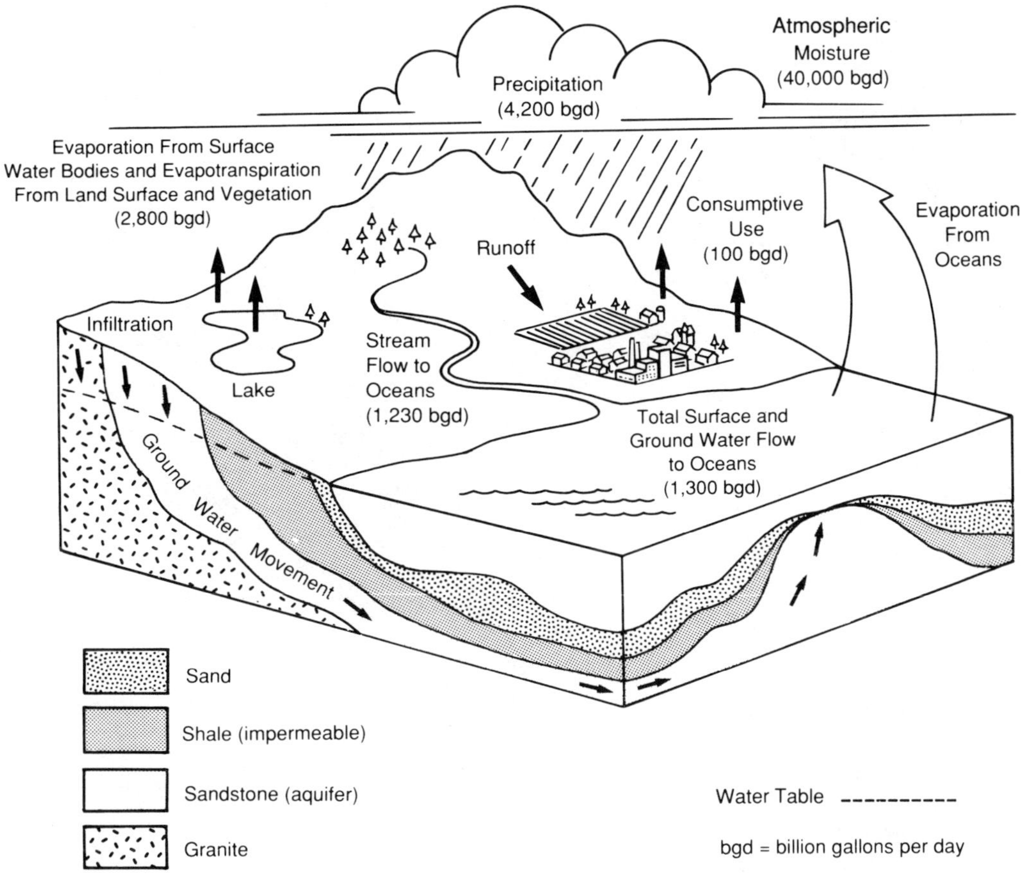

Figure 6-1. Hydrologic Cycle and Water Budget of the Conterminous United States.

6-3. WATER RESOURCES: SURFACE WATER DISTRIBUTION

Figure 6-2 provides a look at the distribution of precipitation within the United States. The eastern portion of the nation is seen to have a consistent rainfall pattern, averaging more than 30 inches of annual precipitation throughout the region. Moving westward into the plains, however, a different situation is encountered, involving less water and more local variation. The West generally receives less than 20 inches of precipitation per year, with portions of the 11 contiguous western states averaging less than 10 inches annually.

The 100th meridian (designating 100 degrees west longitude) has been plotted on Figure 6-2. This line is important to an understanding of water resources in the United States since areas lying west of it generally cannot support modern, dry-land farming. Although some people have succeeded in farming arid regions of the West for centuries without the aid of irrigation, most American farmers require additional water for their crops when precipitation is less than 20 inches a year. As a consequence, when large-scale farming sprang up west of the 100th meridian during the late 1800s, surface runoff—and the irrigation potential it provided—became a key element in the water resources picture.

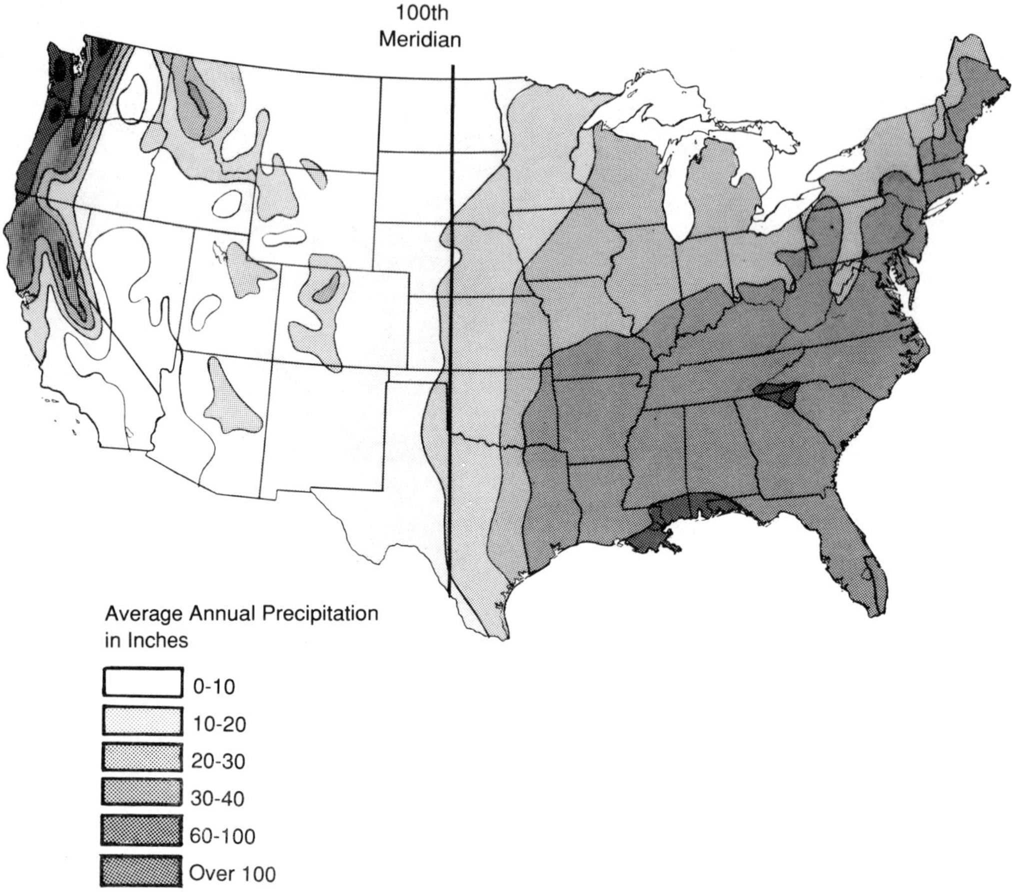

Figure 6-2. Average Annual Precipitation. After U.S.G.S. Water-Supply Paper 2250 (1984), p. 14.

As expected, the surface runoff pattern generally coincides with the amount of precipitation falling on a region. The eastern United States has plentiful water availability, while the West has far less runoff going into its streams and rivers. In fact, significant runoff to feed the region's watercourses exists only in the coastal and mountainous watersheds of the West. With many of the high country watersheds under federal ownership, it is estimated that 61% of the West's water supply arises upon public lands, with more than 95% of the population to some extent dependent upon water from the public lands.

Such an unequal distribution of precipitation and runoff across the nation helps explain why only 3% of daily precipitation is diverted and consumed. A second factor—timing—also comes into play. Not only are the abundant water supplies generally not in the areas of need, but when water does become available in arid regions, the timing of its arrival often frustrates its use.

Stream flow patterns in the West generally reflect a cycle dominated by the influence of snowfall and the subsequent spring thaw. Runoff is dramatically high in the spring and early summer, while quickly returning to low flows as the last of the snow melts in the high country. The low flows last from summer through the next winter.

This runoff pattern was not conducive to meeting the needs of the major users in the West at the turn of the century. Irrigators often required late summer water that simply was not available. Two developments evolved from these needs that have since become major components in the water resources picture: an extensive dam construction program and the use of ground water resources.

6-4. WATER RESOURCES: RESERVOIRS

The year 1902 marks the beginning of the national effort to expand available water resources through the use of major dams and reservoirs. On June 17 of that year, Congress passed the Reclamation Act and set into motion a massive construction program to provide reliable water supplies for western irrigated lands. Under the authority of this Act, the Bureau of Reclamation built a network of dams that by 1970 provided water to 8.7 million acres of cropland—more than one-fifth of the total irrigated acreage in the country. During the same period, programs within the Department of Agriculture were responsible for assisting in the construction of 80 thousand small irrigation reservoirs and over 2 million ponds and pits that supplied water for agricultural use. The U.S. Army Corps of Engineers headed the other major federal effort, responsible for many of the large dams found along the nation's waterways. The Army Corps' reservoir projects generally were in the East, with irrigation often being secondary to other purposes such as flood control.

Reservoirs can increase the availability of usable water in two ways. First, smaller reservoirs are able to capture a portion of the peak seasonal runoff during the spring and to distribute it more evenly during the times of shortage in the late summer. Second, larger reservoirs generally are designed to capture water during wet years and to store it for use during years of little runoff. In fact, some dams in the West are able to hold several years of the total river flow and then to distribute it to users during extended dry periods.

Figures 6-3 and 6-4 summarize reservoir capacity. The maps indicate that the Colorado River basin is the most intensively developed area in terms of dams. Storage reservoirs in this region are capable of holding four times the average annual yield of the basin. The capacity in the Rio Grande basin is also high; dams there can store nearly two years of average flows. While dams are prevalent in the West Coast states, reservoirs there can capture less than half of an average year's runoff.

From 1920 until the 1960s, reservoir capacity in the United States steadily expanded at a rate of about 80% each decade, keeping pace with increasing demands. By 1960, water supply reservoirs across the country had a capacity equal to 204 days of user demands (119 million acre-feet of usable storage capacity with demands of 190 bgd). By 1970, this capacity had grown to 216 days of user demands. In recent years, however, needed withdrawals from reservoirs have grown faster than construction of new facilities. In 1980, the capacity index had dropped to 201 days: the first such decline in 60 years.

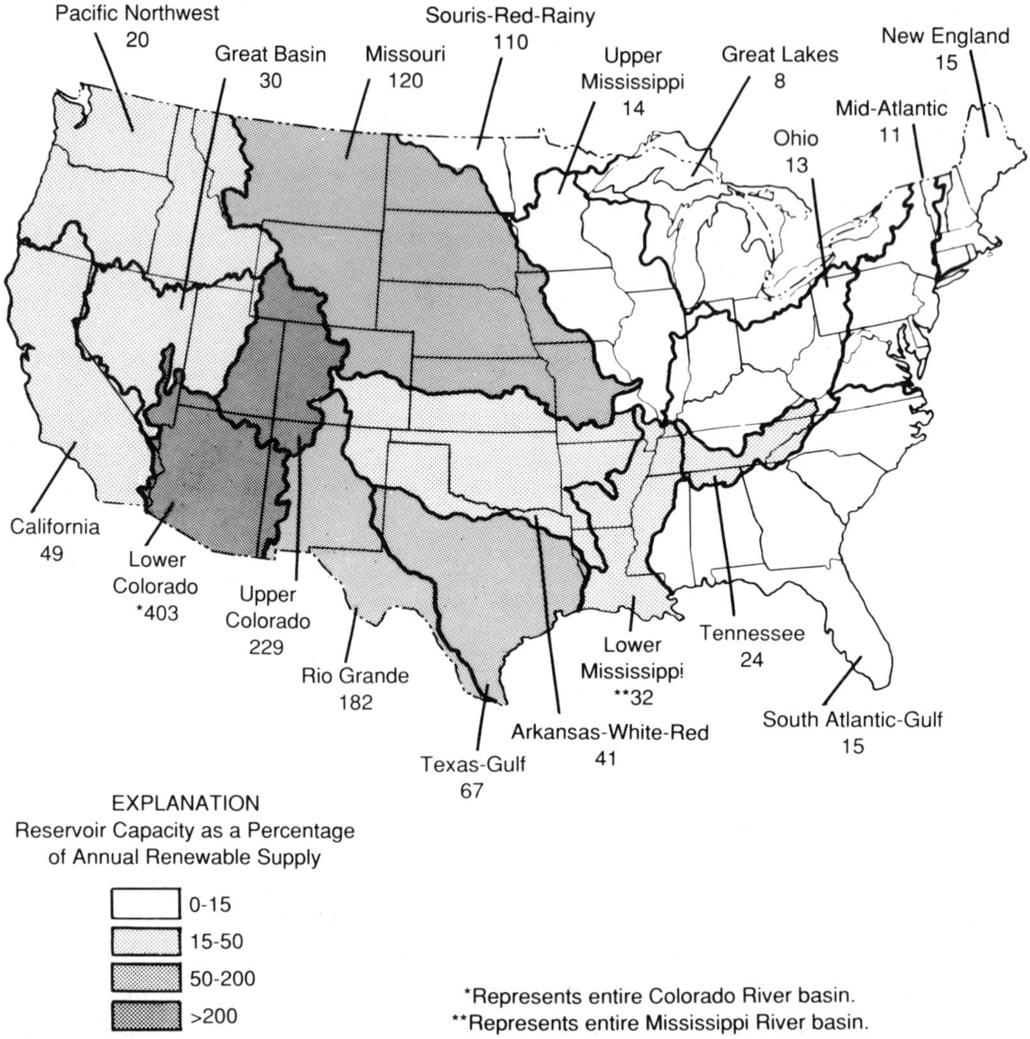

Figure 6-3. Intensity of Reservoir Development in Acre-feet of Reservoir Capacity per Square Mile, by Water-Resources Region. After U.S.G.S. Water-Supply Paper 2250 (1984), p. 32.

The decline in construction of reservoirs has many implications for water resources. It also has many causes. Recent federal fiscal policy is certainly one major factor in explaining the decline in new dam starts. But two physical constraints also face those who wish to build additional reservoirs. The first constraint is simple—the prime sites for reservoirs have already been used. It is increasingly difficult to identify sites for major new dams that can store and distribute water efficiently. The initial dams were located at points where the most water could be stored with the least amount of construction costs. Table 6-1 shows how as these sites were utilized, additional dams became more expensive and bulky relative to the amount of associated reservoir capacity.

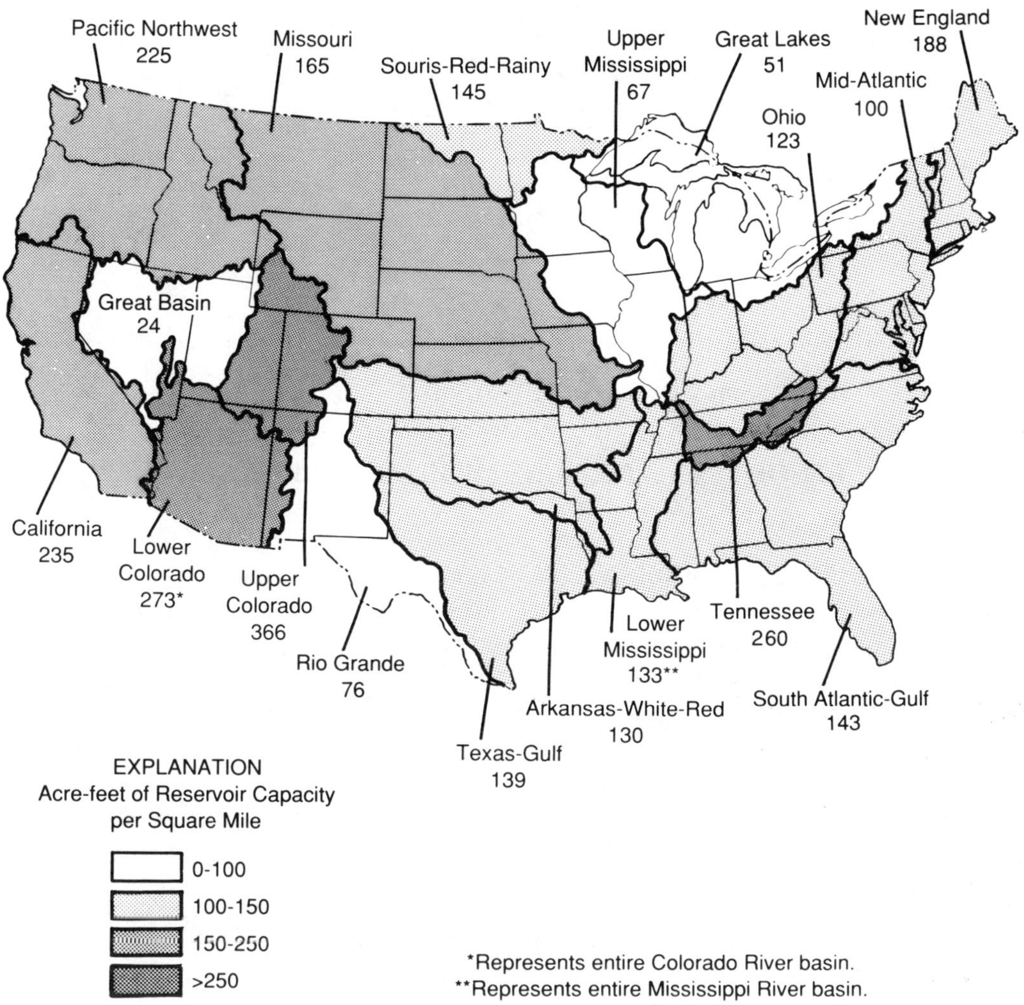

Figure 6-4. Normal Reservoir Capacity as a Percentage of Annual Renewable Supply, by Water-Resources Region. After U.S.G.S. Water-Supply Paper 2250 (1984), p. 33.

A second constraint is that in some basins, existing dams already may be storing and distributing nearly all of the available water yield. In such areas an additional reservoir actually would reduce the amount of usable water from the basin because evaporation loss from the surface of the new reservoir would exceed any gains in available water supply. Concern exists that such a point already has been reached in certain river systems, particularly in the Southwest.

In regions where additional reservoirs are either physically constrained or economically infeasible, water users and planners must look to alternative sources of supply. One such source which has been tapped with increasing frequency over the past decades is ground water.

Table 6-1

EFFICIENCY OF RESERVOIR CONSTRUCTION

Period	*Reservoir Capacity (af) per Cubic Yard of Dam Volume*
Pre-1930	10.4
1930s	2.1
1940s	0.52
1950s	0.45
1960s	0.29

After U.S.G.S. Water-Supply Paper 2250 (1984), p. 33.

6-5. WATER RESOURCES: GROUND WATER SUPPLIES

Quantification of existing ground water resources can lead to optimistic conclusions regarding the potential supply available to thirsty users. Once again, the absolute quantity of existing resources is staggering. Scientists estimate that 50,000 cubic miles of water are trapped in the top 2,600 feet of ground underlying the conterminous United States. Even with only a quarter of this amount being extractable by current technology, it represents an available supply of 46 billion acre-feet. Such an amount of water is equivalent to more than 30 years of total surface runoff in the country and, at current levels of use, would satisfy the entire consumptive water needs of the nation for over 400 years. Is ground water, therefore, the solution to water conflicts and shortages? Unfortunately, the answer is neither simple nor positive.

As with surface water resources, underground supplies are not always in the right place for use. Less than half the nation is underlain by aquifers which can support wells that pump 50 gallons per minute. Not only do some areas of the country lack water, but also the geologic configuration of some aquifers is such that the trapped water cannot be released at a usable rate.

Legal constraints also provide barriers to ground water development. Underground waters are often hydraulically connected to surface flows—flows that people already may have a legal right to use. Pumping of such ground water could deplete the stream flow and rob surface users of their lawful rights.

Water quality can also hamper an aquifer's use. Both natural and artificial sources of pollution may make ground water unsuitable for a particular purpose.

Economic factors may pose the greatest barrier to ground water utilization. The cost of lifting water hundreds of feet in order to water plants may not be economically justified, particularly in light of rising electricity rates. The economics become less attractive when well diversions exceed the rate of recharge to the aquifer, thereby lowering the aquifer's water level. When such water-mining occurs, pumping costs increase and wells need to be deepened or added in order to maintain a constant supply. In the high plains of Texas and New Mexico where water-mining has occurred, the result has been an 11% decrease in average annual withdrawals from the aquifer since 1964. Some irrigators simply can no longer afford to pump, while others have reduced their needs by installing more efficient irrigation systems and shifting to crops that demand less water.

This does not mean, however, that ground water use is past its prime. Despite the potential disadvantages, ground water became and has remained an essential component in the water supply picture in many regions of the country. The pattern of ground water use is summarized in the following section in the context of total water utilization in the United States.

6-6. WATER RESOURCES: HOW ARE GROUND AND SURFACE WATERS USED?

In 1980, ground water accounted for 20% of the nation's total diversions, amounting to 88 billion gallons per day (bgd) of pumping. While most of this water was used for irrigation, it also provided a significant portion of municipal and rural water supplies. But such dependence did not develop overnight. It took many years—and several technological advances—before ground water became a popular source for crop irrigation. Use of the Ogallala aquifer provides a useful example.

Beginning in the 1930s, improved well drilling technology, efficient pumps, and cheap energy enabled water users to turn to ground water when natural surface runoff and reservoir supplies proved inadequate. For instance, in a 25,000-square-mile area in Texas overlying the Ogallala aquifer, only 600 irrigation wells had tapped into the ground water by 1937. In the following 30 years, however, the number grew to over 50,000 wells. The entire Ogallala Formation, stretching from South Dakota to Texas, currently provides 18 million acre-feet annually from 170,000 wells to irrigate 13 million acres of crops.

Regionally ground water diversions are applied to varying uses. Much of the pumping in the East is associated with municipal and industrial demands, while agricultural withdrawals dominate in the West. In fact, more than 50 bgd of the 88 bgd of total ground water use is associated with western irrigation. But such a fact can mislead by diminishing the importance that ground water holds in other sectors as well. Roughly half of the people in the United States depend upon ground water for their household use, and ground water is also essential to much of the nation's livestock.

While ground water fills an important place in the water supply picture, users continue to rely upon the cheaper surface resources to a far greater extent. Well diversions have exceeded surface withdrawals only in the lower Colorado River basin. There the daily consumption of water exceeds the renewable supply from runoff and aquifer recharge. Such a situation, of course, cannot last forever.

It is helpful to analyze the pattern of water withdrawal and consumption in terms of categories of use. At the start of the current decade, cumulative withdrawals by industry, municipalities and other public suppliers, rural use and irrigation totaled 450 bgd, with 22% (100 bgd) of these diversions being consumed and 78% (350 bgd) returning to the oceans, streams and aquifers. Withdrawals increased by about 22%

over the 1970 level, with a 1980 average withdrawal of 2,000 gallons per person each day for all uses.

Industry, at 58%, is by far the largest diverter, although it accounts for only 8% of total water consumption. Municipalities and other public suppliers both withdraw and consume 7%, while rural use (for livestock and domestic purposes) withdraws 1% and consumes 4%.

Irrigation is by far the greatest consumer of water, using 81% of total water consumption. Ninety percent of this use occurs west of the Mississippi. Total withdrawals for irrigation equaled 170 million acre-feet (150 bgd) in 1980, of which 55% was actually consumed. The water was applied to approximately 58 million acres of cropland.

How does unconsumed, diverted water get back to the streams, aquifers and oceans? What happens to water that enters a watershed? How much water in a watershed is consumed, and how much leaves the watershed? What are the impacts of surface and ground water diversions on water quantity and quality? To answer these questions, one must first understand the details of the hydrologic cycle.

6-7. A DETAILED EXAMINATION OF THE HYDROLOGIC CYCLE

One of the goals of hydrologic analysis is prediction. An understanding of the hydrologic cycle gives water managers important data on the water resources within a watershed—data that can be used to predict the hydrologic outcome or impact of a particular development strategy or water resource policy. While prediction is a vital planning tool, it is only as good as the hydrologic data upon which it is based. At this point, starting with surface water resources, the discussion next turns to each component of the hydrologic cycle, the physical processes governing the occurrence and movement of water through the cycle in a watershed, and how the several components of the water cycle are measured. How this information is used in prediction and in water policy formulation is considered after the detailed discussion of the hydrologic cycle.

Surface Water Resources

Precipitation

Precipitation is that part of the hydrologic cycle with which we are most familiar. We read about rainfall amounts and forecasts on a daily basis. As a process, however, most people have very little understanding of both why precipitation occurs and why it occurs where it does. It must be remembered that different types of precipitation exist and that precipitation also varies in *intensity* (inches per hour), *volume* (amount), *duration* (length of storm) and *seasonal distribution*.

Although precipitation's important role in the hydrologic cycle is recognized easily, enough rainfall data seldom exists to plan for a river basin or watershed. Yet rainfall data is essential to such things as flood prediction, the selection of agricultural development strategies, and the distribution of grazing animals on rangelands. Networks of precipitation measuring devices—rain gauges—need to be designed and placed in the field to obtain the necessary rainfall information. This is particularly true on Indian lands.

Rainfall patterns and characteristics are essential pieces of information for planning and water policy formulation. One of the first tasks in rainfall analysis, then, is the identification of both the climatic region in which one is located and the primary mechanisms through which rainfall occurs.

Rainfall occurs when three conditions in the atmosphere are met: (1) the air becomes saturated with water, a condition that depends on moisture availability and temperature; (2) small particles (nuclei) are present in the atmosphere so that condensation can occur; and (3) water or ice particles coalesce enough to fall under the influence of gravity. Saturation results when either the air mass is cooled and reaches its saturation vapor pressure or when moisture is added to the air mass. Rarely does adding moisture to the air result in precipitation; more commonly, precipitation occurs when the air mass is lifted and cooled (1,2,4).

Air masses are lifted and cooled by three processes, and different storm and precipitation characteristics are associated with each process. For example, when air close to the earth's surface becomes warmer than the air above, lifting occurs through a process called *thermal convection*. High intensity, short duration, geographically scattered thunderstorms usually accompany thermal convection. Such storms are typically severe and often cause flash flooding (4).

When general circulation brings together air masses that have different temperatures and moisture content, the air is lifted at the frontal surface where they meet. This process is called *frontal precipitation*. Warm fronts generally produce steady rains over extensive geographic areas. Cold fronts, on the other hand, generally produce less intense rainfall that is more scattered and of shorter duration.

When air masses are forced up the windward side of slopes, hills and mountain ranges, they cool and produce rain through a process called *orographic lifting*. As the air passes the slope's highest point, it begins to lower and warm, leaving a rain shadow on the leeward side.

How much rain does each of these processes produce in a watershed? Several types of rain gauges have been developed to measure rainfall amounts at specific locations. Rain gauge networks are needed to understand the rainfall pattern in a watershed. An effective network is designed consistent with some of the important characteristics of the rainfall. For example, in an area where scattered thunderstorms are common, a network may have more gauges than in an equally sized area where rainfall is generally widespread.

The data obtained from rain gauge networks can be analyzed using different mathematic and graphic methods. Statistical analysis of rainfall data helps to identify rainfall's seasonal reliability and probability of occurrence. Rainfall analysis is a detailed subject of study in its own right, and a complete discussion is not included here. The reader is encouraged to refer to the references listed at the end of this chapter for further information (1,2,4,5).

It is important to note, however, that rainfall data collection and analysis does not need to be complicated. It just needs to be done. Because rainfall is a major input into the water cycle, understanding precipitation is fundamental to understanding the water potential of a watershed. A simple collection method is to place many tin cans throughout the reservation and have nearby residents report the amounts of water collected to tribal water officials. This informal technique for measuring and collecting rainfall will help identify important local patterns.

Once precipitation falls, what happens next? Does all precipitation follow the same surface water path through the hydrologic cycle in a watershed?

Interception, Stemflow and Throughfall

Four processes may occur as precipitation falls on a watershed: (1) the precipitation may be *intercepted* by leaves, twigs or stems and returned to the atmosphere by evaporation; (2) it may follow the stem to the soil surface as *stemflow*; (3) it may fall through the vegetation canopy cover to the soil surface as *throughfall*; or (4) in areas of little vegetation cover, it may fall directly on the land surface (4).

Rainfall is intercepted by the vegetation *canopy* and by *litter*. The canopy includes the leaves, twigs, branches, fruit and stems of plants and trees, while the litter is that portion of the canopy that has fallen to the ground. The extent of interception is determined by the form, density and surface texture of the canopy and litter, as well as by the characteristics of the precipitation (1,4,6).

Interception values usually are reported for a specific period, such as interception during an individual storm event or annual interception. Although forests generally have the highest interception values, well-developed grasses may intercept as much as 10-20% of the rain falling in a single storm. Net precipitation (Pn) is then calculated as

$$\text{Storm precipitation} - \text{interception} = \text{Pn}.$$

What is the importance of interception to the overall water budget or hydrologic cycle in a watershed? In some cases, interception may be considered a loss of water in the sense that interception will increase the amount of water available for evaporation. While interception does not conclusively affect flood development, vegetation cover, with its increased interception, does reduce the speed of rainfall impact and soil erosion. More water may also enter the soil by infiltration, promoting soil moisture accumulation.

Precipitation that reaches the soil or enters the plants may return to the atmosphere as water vapor. That process, and its role in water planning, is described next.

Evapotranspiration

Evaporation occurs when water is changed from its liquid state to vapor by heat (1). *Transpiration* occurs when the water vapor returns to the atmosphere through plants. Both processes often are referred to collectively as *evapotranspiration.*

Evapotranspiration is of great interest to planners and water managers because it strongly affects the water-yielding characteristics of a watershed and can be influenced by forest, range, agricultural and urban land use practices. As discussed earlier, evaporation studies apply to reservoir design. The potential benefits of a reservoir must be balanced against the evaporation water losses that will occur as a result of the creation of an additional lake surface. The irrigation water requirement for any specific crop depends in large part on the evapotranspiration characteristics of the crop and the area in question.

Heat energy converts water to vapor. While the sun is the source of the heat energy, the actual amount of energy available for evapotranspiration depends on the surface it reaches (it's reflectivity), the degree of cloudiness, and the orientation of the watershed (7). For example, if a watershed faces north, less sunlight would be available for evapotranspiration than in a south-facing watershed.

Given the energy available from the sun, the actual amount of evapotranspiration also depends on temperature, humidity, air pressure, wind conditions and the salinity of the water (2). There are several methods for measuring evapotranspiration. Where there is a sufficient supply of water, the methods used measure the *potential evapotranspiration* (PET). Where water may be scarce, the methods used look at the *actual evapotranspiration* (AET) to describe what is occurring under actual field conditions. The method chosen depends on the problem to be solved. For instance, a different method is used to determine evapotranspiration from a crop area than from a snow surface.

The limiting factor in all evapotranspiration calculations is the availability of data on air temperature, wind speed, net solar radiation, humidity and crop-usage patterns. Theoretical estimates can provide rough guidelines for crop selection and reservoir design and can project the change in evapotranspiration when one type of vegetation is converted to another. The water savings achieved by suppressing evaporation from watersheds also can be considered (8).

Infiltration and Soil

The soil is an integral part of the hydrologic cycle. The soil determines the pathways through which water flows once it reaches the earth's surface. The soil condition helps determine the timing and volume of *stream flow* and flooding potential in a watershed. Soil moisture is important to determining plant growth. Any land use practice that affects the soil will have an impact on the hydrologic cycle.

Water movement in the soil is called *infiltration.* The maximum rate at which a soil can receive moisture is known as the *infiltration capacity.* The soil will absorb the maximum amount of water from a rainstorm until its infiltration capacity is reached. At that time, additional water collects on the soil surface and runs over the ground to streams and rivers as *runoff* or *overland flow*. Once in the soil, water movement is referred to as *percolation*, which is generally a slow process. Water in the soil zone moves as underflow to a stream, percolates to become ground water, or is stored in the soil zone where it is subject to either transpiration by plants or direct evaporation (2).

Some hydrologists and water managers want to increase the infiltration rate in a watershed to promote *recharge* of ground water supplies; others want to decrease the infiltration rate to "harvest" water from a rainstorm.

Infiltration can be broken down into three interdependent processes: (1) entry into the soil, (2) storage within the soil, and (3) transmission of water through the soil. Restrictions on any one of these processes will reduce the infiltration rate.

Initial water entry into the soil surface is controlled by the physical and geological properties of the soil as well as by the soil's initial water content. The clay content, salt content, organic matter, root activity and a number of other factors influence water entry as well as the soil moisture content and the movement of water in the soil (4).

Plants draw water for their survival from the soil's moisture storage. The total water stored in the soil is held by capillary forces of attraction between the grains of the soil medium. The volume of water that a freely drained soil can hold for long periods of time is called the soil *field capacity*.

You will recall that water is removed from the soil by *evapotranspiration*, with plants taking water from the soil as if their roots were straws. When plants are unable to take any more water from the soil, the soil has reached its *wilting point*. The *plant available water* is the difference between the field capacity and the wilting point. One goal in agricultural development is to maintain the same amount of plant available water.

Soil infiltration properties affect the design of septic systems, drainage systems for agricultural areas and recharge facilities.

Runoff and Flooding

Runoff occurs when the soil's infiltration capacity is reached—when the soil has absorbed its maximum amount of water. An understanding of the runoff process is critical to water resources planning. Knowledge of the runoff process in a watershed provides water resource planners with a tool to recognize what land is appropriate for development and what land should be protected. For example, an area which easily becomes saturated with water would not be suitable for a housing development, but may be suitable for a water harvesting project. Forestry practices, road construction and range use all affect surface runoff.

Runoff that reaches stream channels within a day of the rainstorm over the watershed causes high rates of stream discharge. Measured in cubic feet per second flowing past a measuring station in the stream, stream discharge is known as *storm runoff* or *direct runoff*. Not all rainwater enters streams as storm runoff. Some rainwater percolates deep into the soil to become part of the ground water recharge.

In some areas, this ground water eventually re-emerges as stream flow and sustains a year-round *base flow* in the stream.

One of the first steps in runoff and stream flow analysis in a watershed is to determine the relationship between rainfall and runoff. A direct relationship between the two usually does not occur; the runoff may vary considerably in a drainage basin during different storms. Initial soil water content, the configuration of the soils in the watershed, and soil characteristics will determine the amount of water that will infiltrate the soil and the amount that will run off the land surface. It should be noted that a stream's peak flow will lag in time behind the highest intensity rainfall. The delay in peak flow is a function of how long it takes the soil to reach its infiltration capacity and the extent that runoff fills small depressions on the land surface before reaching the stream.

Several methods exist to compute storm runoff volume. One method is to try to make a direct correlation with rainfall. The U.S. Department of Agriculture's Soil Conservation Service (SCS) uses a method that predicts volumes of storm runoff from small agricultural catchments. The SCS method considers the hydrologic response of the soils and vegetation cover in a watershed and the soils' moisture content before a rainstorm and establishes a "hydrologic response coefficient" or "Curve number." Another method is the Rational Method, which is used to predict peak runoff volume from data on rainfall intensity and drainage basin characteristics.

Effective watershed management for runoff requires analysis of the lag time between rainfall and peak stream flow, an inventory of land use practices, a continuous record of stream flow measurements, and precipitation data. Such information is particularly critical to flood forecasting efforts.

Flooding from surface runoff warrants special attention here because it is such an important hydrologic problem. The annual losses of crops, property and human life caused by flooding is truly staggering. Flooding problems become more complicated as land use practices alter the watershed and cause flooding to previously unaffected, downstream areas (2). However, a planner can make rough calculations of the runoff effects from a development that are critically important to development planning and flood protection.

Storm runoff in a watershed makes its way to the various stream channels that drain the watershed. Flooding will occur if the volume of water in the storm runoff exceeds the stream channels' carrying capacity. For instance, in a one-square-mile catchment area of a watershed where the soils can absorb a half an inch from a two-inch rainstorm, almost 3.5 million cubic feet of runoff water will be produced in perhaps two hours (2). If the stream channel capacity of that catchment area is exceeded, flooding will occur.

Once in the stream channel, runoff moves downstream in a wave. The shape of the wave may change as it works its way down the watershed. In steep, straight mountainous streams and in desert washes during intense rainstorms, flow velocities are generally high and the waves move downstream with little change in shape. The amount of storage area within a watershed will work to attenuate or dampen the flood wave.

To predict floods and the damage they are likely to produce, the planner may need to assess one or more of the following features (2):

- *Volume of Storm Runoff.* This helps determine the design of storage works for flood control, water supply and irrigation.
- *Peak Flood Discharge.* This is essential for designing bridges, culverts and dam spillways.
- *Flood Height.* This helps the planner determine whether stream banks will be overtopped, the area that will be flooded, and the depth of flooding. Flood depth is particularly important in determining whether crops and structures will survive.
- *Storm and Runoff Time Distribution.* This is important for determining the duration of flooding and the effects of various tributaries. Such an analysis gives the planner the rate of rise of the flood wave, which is essential for the successful design of flood warning and evacuation procedures.
- *Valley Floor Flow Velocities.* This analysis helps determine the survival of structures on the floodplain and the amount of scour (erosion) of agricultural lands.

Ground Water Resources

Ground water resources are interdependent with surface water resources in the hydrologic cycle (9). In many cases ground water originates as surface water; surface water can infiltrate the ground from the natural recharge of precipitation, stream flow, lakes and reservoirs. A ground water system can serve as a storage reservoir for surface water resources. In certain geological situations ground water sustains stream flow. The dynamic interactions between surface and ground water are illustrated vividly by the growing number of ground water pollution incidents that have occurred after a contaminant made its way into the ground water from surface water pollution.

What does the connection between surface and ground water resources mean for the water resources planner? Both resources must be managed together for sound management and protection of either resource in a watershed.

To understand the hydrologic cycle in a watershed fully, the water resources planner must understand ground water geology, storage and movement. Such knowledge will allow the planner to assess more accurately the impacts of surface developments and ground water use strategies and policies.

Geological Considerations

As the name clearly implies, ground water is found beneath the surface of the earth. But what does that subsurface area look like that allows it to hold the vast quantities of ground water? Is it like a giant sponge? What are the rocks like that hold the ground water? Are they all the same? Why do some areas hold vast quantities of clean ground water, and some areas lose more ground water than they gain from precipitation or have undrinkable ground water?

The study of geology is a useful place to begin to find the answers to these questions. Geology is the earth science that studies the rocks of the earth. The type and structure of rocks in the subsurface will control different characteristics of the ground water, such as: (1) the occurrence and amount of water, (2) the water's chemical qualities, (3) the ease with which the water can be withdrawn from the rock material, and (4) the degree to which the ground water supply in the rocks can be replenished through natural and artificial recharge. The areas of the subsurface that contain ground water are called *aquifers*. *Hydrogeology* is the science that focuses specifically on the characteristics and properties of aquifers.

The subsurface rocks have been produced by a combination of forces over a period of millions of years. Rocks are classified into three general categories: igneous, metamorphic and sedimentary. The structural arrangement of these major rock types in large part determines the location and movement of ground water.

Igneous rocks are formed when hot, mobile rock material called magma solidifies. The final texture of igneous rocks is determined by the mineral composition of the magma, the presence of gases in the magma, and the cooling temperature and speed. The texture of igneous rocks is important for water occurrence: there is little water in fine-grained material, but the amount of water in a vesicular (cavity-filled) basalt may be substantial. Examples of igneous rocks include basalt and tuff.

Metamorphic rocks are formed when preexisting rocks are subjected to extreme changes in temperature, pressure and shearing stress forces within the earth. Granite, gneiss, schist, mica and limestone are common types of metamorphic rocks. Generally these rocks are not important aquifers, because they are too fine-grained to hold much water. Limestones are an exception, however, because under proper conditions, water can dissolve limestone and form caves that can store ground water. Fractures within metamorphic rocks may be important for ground water transportation.

Sedimentary rocks are derived from the erosion and transport of other rocks into sediment. Simply stated the sediment is deposited in layers on the earth's surface and under great pressures forms new rock material. Sedimentary rocks are distinguished according to their mineralogic composition and grain size. Sands, gravels, clays, sandstones and conglomerates are typical examples of sedimentary rocks. Sedimentary rocks often are important water-bearing formations.

Why can some rock structures store and transmit water better than others? One important feature is the difference in rock *porosity*. The porosity of a rock is a measure of the extent of the rock's pore spaces. It is these pore spaces, or voids, that can be occupied by ground water. Porosity is expressed as the ratio of the volume of pore space to the total volume of rock, and is commonly given as a percentage. For example, a rock with a porosity of 25% means that one-quarter of the rock consists of pore spaces.

Original porosity, or pore space, is created by the geologic processes that form the rock. *Secondary porosity* is created after the rock is formed, by joints, fractures, solution openings and openings formed by plants and animals. Pores also range in size. Depending on the connection between pores, they may be classified as isolated pores or communicating pores.

The arrangement of the various layers of the rocks in the subsurface is called the *stratigraphic relations*. Information on subsurface stratigraphy is obtained through examination of well cuttings, surface geophysical investigations or gravity surveys. A subsurface stratigraphic picture of a well field is presented in Figure 6-5. The picture may be used to delineate the types of aquifers present, their relative volumes of water, and the intervals that will not produce sufficient or good quality water. An *aquiclude* is a layer that contains water but cannot transmit it effectively. An *aquitard*, sometimes called a "leaky formation," contains water but can transmit it only at very slow rates.

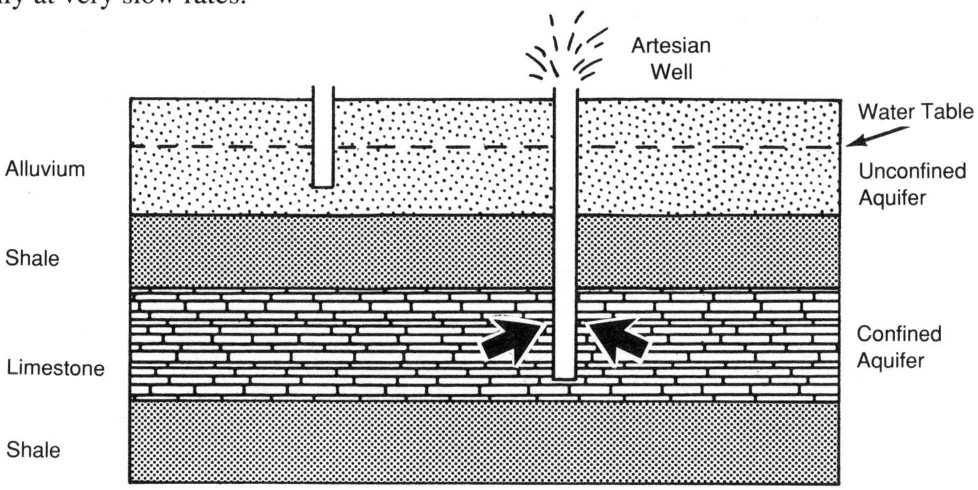

Figure 6-5. Subsurface Stratigraphic Picture of a Well Field Showing Both Confined and Unconfined Aquifers.

Aquifers are either confined or unconfined. Confined aquifers are bounded above and below by impervious layers (aquicludes). The water level in a confined aquifer well would rise to above the top of the confined aquifer. If the water level reaches the earth's surface, it is known as an *artesian* aquifer.

In an unconfined aquifer the water table serves as the upper boundary. This water-table aquifer is recharged directly from the ground by surface water, except in areas where the surface has been paved or the soils do not have a large infiltration capacity.

A good aquifer or set of aquifers may be comprised of many types of formations and alternative configurations. The key factor in assessing the quality of an aquifer is its ability to store and transmit water. Generally, the best aquifers are comprised of unconsolidated materials. These generally consist of the sands and gravels which may fill valley floors and are known as alluvial aquifers. Limestones are probably second in importance as aquifers.

Ground Water Storage and Movement

Water added to or removed from an aquifer represents a change in the *storage volume* of the aquifer. Porosity gives an indication of the total amount of water an aquifer can hold. The *storage coefficient*, on the other hand, indicates how much of the aquifer's water is available for stream flow or well discharge. Grain size, shape and distribution of pores, and overall porosity dictate the aquifer's storage coefficient.

In an unconfined or water-table aquifer, the storage coefficient is equivalent to the *specific yield*, a measure of the volume of water a rock will release upon pumping. Fine-grained materials have low specific yields and consequently yield small volumes of water to wells. The opposite is true of coarse-grained materials. Generally the volume of water released decreases with increasing depth below the land surface because the deeper aquifers are more heavily compacted.

In its natural state, ground water is always moving. The natural movement occurs in response to gravity as well as to temperature and chemical changes. Pumping also induces ground water movement (9).

Water flow through aquifers can be described by a series of equations that begin with Darcy's Law. Darcy's Law states that the rate of flow of ground water through rocks depends on the type of rock and its ability to transmit water, on the length of the flow path, and on the pressure change driving the flow.

The speed at which water moves through the aquifer during a particular time period is called the *hydraulic conductivity* and usually is expressed in feet per day. The hydraulic conductivity of an aquifer depends on a variety of physical factors, including porosity, particle size and distribution, and the shape and arrangement of particles (10). Generally, clay-like materials have low hydraulic conductivity, while sands and gravels display high values. Moreover, within an aquifer the hydraulic conductivity may be greater in one direction than in another. Although most ground water movement in shallow aquifers tends to be nearly horizontal, regional flow patterns can be quite complex.

Well Hydraulics—The Impact of Pumping

Wells inevitably affect the direction and rate of ground water movement as well as the volume of water stored in the aquifer (9). For maximum protection of ground water resources, then, well development must be designed carefully, with a full knowledge of the aquifer's properties in mind.

The same mathematical and physical properties used to describe natural ground water movement can be applied in describing the impacts of pumping on the water table. Figure 6-6 is an illustration of three wells, showing the effect of pumping on the slope of the water table.

When well number 1 begins to pump, water in the aquifer moves to the well from all directions, and the slope of the water table begins to change until it essentially forms a cone. This cone is called the "cone of depression." With continued pumping of well number 1, the water is drawn from an increasingly larger area, called the "radius of influence." The cone of depression also becomes larger—it deepens and widens its area. Eventually, it will begin to affect other wells in the area, dropping their water levels.

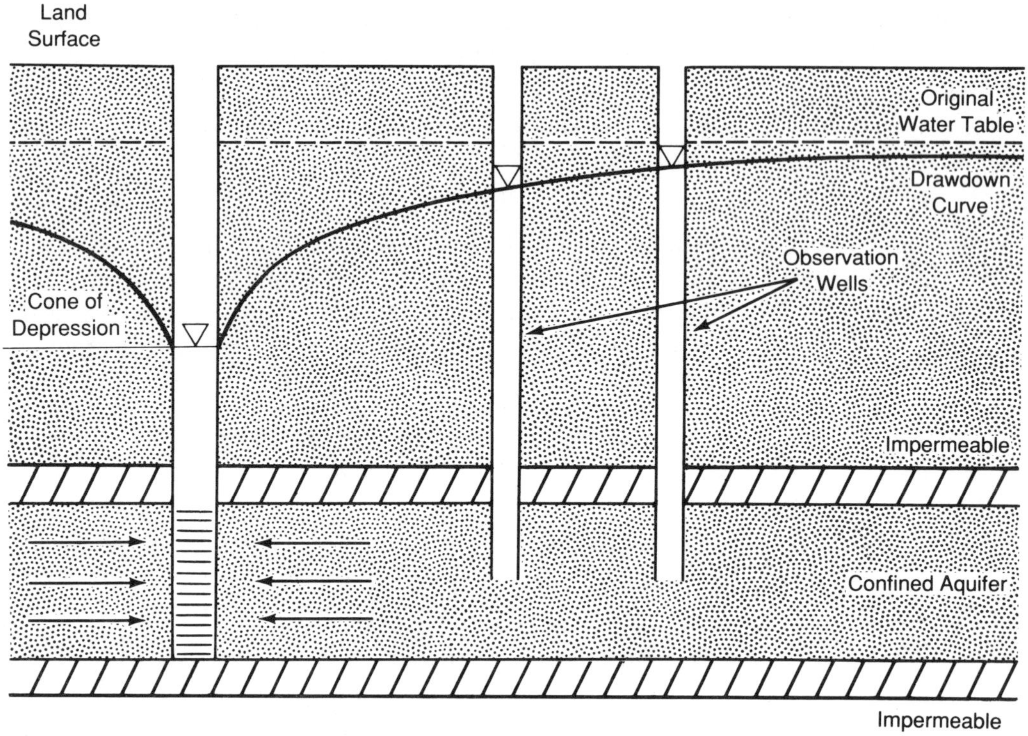

Figure 6-6. Schematic of Drawdown After Pumping Showing Cone of Depression.

The rate at which other wells are affected by the cone of depression is a function of the aquifer material (thickness, specific yield and type of rock), the spacing between the wells, the amount of pumping, and the geologic structural relations within the aquifer. All of the properties of the aquifer must be determined in order to assure proper well development.

The *specific capacity* of a well is a good measure of the well's productivity. To determine specific capacity, divide the well discharge by the drawdown. In a productive well a large discharge is achieved with very little drawdown. Thus, the larger the specific capacity, the better the productivity.

A discussion of ground water geology, storage and movement in the hydrologic cycle would be incomplete if it did not contain a discussion of the natural changes to ground water chemistry that occur as water passes through the aquifer. An understanding of the natural changes that occur in the hydrologic cycle will be helpful when studying water quality relations in the next chapter.

The Influence of Aquifer Materials on Water Quality

The geology or mineralogy of an aquifer exerts a profound influence on the quality of ground water. The connection between the aquifer material and water chemistry is so close that water quality maps (hydrochemical maps) can be constructed based on the mineralogical characteristics of the aquifer.

Several processes change ground water quality during its passage through the aquifer (7,10):

- *Dissolution*—the dissolving of a mineral by water;
- *Hydrolysis*—the decomposition or alteration of a chemical substance by water;
- *Precipitation*—the process that produces a separate solid phase within a liquid medium;
- *Adsorption*—the surface retention of solid, liquid or gas molecules by a solid;
- *Oxidation-Reduction*—the process that changes the electrical charge of an ion and alters its propensity to form chemical bonds with other substances; and
- *Microbiological Activity*—the change in chemical composition of water by the activities of microorganisms.

Because ground water is found in a variety of types of aquifers consisting of sedimentary, igneous or metamorphic rocks, the water chemistry varies according to the type of rock in which the water is found. Enough is known about ground water systems that allows general conclusions to be drawn about natural water chemistry based on the type of aquifer.

Generally water from igneous rocks contains low values of dissolved solids and high silica contents. The waters also may contain small amounts of calcium and sodium. Where mineral veins or ore bodies are present, the waters may contain some of the heavy metals such as lead, zinc, copper, nickel and cadmium. High values of fluoride may also be present in igneous rocks.

Several types of sedimentary rock aquifers exist, and each has a distinct influence on the chemical composition of the water. The sandstones make excellent aquifers and the chemical composition of their waters generally depends on the "cement" that binds the sandstones together. Silica, for instance, results in a low dissolved solids content, while more soluble cements such as calcium carbonate will cause ground water to contain naturally more calcium, sodium chloride and magnesium.

Ground water in clays, marls and silty sedimentary rocks is high in dissolved solids, particularly sulfate and chloride. Iron and fluoride may also be present, and the water generally has a low pH. Carbonate sedimentary rocks are from diverse origins and are very soluble. As a result they generally have large amounts of dissolved solids, particularly calcium, magnesium and carbonate ions. Chloride and sulfate are present in minor amounts.

Evaporites are sedimentary rocks that form as water evaporates and leaves behind salts. Thus, aquifers comprised of evaporites are distinctively high in dissolved solids, particularly the relict salts. Often ground water from evaporite aquifers is unsuitable for agricultural production or for human and livestock consumption.

Ground waters in coal, lignite and peat deposits often release oil and hydrocarbons to the water. The ground waters typically can have a low pH and contain the dissolved gas hydrogen sulfide (an odor producer), ammonia, organic acids, iron, manganese and iodide.

A wide variety of chemical constituents can be found in metamorphic rock because rocks of any kind can be the source of metamorphic rock. While calcium, sodium and bicarbonate can be present in high proportions, generally metamorphic rock aquifers have low concentrations of dissolved solids.

The relationship between aquifer materials and ground water quality provides a general guide for the interpretation of ground water quality. A general idea of expected water quality can be established through an examination of well cuttings alone. When the actual water quality is determined, if it differs from the expected conditions, the water resources planner may have a clue to a pollution problem or reason to believe the aquifer contains geologic material different from the well cuttings.

6-8. THE WATER BALANCE: AN INVESTIGATIVE TOOL

The previous sections reviewed each component of the hydrologic cycle with enough detail to point out some of the implications for watershed planning posed by each component. Now it is time to pull the various components back together to build a tool for water management planning that reflects the unity of the hydrologic cycle: the water balance.

The water balance refers to the balance between the water inflow to a drainage basin from precipitation and snowmelt and the water outflow through evapotranspiration, stream flow, deep percolation to ground water, and withdrawals by people in the watershed.

Simply stated, the water balance is merely an accounting procedure for water. The water balance can be used to understand water in the soil zone, a pond, or an entire watershed. The water balance for ground water resources is represented by the following equation:

$$\begin{pmatrix}\text{Ground Water}\\ \text{Inflow}\end{pmatrix} - \begin{pmatrix}\text{Ground Water}\\ \text{Outflow}\end{pmatrix} + \begin{pmatrix}\text{Natural}\\ \text{Replenishment}\end{pmatrix} - \begin{pmatrix}\text{Return}\\ \text{Flow}\end{pmatrix} + \begin{pmatrix}\text{Artificial}\\ \text{Recharge}\end{pmatrix}$$

$$+ \begin{pmatrix}\text{Inflow from}\\ \text{Streams and}\\ \text{Lakes}\end{pmatrix} - \begin{pmatrix}\text{Spring}\\ \text{Discharge}\end{pmatrix} - \begin{pmatrix}\text{Evapo-}\\ \text{transpiration}\end{pmatrix}$$

$$- \begin{pmatrix}\text{Pumpage and}\\ \text{Drainage}\end{pmatrix} - \begin{pmatrix}\text{Increase in Volume}\\ \text{of Water Stored in}\\ \text{Aquifer}\end{pmatrix}$$

The use and application of the water balance is straightforward. If all but one component of the water balance can be estimated or measured, the remaining component can be determined. For example, estimates or actual data on precipitation, infiltration, deep percolation, and stream flow from a watershed would provide an estimation of the amount of evapotranspiration occurring in the watershed if the inputs from precipitation exceed the stream flow out of the watershed. While this would provide only a rough estimate of evapotranspiration, it is a starting point.

Unfortunately, in practice usually very few measurements of various components of the hydrologic cycle are available. The informational requirements are substantial, as are the staff expertise, and the technical and monetary resources required to complete a hydrologic investigation. In the long run, however, a greater protection and enhancement of Indian water resources is possible only if the effort is made now to develop the comprehensive data base for water management. Tribal water managers must be informed in order to make long-term commitments of reservation water resources that permit the orderly development and conservation of Indian water.

REFERENCE NOTES

1. V.T. Chow, HANDBOOK OF APPLIED HYDROLOGY (1964).
2. Thomas Dunne and L. Leopold, WATER IN ENVIRONMENTAL PLANNING (1979).
3. Werner Stumm and James Morgan, AQUATIC CHEMISTRY (1980).
4. F.A. Branson and G.F. Gifford, RANGELAND HYDROLOGY (1972).
5. R. Linsley and L. Paulus, HYDROLOGY FOR ENGINEERS (1975).
6. Daniel Hillel, SOIL AND WATER: PHYSICAL PRINCIPLES AND PROCESSES (1971).
7. William D. Sellers, PHYSICAL CLIMATOLOGY (1965).
8. American Society of Civil Engineers, INTERDISCIPLINARY ASPECTS OF WATERSHED MANAGEMENT, symposium proceedings, Montana State University, 1970.
9. Jacob Bear, HYDRAULICS OF GROUND WATER (1979).
10. R.A. Freeze and J. Cherry, GROUNDWATER (1979).

SUGGESTED READINGS

In addition to the reference works cited in the text, the reader may wish to consult: Georg Matthess's THE PROPERTIES OF GROUND WATER (1982), and a book by Vernon Snoeyink and D. Jenkins entitled WATER CHEMISTRY (1980).

CHAPTER 7

Water Quality Relations in Watershed Management

7-1. WATER CHEMISTRY AND THE HYDROLOGIC CYCLE

Water quality is of increasing concern to those involved in water management. Water quality refers to the physical, chemical, biological and radiological characteristics of water that affect its suitability for agriculture, industry, domestic consumption, recreation and other uses. As noted in the previous chapter, water in a watershed can contain one or more additional substances such as chemical matter (inorganic ions, dissolved gases and dissolved organic matter), physical matter (silts, solids, clay and colloids), biological matter (bacteria, viruses, algae and protozoa) or radiological matter.

Pollution of a water supply results when a substance is added to water that adversely affects people, plants or animals. Pollution does not come only from man-made sources; natural sources such as increased sediments from erosion can cause pollution.

Because the hydrologic cycle moves water through the environment, the cycle acts as a distribution system by which the substances in water are dispersed easily throughout the environment. Thus, industrial pollutants carried in rainwater can acidify lakes and affect forest productivity and fisheries, even at great distances from where they were initially introduced into the hydrologic cycle. Similarly, a spill of a few thousand gallons of some organic compounds may contaminate many square miles of ground water aquifers and persist for several years. The cumulative and potentially toxic effects of waterborne pollutants making their way into the food chain may pose serious challenges to water managers and policymakers in the years to come.

The hydrologic cycle uses water to move minerals and chemicals between the atmosphere and the earth, the surface and subsurface waters, the geologic material, and the plants and animals. The amount of time that water is stored in a particular component of the hydrologic cycle (*e.g.*, the soil zone or ground water) is called the *residence time* of water. The residence time is critical to the fate and transport of contaminants. The residence time affects both the water manager's prediction of potential impacts to water quality as a result of a future activity and the water manager's estimation of the extent of existing contamination in a particular watershed. The actual transportation of contaminants throughout the hydrologic cycle depends on many factors, such as the geologic mediums in the cycle, the properties and volume of contaminants, and the extent of precipitation.

Commonly, biological microorganisms, sediment load, the diversity of aquatic life and the oxygen content indicate the health of a stream and a watershed. Careful monitoring of water quality on reservation lands can assist the planner in establishing an understanding of the background data that is basic to the design and development activities that will impact water quality. Water quality policy strategy is dictated by the type of pollution from a development activity and the potential pathways of pollution movement in the hydrologic cycle of the watershed.

An early step that must be taken in developing a water quality policy, however, is to ascertain the physical characteristics of the water in the watershed.

7-2. PHYSICAL CHARACTERISTICS OF WATER

Sediment concentration, turbidity and temperature are the most important physical characteristics affecting water quality. For instance, all three characteristics can affect the design and safety of small dams, the effectiveness of water treatment processes and the viability of aquatic life. A water resources planner needs a basic understanding of each of these physical characteristics.

Sediment Load and Turbidity

A natural attribute of a river or stream system is the *sediment load* it can carry. Each river or stream has an energy level that allows it to carry a certain amount and size of sediment. Over time, the sediment load and stream energy level achieve a balance that depends on the watershed's soil, climate and vegetation. The balance leads to a relative stability between the channel bed and the streambanks. Many rivers, such as the "muddy Mississippi," are known for their high sediment loads. Others are famous for water clarity and low sediment loads, such as the Clearwater in Idaho and the Upper Green River in Wyoming.

A decrease in a river system's sediment load will lead to a change in the energy level and will result in downcutting and bank erosion. For example, after the construction of Boulder Dam on the Colorado River, much of the Colorado's natural sediment was trapped behind the dam. As a result, the clear water released from the dam eroded the riverbed for miles downstream, in some places over 15 vertical feet.

On the other hand, extensive soil erosion in a watershed, resulting from logging, overgrazing or urbanization, for example, will increase the sediment load and cause a gradual buildup of the streambed, known as aggradation. This process may lead to a change in the channel pattern of the river or may cause sedimentation of lakes and reservoirs.

An increase in the silt or sediment concentration in streams has several biological effects. Trout, for example, lay their eggs in shallow depressions in the low flow areas of streams. The stream's sediment load is prone to settle in these low flow areas. An increase in sediment load, therefore, not only affects the streambed areas where the eggs are likely to be located, but also may suffocate the young fish whose gill structure is clogged easily by sediments.

Turbidity deals with the extent to which sediments in water interfere with how well the water lets through light. Turbidity causes light to be scattered through and absorbed by the water rather than transmitted directly through it and is measured in Turbidity Units (T.U.).

Turbidity may be caused by a wide variety of materials in differing sizes. Silt, bacteria, algae and humic substances all give rise to turbidity. What creates turbidity will vary from location to location. For example, glacial-fed rivers and streams derive their turbidity from the ground "rock flour" that is produced by the grinding action of the glacier; while water in agricultural areas receives turbidity from eroded soil materials.

The amounts of sediment concentration and turbidity in natural river systems can vary greatly. The geologic and organic material in the watershed, and the size and intensity of precipitation events impact sediment concentration and turbidity levels. Suspended sediment becomes a pollutant when the concentration exceeds the natural background sediment load. Because a streambed, banks and aquatic life will adjust to the background load, often the change from natural conditions is what causes the primary problems.

From a development planning perspective, turbidity and sediment load have four significant impacts that should be considered: (1) both may interfere with the human digestive system; (2) both interfere with the water disinfection process and may actually "shield" harmful bacteria from treatment processes; (3) aesthetically, turbid waters are displeasing; and (4) both turbidity and sediment load interfere with photosynthesis, the process by which aquatic plants make food during growth.

Temperature

River and lake temperatures vary daily and seasonally in response to local climatic conditions. The temperatures normally range from 32° to 77° F, and aquatic ecosystems adjust to the seasonal changes and the constraints that temperatures impose (1).

On a seasonal basis lakes experience temperature stratification. During the early summer, two zones generally are seen, as depicted in Figure 7-1(a). The zones, the hypolimnion and the epilimnion, generally are caused by the summer's intense sunlight and low winds, which prevent mixing. During the summer, dead organic matter and algae settle to the lake bottom, consuming the dissolved oxygen reserve in the hypolimnion. During the fall, a mixing occurs, which cycles nutrients between the surface and deep water as shown in Figure 7-1(b). Some lakes undergo this stratification and mixing process more than once a year.

Although some deep rivers demonstrate temperature stratification, generally turbulence creates even temperature distribution.

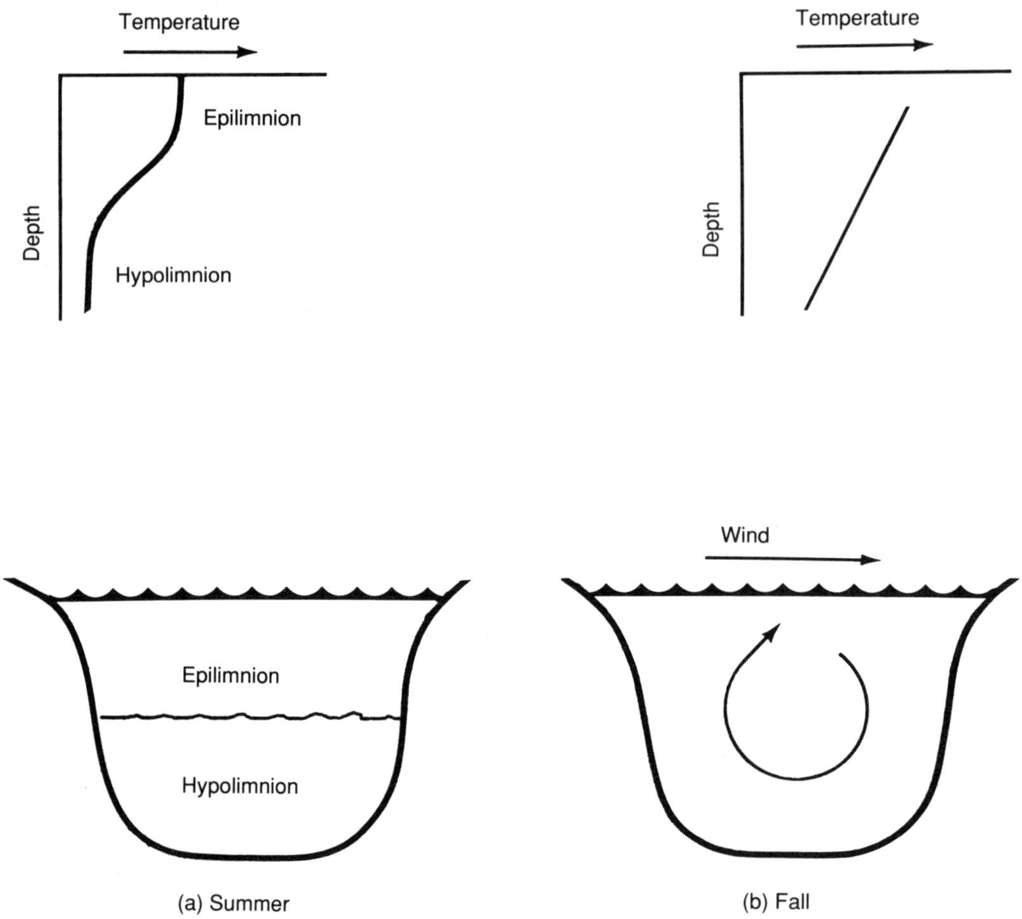

Figure 7-1. Temperature Regime in Lakes as a Function of Season.

Ground water is subject to a geothermal gradient that exists in the earth. Generally, the depth of ground water affected by seasonal and daily temperature changes is not more than 40 feet.

The natural temperatures of streams and lakes can be affected by cooling water from nuclear and coal-fired power plants as well as by heated effluent discharged from industrial plants. Stream temperatures also change when logging operations remove the canopy cover from streambanks.

Adding heated water to streams and lakes can cause a great rise in temperature in the immediate area below where the heated water is added. The rise in temperature depends on the size and volume of the river or lake and the temperature of the heated water. As water moves away from the heat source, it cools. The cooling rate will depend on atmospheric conditions, the characteristics of the water body and the extent of mixing.

Solid particles will settle faster in water at higher temperatures. Moreover, an increase in temperature will decrease the solubility of oxygen in water, a parameter vital to stream life. Temperature also affects the lower organisms in the aquatic food chain, such as plankton and crustaceans, which, in turn, affects the food supply of higher organisms. Some pathogenic bacteria that thrive in warmer waters may be harmful to fish.

In some extreme cases, fish have been killed by lethally high temperatures or by sudden releases of heat below power plants. More subtle effects of such thermal pollution are changes in the feeding and spawning behavior of fish and in their susceptibility to disease. The migration pattern of some fish is triggered by temperature, and this behavior may be disrupted by thermal pollution.

7-3. DISSOLVED GASES, BIOLOGICAL AND CHEMICAL OXYGEN DEMAND

Carbon dioxide (CO_2) and oxygen (O_2) are the most important dissolved gases present in water. Carbon dioxide is responsible for much of a water's initial acidity and thus for the capability of water to dissolve, or weather, the material with which it comes into contact. All living organisms are dependent upon oxygen in one form or another to maintain metabolic processes that produce energy for growth and reproduction. The "atmospheric conditions" of O_2 and CO_2 existing in water are of prime importance to the planner.

All gases in the atmosphere are soluble in water to some degree. Temperature, atmospheric pressure and salinity affect the amount of oxygen in water. Dissolved oxygen in a stream may be considered a resource, and the level of dissolved oxygen is one clear indicator of stream health. Not only do fish and aquatic organisms use dissolved oxygen, but people also use dissolved oxygen for waste disposal. Dissolved oxygen helps render some types of waste innocuous.

Dissolved oxygen can reach a critically low level—the critical oxygen deficit—in streams used for waste discharge. Dissolved oxygen reaches its minimum level at some distance downstream from the waste discharge. Turbulence and mixing will aerate the water naturally and renew the dissolved oxygen reserve in the water at some point further downstream. It is very important, however, that planners be able to estimate the point at which oxygen reaches the critical low, called the critical deficit.

Because every stream channel is different, dissolved oxygen standards are determined on a site-specific basis. Stream geometry, flow conditions, the aquatic life to be affected and the characteristics of the waste are the factors that must be taken into account when establishing the standards.

Quantities closely related to the dissolved oxygen content of water are the biological oxygen demand (BOD) and the chemical oxygen demand (COD). The BOD is the quantity of oxygen required or consumed by microorganisms in the biological decomposition of organic matter. The COD is the quantity of oxygen required to oxidize industrial waste. COD and BOD are used together to estimate the strength of a pollutant in waste water. The measurements of BOD and COD are used to evaluate waste treatment plant design and the potential use of a river or stream for waste disposal.

7-4. CHEMICAL CHARACTERISTICS OF WATER

The chemical constituents in water also affect its suitability for drinking, recreation, irrigation, industry and aquatic organisms. Optimal limits, or standards, for a variety of common chemical constituents are known; however, far less is known about minor elements such as the trace metals lead, selenium, copper and cadmium. Over the last forty years, the expansion of many industries has led to the release of a vast quantity of chemicals into surface and ground waters. Many of these substances are toxic, but the effects of others are almost completely unknown. The ability to detect these elements at low concentrations was developed only in the last twenty years. Many more toxic chemicals presently in surface and ground waters will be detected, and their health effects known, only in the decades to come (2).

The following discussion presents an introduction to the sources of the dissolved constituents—solutes—with a focus on the major elements affected by human activity.

The Acquisition of Solutes by Natural Waters

Chemical constituents are added initially to surface and ground waters by precipitation. What solutes are present in rain depends on where the rain comes from and what it comes in contact with before it reaches the ground. Moreover, the type of material rain comes in contact with when it does reach the ground will impact what chemical constituents are added to ground and surface waters by precipitation.

Precipitation that develops over the oceans contains calcium, sodium and magnesium from sea salt scattered into the atmosphere by breaking waves. Inland precipitation picks up dissolved constituents from dust particles, gaseous emissions from plants and soils, and industrial emissions. Acid rain, for instance, stems from the interaction of water with the oxides of gaseous sulfur and nitrogen compounds released by industries and automobiles.

The chemistry of rainwater also can change when it comes into contact with plants. Rain that falls first onto a forest canopy most likely will bring different chemical constituents to the ground than rain that lands directly on the soil surface.

When rainwater reaches the soil surface processes may occur that alter its chemical character. First, if the water evaporates at the soil surface, it leaves behind its dissolved chemical constituents as a residue on or near the soil surface. That residue may or may not then be redissolved and carried to the subsurface or surface waters by subsequent rainfall. If the rain first runs off the land surface to a stream, its chemical character changes as it picks up and reacts with silt and sediment in the stream channel. Stream water chemistry is influenced substantially by the type of material upon which rain falls and by the material's susceptibility to both mechanical and chemical erosion.

The soil zone is an important biologic and geologic medium that alters the chemistry of rainwater through a number of processes. Water chemistry is altered as the water infiltrates the full soil column of roots, organic matter, clay minerals, weathered geologic material, soil water and dissolved gases.

Some of the dissolved materials in rainwater are leached through to the ground water by deep percolation. The volume and quantity of dissolved materials leached to the ground water can have important implications for agricultural development and for the management of salt-affected soils. For instance, adequate water must be applied to salt-affected soils to leach the salts out of the soil zone to maintain crop productivity. However, salts that are leached from the soil zone may affect ground water quality adversely by raising the salinity or the total dissolved solids.

The actual amount of deep percolation depends on the quantity of rainfall and irrigation water applied, on the extent of evaporation, on the vegetation's characteristics, and on the properties of the soil column. These factors also impact the amount of time soil water is in contact with the soil column.

Ground water's prolonged contact with earth materials creates the largest natural alterations in water chemistry. Ground water, with its dissolved chemical constituents, is largely responsible for the amount and chemical character of the dissolved materials carried to the oceans by the streams (1). The reader is encouraged to review the relation of the chemical character of water to its geologic environment mentioned in Chapter 6. It should be recalled that the significance of this relation lies in its definition of background, or ambient, conditions of ground water quality. A full understanding of background chemical values is important before predictions can be made regarding the impact of proposed development strategies on ground water quality.

Superimposed on the background conditions are, of course, the chemical components affected by human activity. The major human impacts increase the total dissolved solids in both surface and ground water. The examples are numerous. Irrigation, cooling towers for power plants, and municipal waste treatment plants all affect the salt content of water to a great degree. In addition, a change in the ratio of the major ions, such as the sodium to calcium ratio, might render the water unsuitable for agriculture. An increase in the concentration of the major ions, particularly calcium and magnesium, will increase water hardness and scaling and will create soap consumption problems in domestic water systems. Water high in sodium can have health implications, such as affecting the development of cardiovascular disease. Septic tanks, industrial activities and the salting of highways also alter major ion concentrations.

Trace Metals

Small, or trace, concentrations of metals such as iron, zinc, copper and lead are naturally present in water as a result of the rock-weathering process. While many trace metals are necessary for plant and animal growth, excess amounts can be dangerous to plants and animals and highly toxic to aquatic ecosystems. The cumulative effect of trace metals in the food chain can affect human health and reproduction adversely.

Trace metals can be introduced to the hydrologic cycle by direct dumping of industrial waste or by other activities such as mining. Metals become highly mobile and, in their toxic forms, persist as water becomes anaerobic, *i.e.*, devoid of oxygen. Thus, the summertime release of dam-impounded water also may release a host of potentially mobile trace metals into a waterway. Metals in waterways consume oxygen and may suppress much biologic activity that ordinarily would tend to purify the water. Metal loading is particularly acute where an industrial process or a mine uses the entire low flow of a watercourse for waste disposal (1,3,4,5).

Pesticides and Other Organic Compounds

Over the last forty years, there has been a significant increase in the use of complex organic compounds such as insecticides and herbicides. Some pesticides enter aquatic ecosystems by direct fallout or are adsorbed onto solid particles of the soil and subsequently removed by soil erosion. While the concentrations of some of these pesticides in a watercourse may be low, because the pesticides may be soluble in the fatty tissues of some organic matter, they can accumulate in the food chain. Some classes of organic compounds are relatively insoluble in water and are environmentally persistent. These compounds are also a principal source of odor in water.

The toxic effects of many of these compounds are not yet fully known, and water quality standards have not been established for some of them. Moreover, not only can these compounds be directly lethal to an individual animal, but they also can be lethal to an animal population by interrupting the reproduction cycle.

Pesticide effects on people also are not understood fully although pesticides are known to accumulate in our bodies. Many pesticides are known or suspected to cause cancer and/or birth defects. The health implications from long-term exposure to low doses of these chemicals is of particular concern to many people. For instance, epidemiological, *i.e.*, disease-related, studies have shown significant correlations between the incidence of cancer and the origin of certain drinking water supplies. Wells have been closed because of pesticides found in ground water.

Radioactive Materials

Earth materials contain naturally radioactive substances, elements which change spontaneously into other elements by the emission of charged particles from the nuclei of their structures. For example, uranium-238 radioactively decays to radon-222 (a gas) and a number of other products. The uranium decay products are some of the most hazardous materials known to man, and they may persist in the environment for thousands of years. The type of emission, *e.g.*, alpha, beta or gamma radiation, and the strength of these particles are what cause damage to plant, animal and human tissues.

Radioactive materials concentrated through the mining and milling of uranium pose a significant and dangerous threat to the hydrologic cycle. Radioactive dust can be carried by water to streams, lakes and ground water. Uranium mill pond leachate can travel many miles to contaminate ground water resources.

Like pesticides, long-term exposure to low levels of radioactive materials poses a health concern. The tremendous lag time between exposure to radioactive materials and the development of cancer, however, points to the need for long-term epidemiological studies before conclusions can be drawn regarding the danger posed by an activity. Unfortunately, the data are seldom available, yet every development decision requires the planner to define an acceptable level of risk of exposure.

7-5. CONTAMINANT TRANSPORT IN WATER SYSTEMS

The movement of pollutants through the water environment depends on many factors, including the nature and volume of the contaminant, the nature of the medium through which it travels and the capacity of the medium to purify the waste. In lakes, mixing may cause dilution of the pollutant; metals, however, may behave quite differently on the surface and at the bottom of a lake. Pollutants may accumulate in aquatic organisms and in lake-bottom sediments. Microorganisms may consume some of the pollutants; however, in the process they may produce noxious by-products. While decay of a pollutant to a less harmful form is a natural process, that may or may not be among the pollutant's characteristics.

In stream systems, turbulence creates the natural aeration process that may render some harmful substances less mobile and less toxic. Compared to lakes, mixing in a stream or river has greater potential to purify pollutants. On the other hand, streams and rivers can transport waste more rapidly to other areas.

In ground water systems, two processes affect pollutant movement: advection and dispersion. *Advection* is the dominating factor and is the process by which solutes are transported by the bulk motion of the flowing fluid in the ground water system. The hydraulic properties of the aquifer and the gradient, or driving force of water motion, control advection.

Dispersion results from two natural processes: mechanical mixing and molecular diffusion. Microscopic variations in ground water velocity within the pore spaces of an aquifer create mechanical mixing. Molecular diffusion occurs as a result of the inherent random motion of the solute particles and the concentration gradient existing between the ambient ground water and the contaminated water (5,6).

The sediments of the ground water medium also subject contaminants to sorption and retardation action. Coupled with other chemical and biological transformations that retard contaminant movement in a ground water system, how the contaminant spreads within a ground water system may vary. Figure 7-2 provides a simple example of a waste dump that introduces a variety of toxic organic compounds to an aquifer. Contaminant "A" is heavier than water and sinks to the bottom of the aquifer, creating an irregularly shaped plume. If "A" was the only contaminant present, only the deep well (number 3) would be affected. However, if contaminants "B" and "C" were also present, all three wells would be affected.

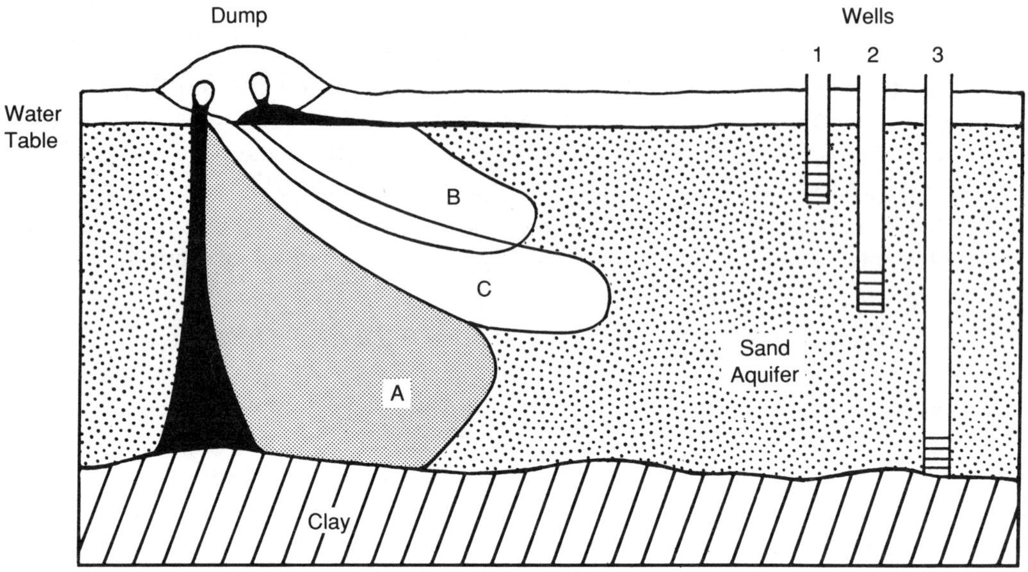

Figure 7-2. Movement of Different Organic Compounds in a Ground Water System.

Several mathematical formulations and models of solute and contaminant transport in aquatic ecosystems currently are available for many compounds. Although this information exists, the reactions, sorption, decay and ion exchange processes for literally thousands of chemical compounds still are undefined. Even for those compounds that have solute transport models, often the sophistication of the models outstrips the ability to gather adequate field data substantiating or refuting the model's predictions. There is also an urgent need to further define the aquifer properties affecting contaminant transport for ground water systems. Field sampling in combination with theoretical approaches would assist such an effort.

To investigate a water quality problem, an initial step is to identify the known pollutant sources and the chemical, biological or radiological elements involved. The next step is to identify the physical properties of the water system and its governing natural processes. Extensive water quality monitoring and the selection or development of a transport model, in concert with field studies, then would follow.

7-6. MANAGING WATER QUALITY

Both surface and ground water resources are linked in the preservation and management of water quality. The specific water quality management policy taken by each tribe will be unique to its own situation. It is possible, however, to outline a few management goals that could serve as potential guidelines for a water quality policy.

An initial goal would be to assure that the total water environment—ground water, lakes, streams and rivers—is protected from environmental pollution. To accomplish this goal the pathways of water movement through the hydrologic cycle must be considered. In protecting ground water, for example, recharge areas would have land use controls, and waste disposal would be prohibited in highly permeable geologic media. To protect the quality of surface waters, land use controls would need to be implemented in contributing watersheds to prevent sediment loading, temperature changes, and contaminated runoff from entering stream courses.

A second goal of water quality management would be to protect and conserve the natural aquatic ecosystem to the greatest extent possible by maintaining the ecological balance and the processes necessary for the natural functioning of the system. For example, the dissolved oxygen resource in a stream is one attribute of the ecosystem that is essential to a self-purifying stream and that would need to be maintained. Moreover, soils that have a large capacity to absorb potential pollutants should be protected (4).

A final goal of water quality management might be to assure the protection of human health and well-being, and the structure and fertility of soils, from exposure to toxic chemicals and pathogenic microorganisms that have acute or chronic effects in domestic, agricultural or waste water systems. A problem with this goal is that new information is required to delineate the chronic and acute effects of toxic chemicals fully. Thus, a water quality policy under this goal should be designed for preventative measures.

The protection and enhancement of tribal water resources over the coming decades depends in large part on a clear definition of the resource's volume, quality and pathways as it passes through reservation lands. The hydrologic cycle is the distribution network through which water and the chemical materials it contains are transported. Hence, the protection of a water supply demands the protection of water quality along with water quantity.

REFERENCE NOTES

1. T. Dunne and L. Leopold, WATER IN ENVIRONMENTAL PLANNING (1979).
2. Veronica Pye, GROUND WATER CONTAMINATION IN THE UNITED STATES (1983).
3. James I. Drever, THE GEOCHEMISTRY OF NATURAL WATERS (1981).
4. John Cherry and R.A. Freeze, GROUNDWATER (1979).
5. Douglas Mackay, P. Roberts and J. Cherry, *Transport of Organic Contaminants in Ground Water*, ENVIRONMENTAL SCIENCE AND TECHNOLOGY, vol. 19, no. 5 (April 1985).
6. Franklin Schwartz, *Macroscopic Dispersion in Porous Media: The Controlling Factors*, WATER RESOURCES RESEARCH, vol. 11, no. 4 (1977) pp. 743-52.

SUGGESTED READINGS

In addition to the chapter references, the reader may wish to consult the following: Samuel D. Faust and J. Hunter, PRINCIPLES AND APPLICATION OF WATER CHEMISTRY (1967); Sawyer and McCarty, CHEMISTRY FOR ENVIRONMENTAL ENGINEERING (1979); Snoeyink and Jenkins, WATER CHEMISTRY (1979); W. Stumm and R. Morgan, AQUATIC CHEMISTRY (1977); W. Stumm and R. Seiver, *Quality of Water: Surface and Subsurface*, in THE SCIENTIFIC BASIS OF WATER-RESOURCE MANAGEMENT (1982); and Forrest B. Wright, RURAL WATER SUPPLY AND SANITATION (1977).

Part III

MAKING THE DIFFICULT CHOICES

CHAPTER 8

Evaluation of Water Use Alternatives

8-1. INTRODUCTION

Evaluation is a key step in the water planning process. Because evaluation by definition means "place a value upon," the perspective of the individual or group doing the evaluation is fundamentally important. For example, a possible water project almost certainly will be evaluated differently by a funding source than it would by a tribe, a city, or a firm proposing the project. Moreover, a funding source that consists of private investors will be concerned principally with the project's financial security and the ability of the responsible party to repay the funds loaned. If the funding source is the federal government, the national benefits and costs of the project and the political value to legislators may be more important than the ability to repay the funds. What gets counted in evaluating the project, then, will differ from one perspective to the next. Although a given project may look attractive to a tribe from an environmental, cultural, and economic perspective, it may not look attractive to others.

What aspect of a project is being "counted" to arrive at a measure of its value? The unit of measurement is called the "metric." For many purposes the appropriate metric is the dollar. That is to say, a potential investor will evaluate the project in terms of its dollar flow. At the outset, what will the project cost in dollars? What revenues, in dollars, will be generated from the project? Even if the project's initial product or service is measured in a unit other than dollars, say kilowatt-hours of hydroelectric power generated, these commonly will be converted into their dollar value to compare all aspects of the project in standard units.

A tribe can use the dollar metric to evaluate a project to determine if it is consistent with some of the tribe's objectives. The dollar metric will work well as a common measure of value for many evaluators. But for others, the dollar metric may not be adequate. Traditional tribal members, for instance, may see water and its use according to spiritual and community values that cannot be measured in monetary terms. If this is the situation, the project should be evaluated by the different metrics.

The different perspectives and the need for different metrics usually means that several evaluations generally must be conducted for all major projects. First and foremost, a water use activity must be evaluated to determine if it is compatible with tribal goals and objectives. As noted in the following chapter, that evaluation will have been discussed to some extent when the planning goals and objectives are chosen.

But other evaluations must occur. If, for example, one water use activity under consideration is an irrigation project, then the irrigation project will have to be evaluated in terms of the market for the agricultural products to be grown in the project: is the opportunity to sell the products at a profit good, or are agricultural market conditions poor? Leasing water to a municipality may be another water use possibility. How should that possibility be evaluated in terms of the willingness of the municipality to pay for the water? What are water and water rights selling for in the marketplace?

So far this discussion has been a bit abstract. Now, to make evaluation more concrete, two evaluation processes will be explained. These processes describe how commodities are evaluated in the marketplace, and how the federal government, through its Bureau of Reclamation or Army Corps of Engineers, evaluates water projects. The discussions are brief and nontechnical, so oversimplification results. The processes, however, are important to tribal water projects, so a basic introduction to them plays a useful role.

8-2. WATER MARKETS

Appropriately enough, the commodity that will be used to illustrate the market mechanism is water itself. Water and water rights are regularly bought and sold in the arid West. The water and water rights markets remain rudimentary when compared to markets for common stock or agricultural products, and their proper role and future in the West are current topics of much public debate. In the following example the idealized version of a water market will be constructed.

Imagine an auction in a barn with an auctioneer standing in front of the room. The commodity to be traded consists of perpetual rights to consume each year one acre foot of water from a stream. A variety of people are in the barn. On the one hand, there are people who have come in, farmers particularly, who currently hold water rights and are interested in selling them. Individually, these people may hold rights to one acre-foot or 100 acre-feet, depending on their particular circumstances. Also in the barn are prospective users, the potential buyers of the water rights. These buyers may be representatives of municipalities, energy companies, or other firms that have some sort of development in mind for which they need water.

Those who came into the barn to sell water rights are called "suppliers"; those who came in with the intent to buy water rights are termed "demanders." The auction process—or market—goes like this. The auctioneer hollers out a price, say, "$500 for the right to an acre-foot." The suppliers then take out paper and write down how many acre-feet of rights they each would be willing to supply or sell at $500 an acre-foot.

Similarly, the demanders from municipalities and industrial firms write down the quantity of water rights, in acre-feet, that they would buy at that $500 price. All of these slips of paper then are passed up to the front where the auctioneer totals them. The auctioneer then knows the total quantity of water rights supplied and demanded at a price of $500.

Assume that the quantity demanded at $500 per right to an acre-foot is 12,700 acre-feet and the quantity supplied at that price is 1,500 acre-feet. At $500, then, the quantity demanded and the quantity supplied are not in balance. The auctioneer then hollers out another price, say $1000, and repeats the totaling procedure. The auctioneer continues to holler out a series of prices and receives the supply and demand data represented in Table 8-1.

Table 8-1

Hypothetical Supply and Demand for Water Rights

Auctioneer Price ($ per right to an acre-foot)	*Quantity of Rights Supplied (in acre-feet)*	*Quantity of Rights Demanded (in acre-feet)*
$500	1,500	12,700
1,000	3,000	11,400
1,500	4,500	10,100
2,000	6,000	8,800
2,500	7,500	7,500
3,000	9,000	6,200
3,500	10,500	4,900
4,000	12,000	3,600
4,500	13,500	2,300
5,000	15,000	1,000

Figure 8-1 shows this data plotted with the vertical axis for the prices that the auctioneer announced, and the horizontal axis for the quantities of rights demanded and supplied at each price. The two line graphs represent demand and supply.

The supply curve slopes upward to the right and shows that at higher prices more suppliers would be willing to supply more water rights. A farmer may not have much interest in selling water rights at $500, but at $5,000 for each right to an acre-foot, the dollar value of the farmer's rights starts to become substantial. If, for example, a farmer has the rights to consume 150 acre-feet each year, then at $1,000 per right to a consumptive acre-foot the farmer would have $150,000 worth of water rights. At a price of $5,000 per right to a consumptive acre-foot, the farmer would have $750,000 worth of water rights.

Table 8-1 also shows the quantity of rights that the municipalities and other potential buyers in the barn would demand at each of the price levels. When plotted on Figure 8-1, this data shows that the demand schedule slopes downward to the right; at higher prices lesser quantities are demanded.

How do these supply and demand schedules interact to determine the prevailing price for water rights at a given time on this stream? The answer is that the point of

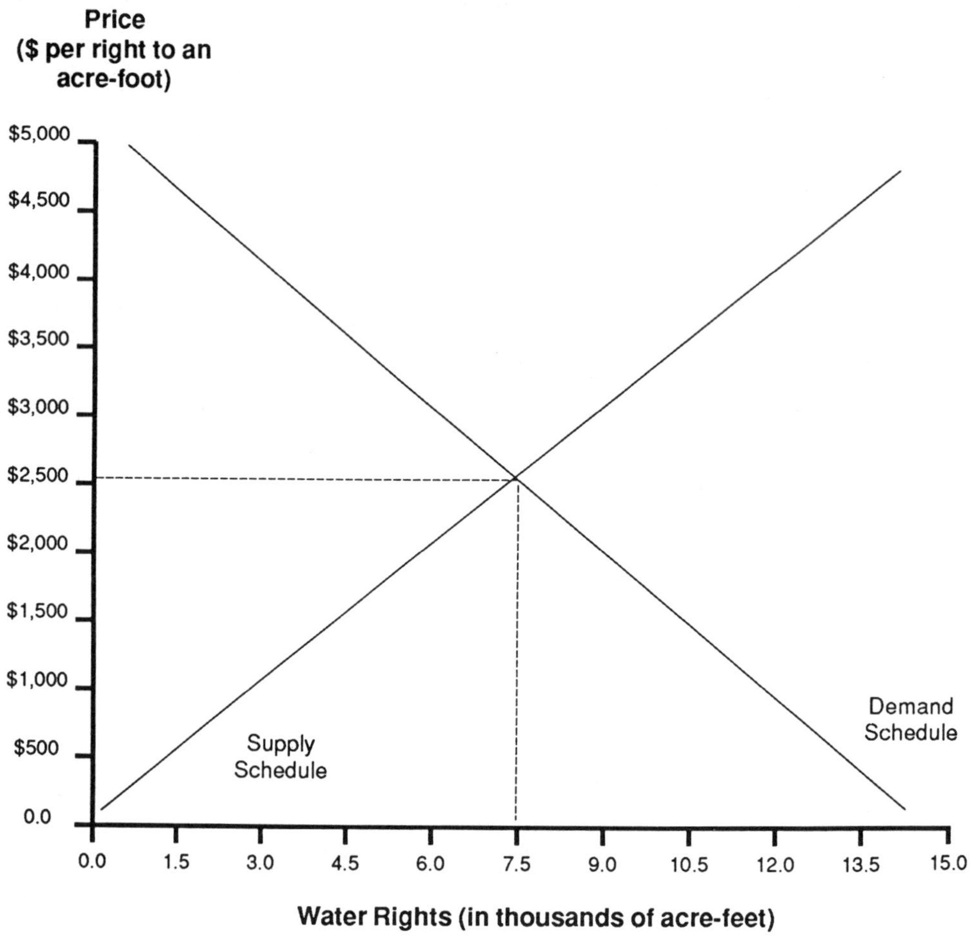

Figure 8-1. Graph of Supply and Demand for Water Rights.

intersection at which the supply and the demand schedules cross is the single price at which the quantity of rights demanded by the municipalities and others is the same as the quantity of rights supplied by the farmers and others. At $2,500 for the right to an acre-foot, 7,500 acre-feet are actually going to be traded between buyers and sellers. This price level is termed the equilibrium price and is the price level that would tend to prevail in the marketplace if supply and demand were to remain constant.

This simplified example is not an unrealistic approximation of what happens in certain markets. In sophisticated market conditions like the New York Stock Exchange, where common stock is bought and sold, technical specialists seek to adjust the price to keep the buy and sell orders in balance. Western water markets are, however, a long way away from the sophisticated competitive conditions of the New York Stock Exchange. Instead of being set by an auctioneer as in our hypothetical example, the prevailing price level in a particular water basin is determined by the practical conditions. If the price is above equilibrium at $3,500, then at least one of the suppliers isn't going to be able to sell water rights because the demand at that price isn't great enough; some suppliers will have to lower their asking price in order to sell. When the price is below equilibrium, the reverse would hold, and the price would have a tendency to be bid up.

Table 8-2

Shift in Demand

Price (\$ per right to an acre-foot)	*Quantity of Rights Demanded After Shift (in acre-feet)*
\$500	18,300
1,000	17,000
1,500	15,700
2,000	14,400
2,500	13,100
3,000	11,800
3,500	10,500
4,000	9,200
4,500	7,900
5,000	6,600

Market conditions are subject to change. Consider what happens when a new group of demanders come into the auction barn because the energy crisis is renewed and the market experiences a sudden increase in the need for water in oil shale extraction processes or for new electrical generating capacity. The effect is to increase the quantity of water rights demanded at any price the auctioneer would holler out. Table 8-2 describes the shift. Before the new demanders arrived, a price of \$500 yielded a demand for 12,700 acre-feet. Now, a price of \$500 yielded a demand for 18,300 acre-feet and a similar shift occurs in all of the other demand numbers at the other price levels. when these new numbers are plotted in Figure 8-2 a new demand schedule is seen to the right of the old demand schedule. What is the consequence of that shift to the right in terms of the prevailing price? The equilibrium price is bid up to \$4,500 at which 10,500 acre-feet of rights are traded. An increase in demand drives up the price. Similarly, circumstances that cause a reduction in the quantity of rights supplied at any price will also drive up the price.

8-3. BENEFIT-COST ANALYSIS

Benefit-cost analysis is a second evaluation procedure that may be increasingly important to tribes. All federally funded water projects must be subjected to benefit-cost analysis. More importantly for tribes, however, the "practicably irrigable" in "practicably irrigable acreage" (PIA) generally is interpreted to mean economically practicable as measured by benefit-cost analysis. Chapter 10 discusses practicably

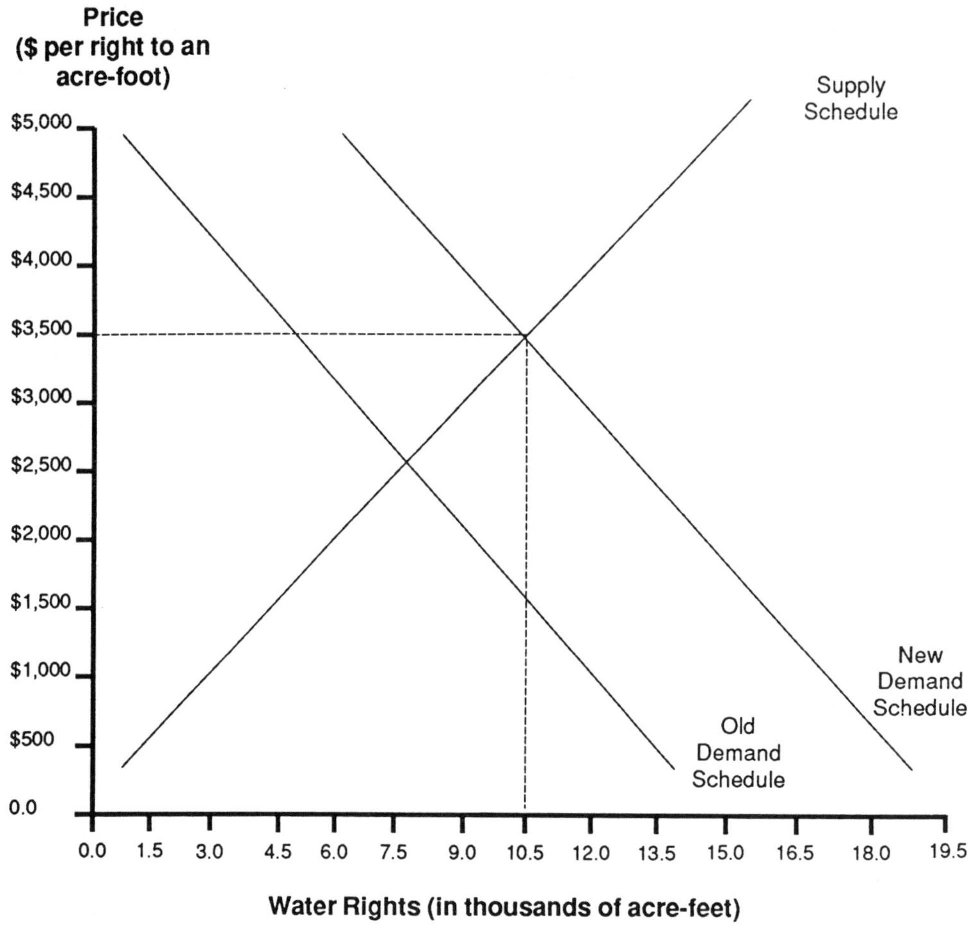

Figure 8-2. Effect of Shift in Demand.

irrigable acreage in detail. For the purposes of this chapter, however, the reader needs to remember only that water rights can be limited by benefit-cost procedures regardless of whether a water project is built or not.

Essentially, benefit-cost analysis tries to simulate a situation in which there is no market. It is designed to evaluate a decision, such as a proposed water project, in a situation where a market does not function or does not function completely. When would a market not, or only partially, function? A flood control project provides an example of when this occurs. Private companies have no real incentive to provide flood control because charging people what would be needed to put the project in place is very difficult, if not impossible. Moreover, if flood control is provided for one person in the floodplain, it is provided automatically for everyone else. Thus, any person who cannot escape being charged for the cost cannot be excluded from the benefits. Congress calls a situation like this a public good, and it is one of the main reasons the government is in the water business at all.

The benefit estimation part of the procedure attempts to simulate a market demand for the products or services of the water projects. The previous section of this chapter introduced the concepts of economic demand and a demand curve; in principle this is what benefit estimation tries to determine. What is the demand for flood control? What, for instance, is the demand for recreation on this particular reservoir? Stated another way, benefit estimation seeks to determine what people are willing to pay to have a particular project put in place.

Estimating Benefits: A Variety of Methods

In practice a variety of methods have been used to determine what people are willing to pay. Sometimes the situation is particularly simple and actual market prices reflect demand for the output. Irrigation is usually that simple. The assumption is made that the amount of crops that will be grown as a result of an irrigation project is not large enough to influence the prices that the market establishes for the crop commodities. Therefore, the evaluation rests on the actual demand that is reflected in transactions in the marketplace. But using actual market prices is not always possible. Return, again, to the case of flood control. No market for flood control exists. Instead, projections of the value of the properties that would be protected by different levels of flood control are developed to establish a demand curve for flood control. Such a procedure obviously assumes that if a market existed flood control would cost, and the owners of the protected properties would pay, at least the amount necessary to cover the cost of the destruction that would occur if there were no flood control. In this way, a demand curve is simulated even though no market actually exists for flood protection services.

Alternate cost is another technique used to estimate a project's benefits. Alternative cost applies when the product being evaluated could be produced by some method other than the one involved in the proposed project. Alternative cost analysis commonly is used with proposed hydroelectric power facilities. The assumption is made that if the hydroelectric power were not produced from a federal multipurpose reservoir, it would be produced by either a fossil- or nuclear-fueled power plant. The difference between the cost of producing the power by means of a power plant and the, presumably, cheaper cost of producing the power from hydroelectric generators at a dam is considered a benefit of the dam and reservoir project.

The Bureau of Reclamation Method: An Irrigation Project Example

Suppose a tribe wants to analyze a potential irrigation project. The arable land will be identified first, then the kinds of crops that can grow on that land will be determined. Next, the tribe will calculate the water needed to grow those crops and an irritation system will be designed to deliver the water. When all of these steps are completed, the tribe will compare the costs and benefits to see if the project is economically feasible. At this last step benefit-cost analysis becomes relevant.

A simplified version of the benefit estimation technique used by the Bureau of Reclamation follows because the Bureau has done nearly every benefit analysis of irrigation that exists outside of the private sector. The discussion centers exclusively on the benefit side of the procedure because benefit calculations are typically more difficult and troublesome than cost calculation. Although problems occur when costs are calculated, generally the cost can be based primarily on engineering studies of one sort or another.

The Bureau makes a distinction between direct benefits and secondary benefits of an irrigation project. It also makes a distinction between national and regional benefits. However, the Bureau's process, illustrated in Figure 8-3, begins with establishing the *gross direct benefits* from the proposed project.

The gross direct benefits consist of two components: the family living increase and the cash income calculation. The family living increase means that some benefits not reflected in the income received from growing crops may accrue to families who settle on newly irrigated land. One example would be the value of food grown for household consumption that would not be available without the irrigation water.

Family Living Increase
+ Cash Income Calculation
= GROSS DIRECT BENEFIT

Cash Income
- Production and Opportunity Costs
+ Family Living Increase
= NET DIRECT BENEFIT
(economic feasibility)

Net Direct Benefit
- Family Living Allowance
= PAYMENT CAPACITY
(financial feasibility)

Figure 8-3. Schematic of Bureau of Reclamation's Benefit Estimation Method.

The cash income calculation is the larger component of gross direct benefits. It is based on the assumed crop yields sold in the marketplace and resulting from the irrigation project.

The Bureau's process next takes the cash income calculation and makes some subtractions from it to determine the *net direct benefit*. All production costs, such as fuels and equipment and charges for depreciation and interest on farm investments, are deducted. An estimate of the opportunity cost of the farmer's labor is also deducted. This deduction assumes that if the farmer had not been working on this particular irrigated land, the farmer would have been working somewhere else; the opportunity cost is what the farmer could have earned in this other occupation. While it is a very low figure in the actual calculations of an irrigation project, the opportunity cost nevertheless is deducted.

This calculation—subtracting the cost item from the cash income and then adding back the increase in family living—produces what is called the net direct benefit, a measure of the project's economic feasibility. In principle net direct benefit is a measure of how much higher the national income would be with this project than without it. On a federal project this concept is important because the federal taxpayer commonly foots a substantial part of the bill. Therefore, if one wishes to have projects that are efficient in the sense that they increase national income, it is necessary to estimate net direct benefit.

Next, the Bureau makes further subtractions from the net direct benefit. In particular, a family living allowance—the cost for a family to live on the land—is subtracted to yield the *payment capacity*. In theory, the payment capacity represents the money that the farmer could afford to pay for the irrigation water and still come out even. The payment capacity is computed to check the financial feasibility of the project—the ability to pay for it. The net direct benefit determines the economic feasibility, but the payment capacity determines the financial feasibility.

Although the Bureau regularly makes the payment capacity calculation, no federal irrigation project has ever paid its full cost. The irrigation water from federal projects is heavily subsidized. One substantial subsidy is that farmers do not have to pay interest on the federal project since the interest is very large on these capital-intensive, long-lived projects. Other purposes of a reservoir, particularly power production in the West, may subsidize the irrigation aspect of a project.

Theoretically, a project is supposed to meet a test of economic feasibility. In other words, the project should make a significant contribution to national income. This project should also meet a test of financial feasibility as reflected by the capacity of the irrigators to pay for the irrigation water. Most irrigation projects that have been built by the Bureau formally have passed the economic feasibility test. For various reasons, however, in the past the economic feasibility test has not been very stringent. In particular, very low rates of interest usually have been used to figure the capital costs of projects, and low interest rates measure the net direct benefits.

The Bureau also calculates each project's indirect or secondary benefits. Theoretically, secondary benefits result from induced effects of the project and are the profits that can be earned from these induced effects. For example, suppose the irrigation project was planned to produce sugar beets. Also assume that sugar processing facilities are to be built in order to process those beets into sugar. Presumably that facility would earn a profit. If a profit is earned then the Bureau's view, at least in the past, has been that the profit also should be counted as a national benefit. The national income, in addition to what results from the production of the sugar beets, also would be raised by the processing of the beets into sugar in terms of the profits that can be made net of cost.

The Bureau's procedure of counting secondary benefits as part of national benefits has a history of controversy. Economists generally have agreed that this computation is not appropriate, the reason being that in a fully employed, competitive economy, if the funds were not expended in constructing an irrigation project, they would be expended somewhere else in the economy where they would have an equal opportunity to earn a net return. Therefore, counting secondary benefits of the irrigation project takes credit for something that would have happened without the project and results in an inflated net direct benefit figure.

Comparing Costs and Benefits: Time Makes the Difference

Once benefits have been calculated and the costs of the project have been developed, it is necessary to make a comparison between those benefits and costs. Although that may seem like a very straightforward thing to do, in practice it is more difficult than it first appears. One reason for that difficultly is the difference in time between when costs are incurred and when benefits are realized.

Consider an irrigation project. If the project is dependent on water storage, a reservoir must be built and filled. Then distribution works must be constructed before water can be brought to the land. The investment costs are substantial and must be incurred well before the return of any benefit from the project. One might ask: Why does the time difference matter? Why not simply add up costs and benefits without regard to when they occur?

The most straightforward answer is based on the existence of interest payments on savings in the economy. In an economic sense, interest implies that a dollar of income, profit or net benefit that occurs earlier is worth more than the same dollar that occurs later. The reason is that the earlier occurring dollar can earn interest in the intervening time period.

The cost side of the ledger behaves similarly. A cost that occurs early in time imposes more burden than the same cost occurring later. If the same cost must be paid a year from now, less must be set aside today because interest will accrue in the interim and make up the difference. At 10% interest, only $10 is needed today to pay an $11 bill one year from now whereas the full $11 would be required to pay the $11 bill now.

Discounting and Present Value

From an economic point of view, the existence of interest in the economy makes it matter when a cost or benefit happens. *Discounting* is the procedure used to compare costs and benefits occurring at different times. This mathematical technique takes account of when costs and benefits occur and weighs costs that occur earlier heavier than costs that occur later. Discounting also weighs benefits that occur earlier heavier than benefits that occur later.

The result of discounting is termed *present value*; and comparisons between benefits and costs are based on discounted present values. A numerical example might help clarify this concept. Suppose a tribe has an opportunity to invest in two projects, either of which will require that it put up $1,000. Suppose further that the first project returns $2,000 in 5 years; the second returns $2,500 in 10 years. Although the cash return from the second project clearly is larger than the cash return from the first, the first project has the advantage of being able to earn interest on its $2,000 return during the intervening 5 years before the second project returns anything.

The discounting procedure provides a means of comparing the returns that would be realized from the two investments. Using a discount rate of 5%, the present value of the first project turns out to be $1,567, and the present value of the second is $1,534. Stated in other words, if $1,567 were put in a savings account that earns 5%, it would be worth $2,000 in 5 years. If $1,534 were put in a savings account at the same 5%, it would be worth $2,500 in 10 years. Both of these projects would be worthwhile investments to the tribe because either would return substantially more money at 5%, as measured by the $1,567 or $1,534 in present value, than the $1,000 the tribe must pay out at the beginning.

If, in our example, then, the tribe has more than $1,000 to invest, it would be worthwhile to invest in both projects because each of their present values is higher than the required initial investment of $1,000. On the other hand, if only $1,000 is available, a choice must be made between the two projects, and it would be wise to choose the first project, which has a higher present value, even though the second yields a higher cash return. Again, the reason is the ability to earn interest on the $2,000 over the interval between the 5 and 10 years in the future.

Discounting, then, is a procedure that gives more weight to something that happens in the near term than to something that happens further in the future, and it applies to both costs and benefits. It also follows from this discussion that if a higher rate of interest, or rate of discount is used, more weight is given to the near future and the less weight is given to the further future. This concept is particularly important in investments like water projects in which much of the cost occurs at the front end while the benefits are strung out over a long period of time. The benefit-cost analysis for these projects is very sensitive to the rate of interest chosen.

A project that clearly qualifies as a 2% rate of interest may not qualify at a 3% rate of interest. And at a 10% rate of interest almost no projects would qualify that have the characteristic of very heavy costs in the near term and a long, strung-out set of benefits.

If a net benefit calculation is computed with a low interest rate, a project may have a benefit-cost ratio of, say, 1.5 to 1. That is, the benefits would be 1.5 times greater than the costs. Such ratios are reported often. But if a 10% rate of interest is used, all of a sudden the costs in the front end weigh heavily and the benefits in the future are light, and the ratio might fall to .5 to 1, or benefits that are only 50% as high as the costs. So the choice of discount rate is critically important to cost-benefit analysis in water project evaluations.[1]

8-4. EVALUATION FROM THE TRIBAL PERSPECTIVE

Even though a project or set of projects may be evaluated favorably according to criteria external to the tribe, ultimately the tribe's own evaluation must be paramount. Is the tribe willing to commit its time, finances, natural resources, and the efforts of its leadership and membership in a particular direction? It must decide what combinations of proposed uses are feasible and desirable to undertake. The tribe must scrutinize the possibilities from technological, legal, administrative, and financial perspectives.

Technologically Feasible Combinations

For each acceptable future feasible use, at least five questions must be asked: (1) How much water will be consumed for such a use? (2) From what source and physical location will that water be drawn? (3) Where will that water be used? (4) For waters used but not consumed (*e.g.*, agricultural runoff, industrial or municipal effluent), what will be the quality of the return flow (thermal and chemical)? (5) Into what receiving waters will that "used water" be discharged? Environmental impacts will be more negative the greater the quantity of water diverted and consumptively used, the further the water is transported, and the greater the degradation in water quality. The uses of water resources for other purposes will be more limited the greater the consumption and/or degradation necessary for any given use. Devoting most of a tribe's water resources to just two or three future feasible uses can make other uses technologically impossible.

Economists refer to water uses made impossible by the choice of some other uses as *opportunity costs*. Technologically speaking, the amount of water available is limited. Therefore, water consumptively used for irrigation and thermal-electric power generation (power plant cooling and steam cycle feeding) may mean not having enough water left to support other uses such as minerals extraction and processing or intensive livestock management. These unsupported uses are the opportunity costs.

It is important to remember that different future feasible uses demand not only different quantities of water resources, but different water *quality* as well. In general municipal/domestic uses demand the best water quality. Fisheries/livestock/wildlife habitat management and recreation come next and are followed by agriculture. Industrial processing and minerals extraction/processing demand the lowest quality water.

The reason for listing these uses hierarchically is that water devoted to any of those uses, except fisheries/wildlife habitat management and recreation, is normally of worse quality after use than before. Thus the technological opportunity cost involved in dedicating large quantities of water to uses that will degrade water quality severely may be the elimination of possible future uses which require high quality water.

To limit the technological opportunity costs, planners often attempt to zone the use of water resources both in place and in time. In other words, planners try to locate uses requiring high quality water upstream from those uses where quality requirements are not as great. They also devote the water first to high quality uses and last to uses where quality needs are relatively low. For instance, municipalities situated adjacent to mountainous areas often try to locate their drinking water reservoirs upstream of livestock feedlots, irrigated agriculture, and industrial plants, because upstream water quality is better.

In areas where all users depend heavily on ground water supplies, the problem is not nearly so simple. In the early 1970s new federal laws[2] began to place serious restrictions on the freedom polluters formerly had enjoyed to dump their effluent into surface water supplies. In response, many pollutant dischargers found it cheaper and easier to inject their wastes back into the ground than to remove the pollutants from wastewater prior to discharging it into surface waters. A gradual effort is now being made to deal with this problem through the implementation of more recent federal legislation.[3] Still, tribes that rely heavily on ground water extraction to meet high quality needs (like domestic use, livestock management, and agriculture) must consider very carefully the technological opportunity costs related to allowing industrial uses that could affect ground water quality permanently.

Legally/Administratively Feasible Combinations

Legal and administrative opportunity costs must be considered in choosing future feasible water uses. Legal and administrative staff time devoted to the management of some uses may inhibit a tribal government's ability to manage other uses. When a tribe contemplates an aggressive, large-scale water development program, the cost of administering the program must be taken into consideration. As with any other public or private sector enterprise, tribes must be sensitive to the need to minimize overhead costs while maximizing revenue.

Financially Feasible Use Combinations

Finally, financial opportunity costs must be considered. In an era of tight credit and diminishing federal support, tribes probably will experience some difficulty in attracting investment capital to *any* large-scale future feasible use alternative. The choice among major development options ultimately may be dictated largely by investor preferences. Regardless, if money is spent in developing a future use—whether that money is borrowed or comes directly out of the tribal general fund—the money will not be available to support the development of other uses.

Defining Feasible Use Combinations: One Approach

Linear programming is one method for deciding how to use limited resources in performing different combinations of tasks. The linear programming technique is used increasingly by planners in various private and public sector situations when they have access to a reliable data base and adequate computer capability.[4] Although a working description of linear programming techniques is far beyond the scope of this chapter, it is worth noting that the method has been used specifically and with some success in large-scale regional water resource management planning. In 1969 for example, international consultants devised a linear programming model for the entirety of India's Ganges-Brahmaputra River system. The model offered alternative "management packages," simultaneously performing functions such as hydroelectric power generation, irrigated agriculture, flood control, navigation, and salinity control.[5] Although most tribal governments would have no need for quite so elaborate a model, practice with this general approach may prove helpful in deciding which use combinations are most technologically feasible. Ultimately, the method chosen to determine feasible use combinations is unimportant. The selected method must, however, provide the tribal planner with a reliable means of revealing which use combinations are feasible and which are not.

The next chapter contains a statement of objectives from a hypothetical tribal water planning committee that has responsibility for deciding what guidelines should be used to develop a water policy. The hypothetical committee's goals and objectives recognize that a certain level of economic self-sufficiency and power is needed to develop the self-determination and self-sufficiency necessary for physical, cultural and political survival. In such a situation, the planner must be sensitive to the need to balance the physical/cultural/political survival goal with the attainment of certain economic objectives that will make continued realization of the survival goal possible. The planner must assemble some alternative future feasible water use combinations and then defer to the tribal leadership—or full membership, depending on the cultural/political organization of the tribe—in terms of the responsibility for deciding which of these use combinations is most in keeping with tribal goals and objectives.

Each of these combinations of future feasible uses represents a *policy option*, or alternative "water policy package," that a tribe can decide to adopt. The planner's chief responsibility lies in presenting to the ultimate decision-makers a variety of options for attaining tribal goals. Table 8-3 shows three hypothetical policy options in terms of how waters would be used consumptively, the probable impact on the achievement of survival objectives, and the anticipated revenues. Either the planner or the tribal leaders themselves can make estimates (reflected in the table by positive and negative numbers) as to whether a given use will aid in attaining a policy objective (+1 through +3), will make the attainment of such an objective more difficult (-1 through -3), or will have no significant effect either way (0).

The policy options in Table 8-3 are purely hypothetical and are by no means intended to encourage real-world planners away from some policy options or toward others. Also, subjective judgment is involved when the positive or negative values are assigned to each use. The process, therefore, is not immune from abuse. If planners or political leaders want to reach a predetermined policy option result, they can manipulate their impact estimates easily. This method, like any other, can either yield reasonable evaluations if used with good faith, or can be employed to mislead decision-makers or the public if used for manipulative political purposes.

Subjective as they may be, the numerical evaluations have been used here as a shorthand way to demonstrate the relationship between attainment of goals such as

Table 8-3

Comparative Analysis of Three Water Policy Options

Uses	*% of Total Supply Used*	*Objectives*			*Net Benefits (mil. $/yr.)*
		Phys. Surv.	*Cult. Surv.*	*Nat'l. Surv.*	
OPTION 1.					
Consumptive Uses:					
Domestic/municipal	05	+3	+3	+3	0
Agriculture	75	+1	+1	+1	5
Minerals/ext./proc.	10	-1	-1	1	8
Hydropower generation	05	0	-1	0	2
Nonconsumptive Uses:					
Fisheries	05	+2	+3	+2	0.5
OPTION 1 TOTALS:	100	5	5	7	15.5
OPTION 2.					
Consumptive Uses:					
Domestic/municipal	05	+3	+3	+3	0
Agriculture	20	+1	+1	+1	2
Hydropower	20	-1	-1	-2	8
Thermal Power	10	-2	-2	0	5
Minerals ext./proc.	25	-3	-3	-2	20
Manufacturing	15	-1	-1	0	15
Livestock	05	0	+1	+1	2
OPTION 2 TOTALS:	100	-3	-2	1	52
OPTION 3.					
Consumptive Uses:					
Domestic/municipal	05	+3	+3	+3	0
Agriculture	50	+1	0	+1	5
Timber & Range mgt.	20	+2	+2	+2	1
Wildlife habitat mgt.	05	+1	+3	+1	.05
Livestock mgt.	10	+1	0	0	2
Nonconsumptive Uses:					
Fisheries	10	+3	+2	+2	4
OPTION 3 TOTALS:	100	11	10	9	12.05

survival and objectives such as sufficient economic development to achieve those goals. Note, for instance, that in these hypothetical options an inverse relationship between revenue and survival tends to occur; that is, if consumptive use patterns and water quality are altered more drastically in pursuit of economic development, the negative impact on goals attainment is greater.

8-5. CONCLUSION

The environmental history of the United States shows that the health of the population and the sustainability of the resource base has been put in danger at times when economic development was the only objective directing policy development. At the same time, data from the 1980 census shows American Indians as a group to be the most economically disadvantaged minority in the United States. Paradoxically, Indian people also inhabit lands containing some of the most sought-after resources in the West—minerals and water.

As stated at the beginning of this chapter, the challenge and the opportunity now facing tribal water policy planners and leaders is to find the means to attain important social objectives—a better way of life, higher standard of living, improved health care, reinforcement of tribal values, or whatever else a tribe defines these objectives to be—without making the same kinds of environmental mistakes that have caused problems for non-Indians and governments.

Those who have tried and failed may argue that the attainment of a perfect balance between economic and environmental well-being is an impossible dream; perfection is often sought yet rarely achieved, and what is "perfect" is also open to question. But, American Indian tribes are in some ways better equipped to find and maintain this balance than their non-Indian neighbors.

Non-Indian governments are fractured into a bewildering array of local, regional, state, and federal agencies all claiming jurisdiction over various aspects of water resource allocation and quality control. Each tribe, on the other hand, is its own semi-sovereign nation. Non-Indian people are also divided into an array of subcultural units, political and economic interest groups, and social factions. While many tribes are also admittedly subject to divisions within themselves over issues such as whether and how natural resources ought to be developed, each tribe is—or can be—drawn together and strengthened by powerful unifying forces: tribal tradition and heritage. The purpose of this chapter has been to help planners define alternative water policies which arise from and strengthen, rather than weaken, these unifying forces. The technical information in this and other chapters is presented to help managers and decision-makers achieve a broad purpose: the adoption of water policies which will sustain the health of tribal members, safeguard the heritage of its cultural traditions, and support the hope for a brighter economic future.

Once a tribe has achieved some threshold level of unity over its water policy, tribal leaders can decide which options will prove most viable from the standpoint of relations with non-Indian governments and how to finance these options. Moreover, the tribe can begin the legal and administrative implementation of the chosen options by developing a water code. These next steps are discussed in the following chapters. But unity over water policy comes first. The next chapter outlines the planning elements that facilitate obtaining that unity and defining acceptable options.

REFERENCE NOTES

1. *See In Re the General Adjudication of All Rights to Use Water in Big Horn River System and All Other Sources, State of Wyoming*, 750 P.2d 681, 709 (Wyo. 1988) for a discussion of how different parties argued for different discount rates in a recent major river system adjudication, and how the Wyoming Supreme Court resolved the issue.
2. Clean Water Act, 33 U.S.C.A. § 1252 *et seq.* (1980 & Supp. 1984).
3. *E.g.*, Resource Conservation and Recovery Act of 1976, 42 U.S.C.A. § 6901 *et seq.*
4. *See* E. Stokey and R. Zeckhauser, A PRIMER FOR POLICY ANALYSIS at 177-200 (1978).
5. P. Rogers, "A Game Theory Approach to the Problems of International River Basins," WATER RESOURCES RESEARCH 5, No. 4 at 749-60 (1969).

CHAPTER 9

The Elements of Water Policy Planning

9-1. INTRODUCTION

As earlier chapters have noted, tribal governments are now at a historic turning point regarding their use and management of water resources. It is a point marked by formidable challenges and by unprecedented opportunities. The challenges already have been well documented. Especially in the West, water uses gradually are shifting away from many forms of irrigated agriculture and toward more extensive municipal and industrial applications. The economic significance (and therefore, the dollar value) of water is rising dramatically; as a result, we are also witnessing aggressive legal and political efforts to divest Indian people of their water. The opportunities for tribal governments arise from the fact that as the tribes gradually assume more actual control over the water resources now in dispute, they can adopt water policies created to meet specific tribal needs and avoid some of the fundamental problems that now plague water policy implementation by non-Indian governments.

What water policy problems should be avoided? Some such problems were outlined in a 1973 report to Congress by the National Water Commission (1) and two are of particular concern here. First, the Commission reported pervasive lack of coordination in water policy planning among federal, state, regional, and local governments. Each level of government had its own priorities to determine which users should get what quantity of water, at what time, at what prices, and for what uses. Second, the Commission identified a nearly total lack of coordination between governmental decision-makers regulating land use, those allocating water resources, and those regulating water quality. The toxic contamination of drinking water supplies in many areas of the United States—a problem that seems to grow with each passing day—is one tragic effect of this inattention to the water quality impacts of various land uses.

Many tribes now have the opportunity to create a unified water policy uniquely tailored to their needs as semi-sovereign nations and within which issues of land use, water resource allocation and conservation, and water quality control are all considered simultaneously in an integrated fashion. With a little luck and a lot of effort, the fragmentation of authority, the lack of use/effect coordination, and the growing public health threats besetting non-Indian water policymakers will be problems that Indian tribes can circumvent.

This chapter describes one approach a tribal government can take to define water policies that will help attain tribal goals and avoid some common and serious errors in the planning process experienced by non-Indian governments. What follows is an introductory overview of water policy planning, using one suggested planning model as an example. Since this is not a comprehensive treatise on the subject, citations to various reference works that provide a more detailed "how to" description of the planning process are provided.

Generally, the suggested water policy planning method consists of:

- a definition of tribal goals and objectives;
- an inventory of all existing reservation resources;
- the identification of all future feasible water uses on and off-reservation;
- a projection of all future feasible use impacts on existing reservation resource inventories;
- the elimination of those water use activities that are inconsistent with tribal goals and objectives;
- an evaluation of the remaining activities in light of the economic, legal, and political environment outside the reservation (what is feasible?) and tribal goals (what is desirable?); and
- a choice of specific combinations of water use activities for possible implementation.

A systematic overview of the entire process of planning, evaluating, choosing and implementing a tribal water policy is depicted in Figure 9-1. Figure 9-1 and the text that follows portray water policy planning and implementation as a dynamic, cyclical activity.

Once a policy is chosen and implemented, it must be re-evaluated continuously to assess how well the policy is assisting in the attainment of tribal goals and objectives and to determine when and how it may need adjustment (Figure 9-1, step 10). The re-evaluation is accomplished by going through the cycle again and doing such things as updating the inventory; re-evaluating the legal, technical, and economic feasibility of chosen water uses; measuring the actual impacts of chosen water uses; and evaluating the internal consistency of uses comprising the policy in terms of water quantity and quality.

9-2. DEFINING TRIBAL GOALS AND OBJECTIVES

In the battle for western water, water policy tends to be seen as an end in itself—as justification for legal claims made on the resource. But at the initial stage of policy planning, water policy formulation should be seen as a *means* to achieve some fundamental tribal goals and objectives. Before making decisions as to *how*

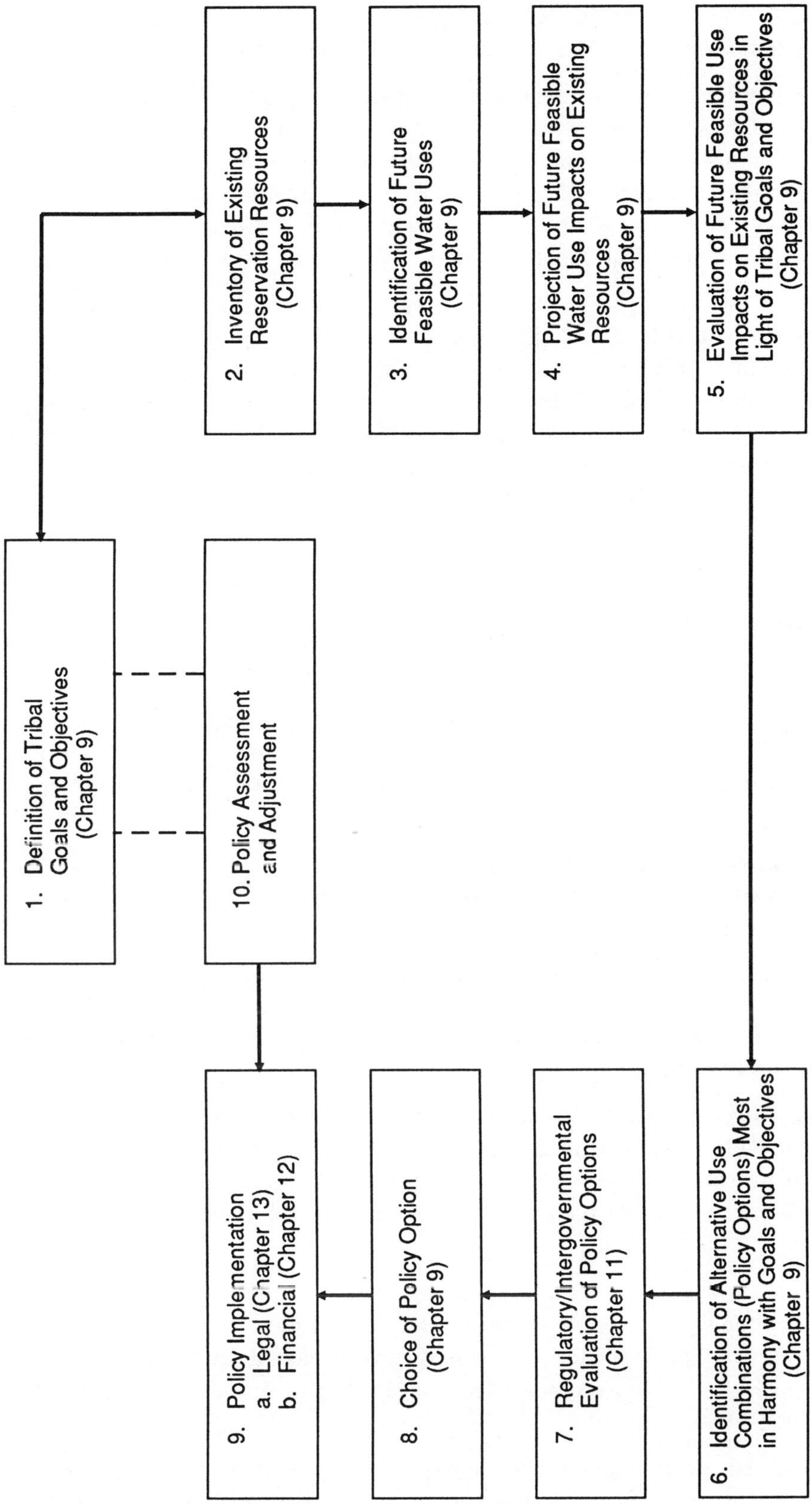

Figure 9-1. Steps in the Water Policy Cycle.

water resources should be managed, it is crucial that a tribe understand *why* it wants to undertake the development of its water or of any other resource.

No one universal process determines a tribe's ultimate goals and objectives. Decisions about goals and objectives may be made by a council of elders in one tribe, by elected tribal government leaders in another, or by general membership meetings in another. Likewise, each tribe draws on its own unique cultural heritage and traditions when it envisions what it wants its future to be. However, the following is a hypothetical example that illustrates how tribal goals and objectives could be defined.

Assume that the task of defining the goals and objectives of a hypothetical tribe has been given to a "tribal water planning committee." The committee is comprised of traditional and political leaders and has been asked to study what goals and objectives should underlie the tribe's water policy. The report developed by the committee contains the following conclusions:

1. The ultimate goal of the tribe is survival. By "survival," three things are meant:

    - *physical survival*—the continued existence of the tribe on its reservation homelands;
    - *cultural survival*—the perpetuation of traditions and beliefs that are essential to the tribe's self-identity and the unity of its membership; and
    - *political survival*—the ability of the tribe to endure as a sovereign nation.

2. In defining this survival goal, it becomes clear that certain conditions—stated as policy objectives—must be met to achieve that survival goal:

    - *physical survival* depends on the ability of tribal lands and water resources to continue to sustain life, and requires that resources be developed in a way that does not threaten the lives or health of present or future tribal members;
    - *cultural survival* depends on the tribe's ability to preserve those institutions and practices that sustain, strengthen, and renew the tribe's fundamental sense of identity. This objective implies some degree of control over the nature and extent of tribal contact with non-Indian cultures; and
    - *political survival* involves having enough control over both the economic and the legal aspects of reservation life to assure the perpetuation of tribal sovereign governmental authority and to defend the tribe politically and legally from the hostile actions of non-Indian governments.

3. To satisfactorily attain the above objectives, however, the self-determination, self-sufficiency, and self-protective capability of the tribe

must be improved. This, in turn, will require a certain level of thoughtful, effective economic development.

4. Therefore, the guiding principle behind the development of all resource management policy must be that the policies provide the tribe with enough income to attain its goals, but not threaten the tribe's physical, cultural, or governmental survival.

The primary reason why identification of these principles is the first step in policy planning is to ensure that a tribe will understand fully why a particular water policy is being developed. Such information will become critically important at a later stage in the planning process once resources have been inventoried, future feasible water uses have been identified, and the impacts of future feasible uses on existing inventories have been projected. These objectives assist the planner in deciding what combinations of future water uses will be wise for the tribe to undertake. Figure 9-2 is a flowchart that depicts a process for determining goals and objectives.

9-3. INVENTORY OF EXISTING RESERVATION RESOURCES

One prerequisite for good planning is good information. After defining goals and objectives, a tribe needs an inventory of existing reservation resources. The term "resources" is used here in a very broad sense, and includes: (1) natural resources (land and land use, timber and range, wildlife and fisheries, minerals, water, air quality, sacred areas); (2) human resources (tribal population size, age composition, geographic distribution, health status, cultural practices and institutions); and (3) financial and governmental resources (sources of tribal income, credit status, relations with the external financial community, legal status of control over natural resources, tribal resource management capability, and relations with non-Indian governments). Figure 9-3 depicts an inventory and assessment process for tribal water resources planning.

Natural Resources

The inventory or survey of natural resources is accomplished by creating as complete a description as possible of their condition at a point in time. This *Handbook* provides insights on how to do this with regard to water resources, including the elements of a hydrologic survey. Chapters 6 and 7, for instance, provide an introductory explanation of how to determine the location, quantity, quality, and interaction of ground and surface water supplies and how to assess the current management of such supplies. (*See also* reference notes 2-5.)

Fairly elaborate techniques exist for inventorying land and land use (*e.g.*, soil surveys, air-photo surveys), timber and range, wildlife and fisheries, minerals, and air quality. General textbooks on the management of each of these resources contain descriptions of how to undertake a qualitative and quantitative assessment of a given resource. Tribal religious leaders can provide guidance on the location and preservation of sacred areas on or near tribal lands.

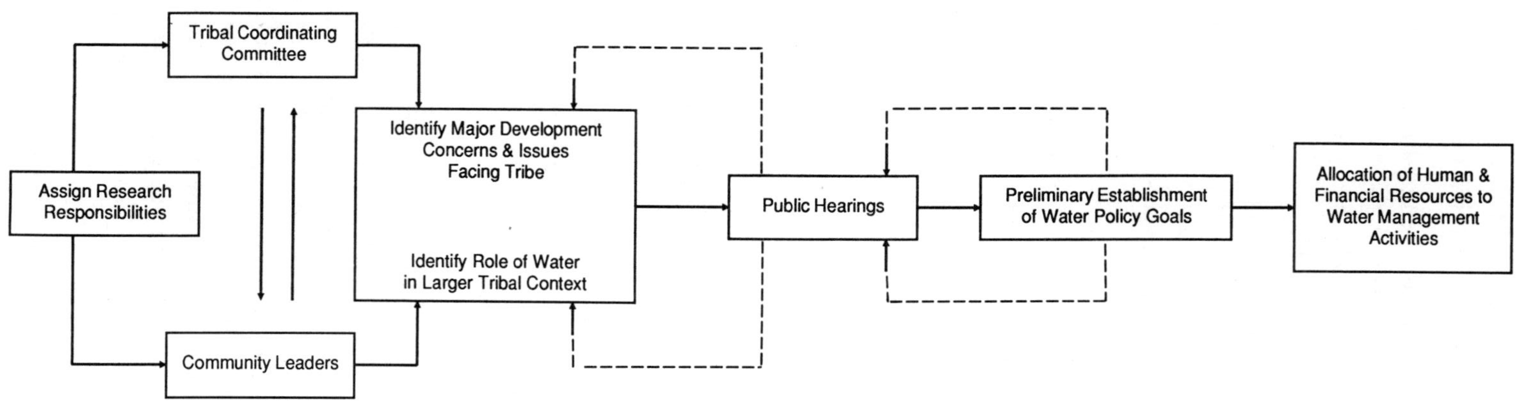

Figure 9-2. Preliminary Determination of Priority for Water Management.

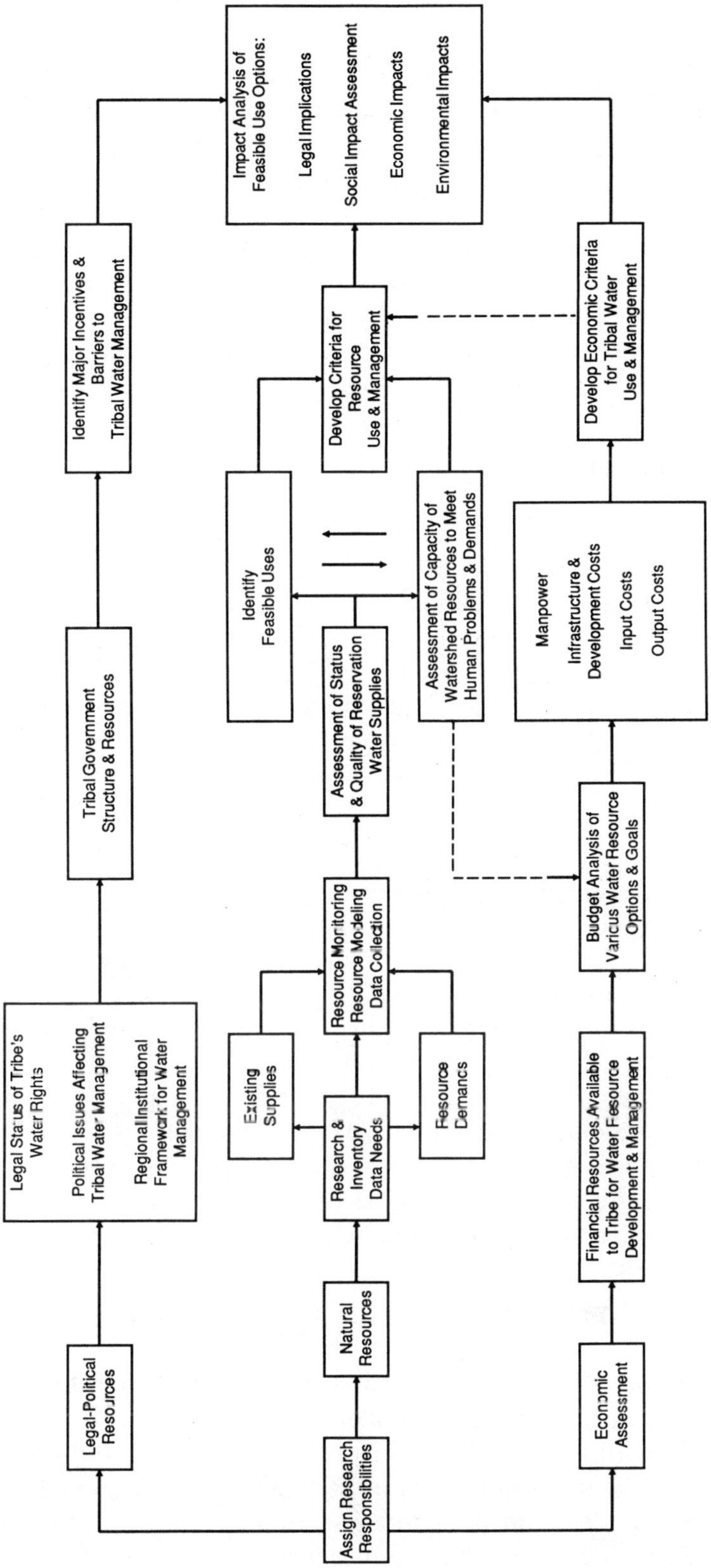

Figure 9-3. Resource Inventory and Legal, Economic and Political Assessment.

Human Resources

A human resource inventory involves a close look at tribal members as a group. How large is the tribe? How are the members distributed on the reservation? Is the tribe growing larger, smaller, or staying the same size? Is there a high concentration of youthful or elderly tribal members? What percentage of members live off-reservation, and is that percentage growing or declining? Do significant health problems affect the tribal population? What cultural practices and institutions are seen as vital to the tribe's continued existence and self-identity (*i.e.*, what qualities of the tribal character, beliefs, or traditions have enabled the tribe to withstand four centuries of Euro-American cultural pressure and still survive)?

Financial/Governmental Resources

The financial and governmental inventory includes an examination of: the tribe's current ability to manage its natural resources (*e.g.*, personnel, facilities); the legal status of water and other natural resources to which the tribe is laying claim; and the tribal government's relations with local, state, and federal governments (*e.g.*, interagency agreements, pending lawsuits). An economic survey requires: a review of tribal assets and sources of revenue; a review of the income sources of tribal members; a look at trends in the non-Indian economy that may influence tribal well-being (*e.g.*, market trends for goods the tribe produces); and a look at credit availability.

Significance for an Integrated Perspective

In the implementation of various governmental programs, many tribes gather the kind of information previously discussed. Assembling the data on natural, human, and governmental/financial resources in one place at one time is helpful because changes in water policy inevitably will have an impact in each of these other resource areas. That impact may be seen as positive, negative, or neutral; it may be direct or indirect; it may be profound, moderate, or insignificant; and it may be short-term or long-lasting. Regardless, some impacts will occur. The tribe that has better information on its current condition will be better able to benefit from the positive impacts and to minimize the negative ones.

9-4. IDENTIFYING POSSIBLE WATER USE ACTIVITIES

Once the resource inventory is completed, policy planners can turn to identification of all future feasible uses of their water, on- and off-reservation. Future uses are not evaluated in terms of whether they are in keeping with tribal goals and objectives; initially, the kinds of water uses that could feasibly be undertaken on the reservation simply are determined. Various sources for the water use activities may be examined. Perhaps the tribe has been approached by a city or a firm with a specific project in mind, or a tribal member has raised a possibility. At this point the focus is on creating a list of possibilities and subjecting them to an initial scrutiny for feasibility.

As with other terms used here, "feasible" has a broad meaning, and includes *technological*, *legal/administrative*, and *economic* feasibility. Doing the initial feasibility assessment, therefore, involves asking questions such as:

- *Technological*—Does the hydrologic survey indicate there is enough water to support a specific proposed future use? What technologies and management practices are necessary to make a proposed future use possible, and can tribal personnel be trained to make use of these technologies and practices?

- *Legal/Administrative*—Does the tribe have a sustainable legal claim to the water it wants to devote to a future use? Or can it develop such a claim? Will licenses, permits, or other forms of intergovernmental agreements be needed, and how difficult will it be to obtain such agreements? Does the tribe have, or can it develop, the administrative capability to oversee a proposed new use of water resources responsibly?

- *Economic*—Will it be possible to obtain funding for developing a proposed future use? Is there a market for the products or services arising from the possible water use? Can the operation be made profitable or at least self-sustaining?

At the initial feasibility assessment stage, each of these questions, or some variation of them, must be asked of any proposed future use of tribal waters. The possible uses, of course, may vary widely from tribe to tribe because of the great variation in the size of reservations and in the available water resources, as well as the degree of existing economic development and technological and governmental management capability. Some of the general uses to which water resources now are being devoted are listed in Table 9-1; most, if not all, of these water applications already exist on many reservations. After answering each of the questions listed above concerning each of the uses listed in the table, planners then will have identified initially their tribe's future feasible water uses.

The time, effort and money that a tribe can afford to commit to develop the initial feasibility studies also will vary from tribe to tribe. A thorough job, however, needs to be done at the initial feasibility stage to ensure that planners do not waste additional time, effort, and money on ideas which ultimately prove unworkable. At a minimum, advisory opinions are needed from trusted experts in each of these areas to determine whether a specific proposed future use is worth further consideration. Some clearly infeasible proposals may be eliminated at this stage, and attention then can be focused on proposed uses which appear most technologically, legally/-administratively, and economically workable.

Table 9-1

Some General Uses of Water Resources in the United States

1. *Domestic and Municipal*—drinking, cooking, washing, sanitation.
2. *Agriculture*—irrigated and dry, food and fiber for on-reservation consumption or export, hydroponics.
3. *Hydroelectric Power Generation*—high or low-head, in conjunction with irrigation or alone, pumped storage, instream or diverted.
4. *Thermal and Geothermal Electric Power Generation*—for cooling and stream cycle feeding in conventional fossil fuel or nuclear power units; deep-well injection in "dry rock" geothermal units.
5. *Minerals Extraction and Processing*—deep-mining and milling of uranium, precious metals, fossil fuels; surface mining and processing of same; synthetic fuels development.
6. *Manufacturing*—examples include synthetic chemicals (solvents, fertilizers), electronic components, clothing, tools and equipment.
7. *Navigation*—commercial (stream channelization, dredging).
8. *Livestock Management* (concentrated)—feedlots, packing houses.
9. *Fisheries Management* (concentrated)—hatcheries.
10. *Timber and Range Management*—logging, livestock.
11. *Wildlife Habitat Enhancement*—species preservation, hunting.
12. *Waterborne Recreation*—fishing, boating, swimming, still and white water.

Source: Derived from Viessman & Welty (5) p. 596-606.

9-5. PROJECTION OF THE IMPACT OF WATER USE ACTIVITIES ON EXISTING RESERVATION RESOURCES

Having generated a list of future feasible uses, the next step is to evaluate the probable impacts of these uses on existing reservation resources. To repeat an earlier observation, no change in reservation water use will be without impacts. Whether these impacts will be seen as positive, negative, or neutral depends heavily on the perspective of the planners doing the impact assessment.

Choice of Methods

A description of an evaluation method follows. This is a method commonly used to prepare environmental impact reports (6), but it is expanded here to consider the effects of proposed future water uses on human and governmental/financial resources. Other more elaborate impact assessment models and techniques exist (7-10), but space limitations preclude their review here.

Figure 9-4 is a simplified sketch of the mode of analysis, known as a *cross-impact matrix*. The matrix provides a way for the planner to consider systematically the impacts of all future feasible water uses on all existing reservation resources. Across the top of the matrix is an abbreviated list of the reservation resources inventory described earlier in this chapter—a catalog of the overall condition of the reservation at present. On the left-hand side of the matrix is the list of future feasible water uses identified in the previous step of the planning process. The matrix helps the planner predict or "map out" the probable impact of each future feasible use on each existing reservation resource.

Future Feasible Water Uses / Existing Reservation Resources	1. Surface Water Quantity	2. Ground Water Quantity	3. Surface Water Quality	4. Ground Water Quality	5. Timber	6. Rangeland	7. Arable Soils	8. Minerals	9. Wildlife & Fisheries	10. Air Quality	11. Sacred Areas	12. Population Distribution	13. Population Size	14. Population Health Status	15. Cultural Practices & Institutions	16. Tribal Income	17. Intergovernmental Relations	18. Tribal Administration
A. Domestic & Municipal																		
B. Agriculture									9-B							16-B		
C. Hydroelectric Power									9-C							16-C		
D. Thermal Electric Power																		
E. Minerals Extraction/Processing			3-E	4-E							11-E			14-E				
F. Manufacturing																16-F		
G. Navigation (commercial)																		
H. Livestock Management																		
I. Fisheries Management															15-I	16-I		
J. Timber & Range															15-J	16-J		
K. Wildlife Habitat															15 K	16 K		
L. Waterborne Recreation																		

Figure 9-4. Cross-Impact Matrix for Projecting the Impact of Future Feasible Water Uses on Existing Reservation Resources.

An Example

As used in this hypothetical planning situation, the matrix in Figure 9-4 shows a total of 216 cells or "impact intersections" at which some evaluation is needed. As suggested earlier, the impact of each use on each resource can (and should) be evaluated in terms of whether it is seen as positive, negative, or neutral; whether the impact is profound, moderate, or insignificant; and whether it is short-term or long-lasting.

In doing the evaluation at each intersection, one way to predict the impacts of future feasible water uses on existing resources is to look at what the impacts of those uses have been elsewhere. If, for instance, tribal planners learn from feasibility studies that one possible use of the reservation's ground water could be for minerals extraction and processing, an investigation should be undertaken of the water quality impacts of such operations already being conducted in similar environments.

For example, a dam holding back radioactive liquid mill tailings at a uranium ore processing facility near the southeastern border of the Navajo Reservation failed in 1978, spilling contaminants into streams that tribal members used to water their livestock. Since the possibility of another similar accident cannot be discounted totally, possible surface or ground water contamination arising from the use of water resources for minerals extraction and processing must be addressed by the planner. Thus, negative impacts on ground and surface water are noted at cells 3-E and 4-E of the sample matrix. Possible human health impacts are noted at cell 14-E. At the same time, however, estimated positive impacts on tribal income resulting from a mining and milling operation should also be taken into account and are noted on the matrix at cell 16-E.

In another hypothetical situation, a planner might determine that water uses that enhance wildlife habitat management, fisheries, timber and range would result in generally positive impacts on tribal cultural practices. This would be noted in cells 15-I, -J and -K. At the same time the planner might find that these water uses would provide a less positive impact on tribal income than would activities like minerals extraction, and would make note of this in cells 16-I, -J and -K.

Analysis would proceed using this method until information had been gathered for each of the 216 cells in the Figure 9-4 matrix. In a real-world planning situation, feasibility studies probably would yield no more than half of the future feasible uses listed on the left side of the matrix. A larger range of uses has been included here simply to demonstrate the array of interactions that conceivably could occur on a resource-rich reservation.

9-6. ELIMINATION OF THOSE WATER USE ACTIVITIES THAT ARE INCONSISTENT WITH TRIBAL GOALS AND OBJECTIVES

The next step is to judge possible water uses according to the criteria developed in the earlier definition of tribal goals and objectives. First, the planner must determine whether any individual future feasible uses actually might prevent the attainment of those goals and objectives. For instance, would any future use threaten the ability of tribal lands and water resources to continue to sustain life? Will any proposed new uses create serious long-term public health effects? If agreements with non-Indian governments are not kept, is there a significant possibility that the tribe could lose control over its existing land and water resources? Would any proposed uses have a serious negative impact on tribal culture or social organization, or on sacred areas on or near the reservation? Would any future uses involve giving over so much control of resource or financial management to non-Indians that the tribal government's authority would be weakened substantially or permanently ?

If the answer is "yes" to any of these questions regarding any future feasible use, that use is a candidate for elimination from further consideration in the policy planning process for the hypothetical tribe whose goals and objectives are being used in this example. For if this tribe (or any other) becomes financially dependent on a water use that prevents the attainment of fundamental goals and objectives, the effect can be to make the tribe a prisoner of its own reservation. The inconsistencies between objectives and uses must be weeded out before planning can proceed to a successful conclusion.

REFERENCE NOTES

1. National Water Comm'n, WATER POLICIES FOR THE FUTURE—FINAL REPORT TO THE PRESIDENT AND TO THE CONGRESS OF THE UNITED STATES (1973).
2. V. Chow, ed., HANDBOOK OF APPLIED HYDROLOGY (1964).
3. T. Dunne & L. Leopold, HYDROLOGY FOR PLANNERS (1981).
4. W. Viessman et al., INTRODUCTION TO HYDROLOGY (2d ed., 1977).
5. Viessman & C. Welty, WATER MANAGEMENT—TECHNOLOGY AND INSTITUTIONS (1985).
6. L. Leopold, et al., A PROCEDURE FOR EVALUATING ENVIRONMENTAL IMPACT, U.S.G.S. Circular No. 645 (1971).
7. Environmental Impact Center, FINAL REPORT ON A METHODOLOGY FOR ASSESSING ENVIRONMENTAL IMPACT OF WATER RESOURCES DEVELOPMENT (1973).
8. R. Munn, ENVIRONMENTAL IMPACT ASSESSMENT—PRINCIPLES AND PROCEDURES (2d ed., 1979).
9. D. Keyes, LAND DEVELOPMENT AND THE NATURAL ENVIRONMENT: ESTIMATING IMPACTS (1976).
10. W. Marsh, ENVIRONMENTAL ANALYSIS: FOR LAND USE AND SITE PLANNING (1978).

SUGGESTED READINGS

Many of the references gathered for this chapter were selected specifically for their value as additional general reference readings. In the overall category of water policy planning, the most highly recommended single work is Viessman and Welty's WATER MANAGEMENT—TECHNOLOGY AND INSTITUTIONS (5), especially chapters 3 and 4, on water policy and institutions and on water resources planning. A companion work not listed above is Viessman and Hammer's WATER SUPPLY AND POLLUTION CONTROL (4th ed., 1985), which can be of enormous value in estimating water quality impacts of proposed developments. Stokey and Zeckhauser's PRIMER FOR POLICY ANALYSIS (1978) is basically a "tool kit" of techniques for public administrators to use in making complex policy implementation decisions. For an example of how economists have applied their own modes of analysis to American Indian water resource management in the southwestern United States, *see* Kneese and Brown, THE SOUTHWEST UNDER STRESS—NATIONAL RESOURCE DEVELOPMENT ISSUES IN A REGIONAL SETTING (1981).

Chapter 10

Identifying Practicably Irrigable Acreage (PIA)

10-1. THE NEED TO UNDERSTAND PIA

If each reservation had unlimited water resources, there would be no need to make the difficult choices between various water uses. Water abundance, however, is the exception rather than the rule on reservations throughout the arid West. As a consequence, a limited water supply must be allocated in accordance with priorities developed by the tribe and its use fostered and administered in compliance with those priorities.

A basic first step, however, needs to be taken prior to developing and implementing a water policy for the reservation. That step involves assessing how much water is available to the tribe for its use. An initial element of this assessment is physical measurement of on-reservation water resources. But physical availability does not translate always into availability under the law. Far more water typically runs through a reservation than tribal members legally are entitled to put to use. It is, therefore, essential to understand the components of the quantification of *Winters* rights.

In its 1963 decision in *Arizona v. California*, the United States Supreme Court set forth "practicably irrigable acreage" (PIA) as the test with which to quantify reserved water rights on a reservation established with the intent that its inhabitants pursue agriculture.[1] Under the PIA test, tribes legally are entitled to as much water as is needed to irrigate all practicably irrigable acreage within their reservation boundaries. The Court, however, failed to provide much guidance regarding specific aspects of what acreage was to be considered practicably irrigable. Does it mean all acreage where the soil will support crops; or must a water supply be available physically as well? Does economic feasibility play a role in the analysis? And should the assessment be made under the technology existing at the time the reservation was established or under current practices?

These types of questions regarding PIA are being raised in courts throughout the West as more tribal governments quantify their *Winters* rights. Answers to these questions are slow in coming, and it is not the purpose of this discussion to speculate on the validity of various interpretations of PIA (*e.g.*, the role of economic factors). Rather, this chapter introduces the basic concepts that typically go into a PIA analysis—concepts that a tribe will need to understand in order to assert its own position as well as to counter those positions with which it disagrees.

10-2. THE PIA ANALYSIS

Identifying practicably irrigable acreage is a complex and costly task. It involves extensive investigations by hydrologists, soil scientists, economists, agronomists and engineers who must coordinate their efforts in the laboratory, office and field. Although various strategies for assessing PIA can be formulated, each usually embodies the following components:

- Identifying arable land on the reservation (*i.e.*, land amenable to sustained agricultural use).
- Determining feasible cropping patterns on the arable land.
- Calculating the amount of irrigation water needed by the crops.
- Designing an irrigation network sufficient to deliver the required water.
- Comparing the costs of production to crop income in order to establish the acreage that it is economical to irrigate.

Step 1: Identifying Arable Land

The Three Suitability Factors

The initial task in a PIA assessment is identifying land which can be farmed over a period of years. Three basic factors determine whether particular land is in fact arable. First, the soil must be suitable for crop growth. Features such as salinity, texture, moisture retention, depth, composition and alkalinity determine whether certain soil is amenable to cultivation. The second factor in an arability assessment is slope. Simply stated, if a piece of land is too steep, it should not be cultivated.

Finally, the acreage must have proper drainage characteristics in order for it to support sustainable agriculture. Thousands of acres of irrigated land in the United States and throughout the world have gone out of production due to inadequate drainage that leads to a buildup of salt in the soil. The most important parameters influencing drainage that must be considered in an arability assessment are the hydraulic conductivity of the soil beneath the root zone and the depth of soil to an impermeable barrier.

Field and Laboratory Analyses

To assess the characteristics of the soil, many samples of it must be collected and analyzed. A typical field program involves several types of investigations. Shallow augers (5 to 10 feet) are used to collect and log soil strata under the root zone. Digging of backhoe pits also is used to understand the soil profile and root zone. Drilling programs commonly are undertaken as part of the investigation to gain additional information about soil further beneath the surface. Samples from each of these tasks then are analyzed in soil chemistry, infiltration and hydraulic conductivity tests.

Ideally, each parcel of land being studied in a PIA analysis should undergo field investigations and testing in order to establish its arability. This level of detail is generally impractical from both time and cost standpoints. Although there is no strict rule as to the level of detail required, field sampling at about half-mile intervals usually proves adequate for reservation assessment. Where extreme diversity of terrain and soil type occurs, however, more detailed sampling may be necessary.

Land Classification

Once the soil, slope and drainage characteristics of reservation lands are analyzed, the acreage can be classified to reflect relative arability. The set of categories applied to the Big Horn River system adjudication[2] in Wyoming serve to demonstrate the type of delineation used:

Class 1 — Lands of high quality for irrigation that will yield high returns with minimum production and management costs.

Class 2 — Good quality lands with only minor deficiencies.

Class 3 — Fair quality lands having more serious deficiencies than Class 2 lands.

Class 4 — Lands of marginal quality for irrigation, used mainly for shallow-rooted crops or pasture.

Class 5 — Lands placed in a deferred status pending further investigation.

Class 6 — Lands that do not meet the minimum requirements for arability.

The state of Wyoming attacked these categories, asserting that they failed to consider economic factors and were too vague. The Wyoming Supreme Court, however, upheld the system as "reasonable and fair to the parties" because the arable acreage determined by the system was subjected to an engineering analysis to calculate irrigable acreage, and these acres were in turn subjected to a "stringent economic analysis."[3]

Step 2: Establishing Cropping Patterns

Once the arable acreage is identified and classified, the next step in the PIA analysis is to determine what crops can be grown on the land. Perhaps some acreage will be suitable for corn, some for alfalfa, and other acreage for small grains such as barley. The main factors influencing this suitability are climate, elevation and soil characteristics. Agronomists analyze the arable acreage in light of these factors and come up with projected amounts of land dedicated to each crop type. In order to make a more realistic estimate of cropping patterns, the analysis should include consideration of local demand for farm products, ease of transportation and preferences of the local farmers.

Step 3: Calculating Water Requirements

With the number of acres identified for each crop type, a straightforward process is used to calculate the associated water needs. Evapotranspiration (the amount of water consumed into the atmosphere) by different crops can be estimated using several methods (*e.g.*, Blaney-Criddle). For instance, at a particular location, a stand of alfalfa may evapotranspire 1.8 acre-feet of water per acre during the growing season. If one assumes that during the summer, only 4 inches (0.3 feet) of rain are available to the crop, then the total consumptive use of irrigation water will be 1.5 acre-feet per acre (1.8 - 0.3 = 1.5). If there are 1000 acres of arable alfalfa land on the reservation, the associated consumptive water needs would amount to 1500 acre-feet per year.

Consumptive use, however, is only part of the picture in determining water requirements. Due to ditch losses and other inefficiencies, more water must be diverted and delivered to the field than simply the amount consumed by the crops. In many areas of the West, less than half the water diverted for irrigation actually is evapotranspired by crops. If, in the above example, the reservation irrigation practices resulted in half the water diverted being consumed (a 50% efficiency), then the diversion requirement would be 3000 acre-feet. If the efficiency were only 33% (*i.e.*, two-thirds of the diverted water was lost in transit or not used by the crops on the field), then the diversion need would equal 4500 acre-feet. An additional water requirement is the leaching fraction—that portion of water that must be applied in excess of plant requirements to maintain an adequate salt balance in the field.

The previous example shows that efficiency will play a major role in determining the quantity of tribal water rights. Furthermore, the role can be controversial. States can be expected to argue that future reservation irrigation should be assumed to be very efficient (thereby decreasing the diversion right), while tribes wishing to maximize their *Winters* rights might argue that the assumption of highly efficient systems is wrong.

Step 4: Designing the Irrigation System

After calculating the water needs for crops on particular arable lands, agricultural engineers then are able to design the facilities needed to irrigate the land. The irrigation network should be designed to deliver water to the acreage in the cheapest way possible, including an efficient diversion system, distribution network, on-farm delivery system, drainage facilities, and wells and pumping plants where needed.

The analysis incorporates a detailed estimate of capital costs for the system as well as other expenses associated with water delivery. Included are costs for engineering, annual operating and maintenance costs (including power and labor), and replacement costs for each component. Cost calculations then are used by an economist to take the PIA analysis through its fifth, and final step.

Step 5: Analyzing Economic Feasibility

In the world of engineering and economics, a benefit-to-cost ratio of greater than 1.0 is said to demonstrate the economic feasibility of a project. Such a benefit-cost analysis generally is applied by courts to arable reservation acreage in order to determine if it is practicably irrigable. In other words, the costs of delivering the water (including the initial capital costs) and of raising the crops on a particular parcel of land are compared to the economic benefits (*i.e.*, the income) derived from selling the crops. If the income from the crops on a certain parcel exceeds the total costs, then the acreage is considered part of the tribal PIA land. If, however, the parcel's irrigation and production costs exceed the benefits derived from selling the crop, courts generally consider the acreage not to be practicably irrigable. The parcels that pass this economic test are then totaled to establish PIA on the reservation. Finally, the associated water needs of the practicably irrigable acreage (in terms of consumptive requirements or total diversions) becomes the quantity of the tribal water right.

10-3. AREAS OF CONTROVERSY

Areas of potential dispute arise throughout the PIA analysis as tribes attempt to maximize their *Winters* rights and states try to minimize tribal claims. In each of the five steps discussed above, litigants can be expected to argue over assumptions and decisions made, ranging from those involving classification of soil types to the selection of appropriate water efficiency rates.

It is in the area of economic feasibility, however, that the dispute gets the most complex. Recall from Chapter 8 that the present worth of future economic benefits is established to determine if such benefits outweigh the current costs of building an irrigation system. A particular controversy is posed by the process used to determine present worth, because that figure can be easily manipulated depending upon the assumption that a party makes regarding the so-called "discount rate." The discount rate, which is related to interest and inflation rates, is difficult to predict accurately; yet it holds tremendous power over a project's economic feasibility. The following example demonstrates its impact on the PIA analysis.

Assume that a tribe has arable acreage on which they plan to grow irrigated alfalfa. They calculate that for each of the next 25 years, they can make $100 per acre after subtracting the annual production costs from the gross income. If there were no inflation or interest rate, then the present worth of $100 per year for 25 years would equal $2,500. But under real circumstances, the present worth of future money must be reduced by the discount rate to account for interest and inflation. Assuming a discount rate of 4%, then $100 for 25 years is equivalent to a present sum of $1,562. Consequently, the tribe economically could justify irrigating the acreage only if the initial capital cost of building the irrigation system were less than $1,562 per acre. If so, the future benefits from irrigating the land would exceed the cost, and the acreage would be considered practicably irrigable.

A 10% discount rate, however, changes the situation drastically. Under this higher interest/inflation rate, the present worth of $100 per year for 25 years equals only $908. Consequently, only those parcels for which an irrigation system could be built for less than $908 per acre, rather than $1,562, are considered practicably irrigable. Much less land will be considered PIA under the 10% discount rate than under the 4% rate; yet honest differences of opinion exist regarding what estimate will prove most accurate over the coming 25 years.[4]

Additional controversy arises in the benefit-cost ratio when determining PIA. For instance, many tribal advocates assert that the secondary benefits derived from increased irrigation activity on the reservation should be considered in the analysis. This would include as benefits the income from additional stores and other services spawned by the economic activity associated with additional irrigation. Opponents to this approach assert that such secondary benefits should not be considered in the equation. As noted in Chapter 8, many economists have argued against the Bureau of Reclamation practice of including secondary benefits in the benefit-cost calculations. One primary reason for their opposition, however, may not be applicable to tribes. These economists argue that the funds should not be counted as part of the national benefits because they would be spent elsewhere and have an equal opportunity to earn a net return in a fully employed economy. A fully employed economy, however, is an uncommon situation in Indian Country.

The economic analysis is obviously a complex component of a PIA determination—and controversy is expected to continue. The Supreme Court has yet to rule on the extent to which economic feasibility should be incorporated into a PIA analysis, let alone on what discount rates or secondary benefits potentially apply. It is helpful, however, to look at how the controversies associated with PIA were handled in other courts, including the recent Wyoming adjudication involving the Wind River Reservation.

10-4. LESSONS FROM WYOMING

The Wind River Indian Reservation encompasses approximately 2.5 million acres in the Big Horn River system of western Wyoming. In 1988, the Wyoming Supreme Court generally upheld the findings of a Special Master and a district court in a general stream adjudication of the Big Horn River system.[5] In the end, the supreme court held that 54,216 acres of historically irrigated lands of the reservation were PIA[6] and that an additional 54,005 acres were also practicably irrigable. These findings extensively reflected the lengthy analysis and conclusions by the Special Master, from whose report many lessons regarding PIA can be gleaned.

Estimating Costs of the Irrigation Network

Three major parties were involved in litigating the amount of reserved water rights associated with the Wind River Indian Reservation. The tribes of the reservation represented themselves, the state of Wyoming opposed the tribal claims, and the United States appeared on behalf of the tribes although it often disagreed with the tribal position. Each of the three parties acknowledged that practicably irrigable acreage is defined as "those acres susceptible to sustained irrigation at reasonable costs."[7] From there, however, very little agreement was seen.

A key component in the analysis of PIA that proved controversial was the cost of building the irrigation system. The United States calculated that the cost for developing the network would average about $2,000 per acre. The tribes, however, estimated this figure to be more on the order of $1,500 per acre. The parties each relied on different assumptions.[8]

First, the tribes reduced the federal figure for energy cost by 10% by assuming lower sprinkler irrigation pressures. Improved performance of low pressure sprinklers (at 40 to 48 pounds per square inch (psi)) is making replacement of the higher pressure models (55 psi) possible in some instances. The tribes also significantly reduced on-farm costs and pipeline expenses when they assumed that volume discounts could be received for materials. The tribes' experts also disagreed with the United States regarding the need for "elaborate" pumping facilities, and, therefore, showed a 60% reduction in those costs. These experts asserted, as well, that the drainage system was overdesigned and cost nearly one-third more than necessary.[9]

The final area of disagreement involved the estimate for engineering fees and contingency costs. The tribes assumed that engineering fees would equal 10% of the total costs of building the irrigation network, with an additional 10% budgeted for contingencies. The United States, however, estimated these two factors to equal 25% of the total cost, while the state asserted that 35% was the appropriate figure. The high value used by the state, along with a few other assumptions that differed from the analysis of the United States, resulted in an estimated development cost of about $2,400 per acre by Wyoming, compared to the $2,000 figure of the United States and the $1,500 value asserted by the tribes.[10]

The Importance of Objective Consultants

The Special Master accepted the $2,000 per acre development cost estimate of the United States in his findings—and his reasons for doing so provide an important lesson:

> It is not an easy task to assign a development cost to a given project when experts in the field cannot agree on what is an accurate estimate. While I respect the experience, education and expertise of those witnesses testifying on this matter, I conclude that the conclusions presented by the United States . . . are reasonable and realistic and are the figures I adopt in determining the feasibility of future projects. A brief discussion follows explaining my conclusion.
>
> The experts who appeared on behalf of the State of Wyoming and the Tribes gave a partial impression that they were advocates of positions favorable to their clients rather than experts doing an independent, unbiased analysis of the feasibility of constructing irrigation projects. This is not a

> condemnation of their work or opinions and it is understandable how a certain degree of advocacy could develop during lengthy and important proceedings. It is, however, significant enough to warrant the conclusion that the preponderance of the evidence supports the position of the United States.[11]

Consultants must walk a difficult line between representing their client and being objective experts before the court. Tribal and state experts apparently overstepped this line to the detriment of their clients in the Wyoming case.[12] Likewise, an expert easily can appear to be too much of an advocate in other aspects of the PIA analysis, as demonstrated by the following findings of the Special Master:

> In considering . . . potentially irrigable acres, [the State economic expert] made several assumptions which are clearly at odds with the reality of the circumstances now existing in the Division and likely to exist in the future. He assumed all of these parcels would be worked by existing irrigators and no unemployed labor would be used. This is possible, certainly, in some instances, but not all. . . .
>
> Further afield, he assumed each tract of this land placed in production would require a full complement of new machinery fully costed. He assumed . . . the maximum size of a farm in the area would be 320 acres. Though acknowledging that Indian irrigators in the area are not held to this limitation, and admitting that some efficiency could be achieved on a larger unit, he held to this farm size through cross examination. . . . When asked to assume a bean planter could be operated ten times more efficiently if there were no acreage limitations, he felt the savings would be negligible and declined to consider that assumption realistic. Essentially, he refused, even hypothetically, to consider a larger farming unit. . . .
>
> I find the assumptions of the State's economist hard to apply to the real world. In taking an inflexible position, he has biased his costs to the detriment of his analysis, which I must consider inadequate to advance the State's claim. . . .[13]

Appropriate Use of Expert Witnesses

The previous quotes of the Special Master highlight the need for care in the selection and use of consultants in order to insure the credibility of the tribal position at trial. Objectivity is indeed important; yet a further pitfall in the use of expert witnesses must be avoided as well:

> Continuing, the State called Mr. [Doe], a respected man of good professional reputation. In this instance, however, the State used him so broadly that his testimony was not always solid. While excellently qualified as a civil engineer in the field of highway construction in Wyoming, and also in the area of photo interpretation, he often was asked to testify outside his expertise, offering opinions as a soils scientist, an

irrigation engineer, an agricultural engineer, an economist, and a statistician.[14]

All too often expert witnesses go beyond their areas of expertise when testifying in court. Although the lawyer should be prepared enough to know not to ask a witness the wrong type of question, it is ultimately the consultant's responsibility to draw the line on where his or her expertise ends. Failure to do so can not only prove embarrassing, but can also be very detrimental to the client's case.

The Need for Field Work

The tribal and federal positions in the Wind River litigation were obviously furthered by the fact that, in some instances, Wyoming's use of consultants undermined its assertions. The Special Master also found the state's position to be less compelling because more field investigations had been undertaken by the other parties. The Master recognized that, in undertaking a classification of land in a PIA analysis, there is no substitute for on-the-ground verification:

> State expert [Jones] pursued his analysis by counting [test] holes shown on various documents and in some instances observing parcels from the road as he drove by. When asked which portion of a particular tract was arable, and the acreages of both the arable and nonarable portions, Mr. [Jones] said he thought one would have to really visit the tract to tell exactly. Another State expert [Mr. Smith] agreed field investigations are necessary and found it not good practice to make acreage determinations in the office without the basis in reality that comes from field review. This was the point raised by experts who actually went onto each tract in doing the Federal and Tribal studies. It is also one of the reasons I find the Federal and Tribal studies generally more credible. . . .[15]

The Limitations of Data Gathering and Analysis

Even though the state's position was undermined by its lack of field work, Wyoming nonetheless continued criticizing the other parties for failing to support their claims adequately. A recurring theme in the state's attack on the reserved water rights claims involved the assertion that the United States and the tribes had failed to gather sufficient technical data upon which to draw conclusions. Such attacks were aimed at the land classification methodology (*i.e.*, too few soil sample and test holes) as well as at the subsequent analysis of cropping patterns. In the latter instance, the state questioned the reliability of the climatological data since it was gathered from only seven locations and, therefore, was not sufficiently accurate over the entire reservation. The Special Master responded as follows:

> As I stated in my arability discussion, an optimum approach can be envisioned for any aspect of an analysis which, when compared to the study actually done, makes the effort appear far from complete. Climate data gathering stations could have been set up in hundreds of locations on the Reservation to get a better sampling of the variance in climate from one

> study area to another. Particularly detailed measurements of solar radiation could have consumed thousands of hours of work. Even with that effort, the data could be criticized for not representing the average or norm for the area for a given cycle of years. This entire adjudication could have been delayed for ten years while a complete study was done for a ten year cycle.
>
> Obviously, it is unfair to require such an unrealistic test when there is no evidence, and only speculation, that the data used by [the United States] was unreliable or that any greater effort would produce different results. Reason and common sense, together with the inevitable restrictions of time and budget, dictate that something less than perfection should warrant the conclusion that an adequate, professional job has been done in compiling data reliable enough to use with reasonable certainty.[16]

The Special Master referred to "the inevitable restrictions of time and budget" that tribes will face in any PIA analysis. This statement highlights the fact that care must be taken in allocating limited tribal financial resources among consultants. Several such professionals will need to be hired within a limited budget, and it is necessary to avoid allocating too many dollars to a particular person or task. Tribes should be on the lookout for proposals that offer to undertake work in more detail than will be required, thereby making fewer dollars available for other necessary tasks. On the other hand, inadequate field data and analysis can undermine a tribe's *Winters* rights claim severely, so there is no easy solution to this dilemma.

The bottom line, however, is to insure that consultants are hired to undertake work only in their field of expertise; that they are able to present a credible case as an expert witness before the court; and that they are willing to explain the details and rationale behind their proposed methodology prior to being hired by the tribe.

A Final Lesson

The previous sections have demonstrated several ways in which Wyoming and the tribes differed in their approach to identifying PIA. One further difference existed which provides a useful lesson for future application. Wyoming asserted that the tribes failed to analyze existing irrigated land under the PIA standard, therefore such lands should not be part of the PIA total. The tribes countered that lands already under irrigation were obviously practicably irrigable. They also asserted that certain other types of land should be deemed PIA without having to undergo the whole analysis. These included lands previously irrigated but currently idle, trust lands with state-adjudicated water rights, Indian fee lands, and lands not in use but irrigable from existing canals. The court agreed that testing currently irrigated land was unreasonable, and that some of the other lands also should be faced with a less stringent analysis for determining PIA.[17]

The lessons from Wyoming demonstrate one court's approach to PIA and, although its findings are useful to an understanding of the PIA concept, other courts may arrive at different conclusions for other reservation lands. Also, there is much flexibility embodied in the five-step procedure set forth in this chapter for identifying PIA, and the procedure can be modified to suit a specific situation. In particular, the steps described do not proceed necessarily in independent, discrete order. Rather, tasks often proceed concurrently with significant interaction between the experts.

Whatever the procedure, however, at the end of the PIA litigation or negotiated settlement, a tribe will know how much water legally is available to it. With this knowledge and this legal right, the nineteenth century promises of permanent tribal homelands is a step closer to fulfillment.

REFERENCE NOTES

1. *Arizona v. California*, 373 U.S. 546 (1963).
2. *In Re the General Adjudication of All Rights to Use Water in the Big Horn River System and All Other Sources, State of Wyoming*, 750 P.2d 681 (Wyo. 1988).
3. *Id.* at 707.
4. *See* 750 P.2d at 709 for a discussion of how different parties argued for different discount rates in the Big Horn River system adjudication and how the Wyoming Supreme Court resolved the issue.
5. *In Re the General Adjudication of All Rights to Use Water in the Big Horn River System and All Other Sources, State of Wyoming*, 750 P.2d 681 (Wyo. 1988).
6. *Id.* at 712-16.
7. *Id.* at 706.
8. The following discussion is based on the report of the Special Master. The Wyoming Supreme Court's discussion of the economic issues is presented at 750 P.2d 709-11.
9. Report of the Special Master Concerning Reserved Water Rights Claims by and on Behalf of the Tribes of the Wind River Reservation (Dec. 15, 1982), *In Re the General Adjudication of All Rights to Use Water in the Big Horn River System and All Other Sources, State of Wyoming*, Civil No. 4993 (5th Jud. Dist., Wyo., May 10, 1983), at 173-74.
10. *Id.* at 176.
11. *Id.* at 176-77.
12. For instance, the Wyoming Supreme Court noted that the tribes' irrigation engineer witness was not credible because he "admitted he sometimes followed instructions, not his conscience." 750 P.2d at 712. On the other hand, the Special Master praised one of the federal government's witnesses because he was "detached from any preconceived estimates of what should be the result." Special Master quoted by Wyoming Supreme Court at 750 P.2d at 707.
13. Master's report at 104-05. For additional criticisms of the state's experts, *see* the state supreme court's decision at 750 P.2d at 709-10.
14. Master's report at 102.
15. Master's report at 101-02. The tribes' claims to two parcels were denied in part because of inadequate field work by one of their experts. The Wyoming Supreme Court found that the irrigation and drainage engineer and field investigator for the tribes "spent an inadequate amount of time in the field" resulting in a "hasty investigation." 750 P.2d at 711-12.
16. Master's report at 168-69. The Wyoming Supreme Court quoted with approval the statement by the Special Master that the state could not force the federal government to have to prove more "merely by asserting that greater efforts could have been made in the data collection"; a party must do more than merely allege that more studies could have been done. 750 P.2d at 708.
18. Master's report at 89.

SUGGESTED READINGS

An article by Burness, Cummings, Gorman and Lansford, *Practicably Irrigable Acreage and Economic Feasibility: The Role of Time, Ethics and Discounting*, 23 NAT. RES. JOURNAL 289 (1983) discusses PIA with a sympathetic bent toward maximizing tribal claims. The opposite approach toward PIA is taken in Brookshire, Merrill and Watts, *Economics and the Determination of Indian Reserved Water Rights*, 23 NAT. RES. JOURNAL 749 (1983). For the closest thing to a discussion of the elements of PIA by the Supreme Court, *see* Report of Special Master Elbert P. Tuttle, *Arizona v. California* (Feb. 22, 1982), from page 88 through 103.

Chapter 11

Regulatory Implications of Water Use Options

11-1. THE FRAMEWORK OF GOVERNMENT REGULATION

The United States is a nation of regulation. When a person decides to pursue an idea or project within this country, countless procedures, standards, ordinances, rules, permits, guidelines, statutes, licenses, and other forms of regulation seem to demand compliance. The barrage of requirements comes not only from the federal government, but state and local laws generally must be understood and followed as well.

Regulation is not intrinsically bad; in fact the rationale behind implementing so many requirements often is well motivated. A majority of regulations are designed to keep development from infringing on the rights of others, from undermining public safety, and from harming the environment. Some people, however, believe that regulation has been taken too far and rhetorically espouse the need for government to reduce its demands on the citizenry. Regardless of personal beliefs on this topic, one fact remains clear: government regulation is currently prevalent in this society, and it must be considered when planning a major project.

The importance of considering the implications of government regulation is particularly great when planning a water project. In few other areas is a developer faced with so many requirements before being allowed to construct the facility. For instance, prior to building a dam, the developer must get a license from the Federal Energy Regulatory Commission, obtain permits from the U.S. Army Corps of Engineers, participate in extensive assessments under the National Environmental Policy Act, ensure that the project does not harm endangered species and historical sites, comply with relevant dam safety provisions, and jump through a variety of other potential hoops mandated by local, state, and federal law. All regulatory requirements should be identified and assessed early in the planning process—for they may prove so burdensome as to make the option of building a dam unattractive to the developer.

Even less obtrusive water use options that do not include dams or other structures face a number of regulations. Water used in industrial or municipal systems must be assessed and permitted prior to its discharge under the Clean Water Act. Likewise, federal regulations and restrictions may face those simply wanting to use the water for drinking (*i.e.*, under the Safe Drinking Water Act). Indeed, water can be used for very few purposes that do not face some sort of regulatory hurdle. For tribes, the assessment of regulatory requirements can get even more complicated due to unique jurisdictional issues on reservations. Many laws, particularly those of state and local governments, have no effect on tribal affairs; and controversy persists over what regulations actually do or do not apply on reservations.

This chapter lays out the elements of the regulatory controversy, and where possible, suggests conclusions regarding the applicability of federal and state regulatory jurisdiction over tribal affairs. Next, specific federal requirements that face Indian water projects are explained in order to assist tribes in the planning process. The chapter then concludes with recent policies of the U.S. Environmental Protection Agency that impact tribal water use.

11-2. REGULATORY JURISDICTION ON INDIAN RESERVATIONS

Ever since Indian reservations were established, conflicts have existed over jurisdiction within their boundaries. Over the past two centuries, the United States Supreme Court has handled dozens of cases involving fights over whose laws had effect within the reservation. Controversies have centered around taxation matters, criminal jurisdiction, and the regulation of various reservation activities.

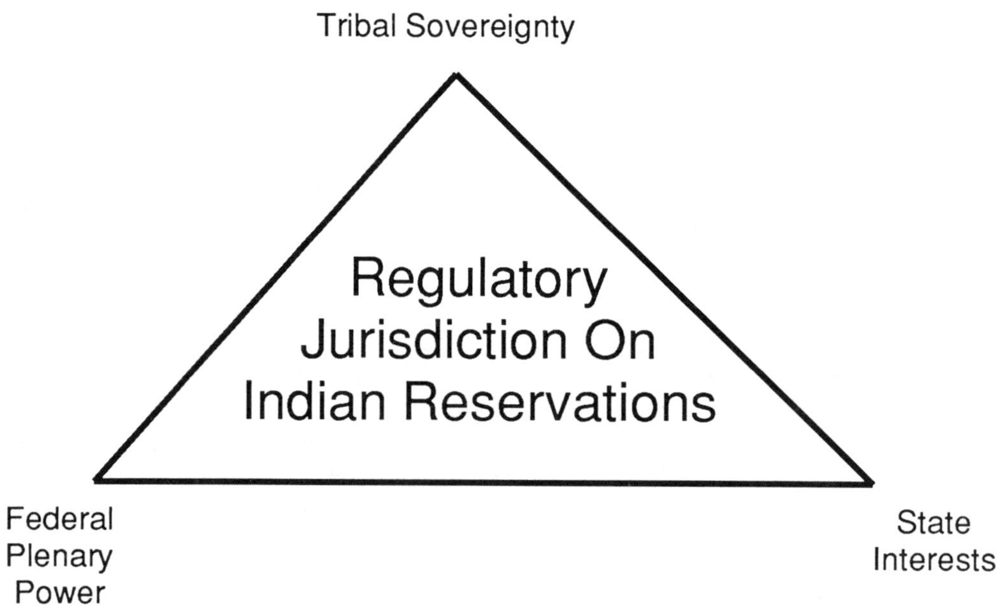

Figure 11-1. Schematic of Regulatory Jurisdiction.

Figure 11-1 demonstrates the three major forces weighed by the Court in deciding these jurisdictional disputes in Indian Country. At the top of the triangle lies "TRIBAL SOVEREIGNTY," which acts to keep regulatory jurisdiction with the tribe to the exclusion of state law and, to a lesser degree, of federal law. The next component of the triangle is "FEDERAL PLENARY POWER," a concept that provides Congress with broad discretion to impose laws and regulations upon tribal activities. At the third vertex lies "STATE INTERESTS," which the Supreme Court has determined should also be considered in the jurisdiction assessment. Although no simple or sure answers are available, the following sections describe these three elements and assess their respective roles in determining regulatory jurisdiction over reservation water projects and other tribal activities.

Tribal Sovereignty

The concept of tribal sovereignty was summarized recently by the Supreme Court:

> Indian tribes are unique aggregations possessing attributes of sovereignty over both their members and their territory; they are a "separate people" possessing "the power of regulating their internal and social relations. . . ." [Cites omitted.][1]

This important legal tenet developed during the early days of Indian law when states attempted to assert jurisdiction over tribal lands. When the state of Georgia tried to impose its laws on the Cherokee Nation in the early 1800s, the Supreme Court struck down the state's attempt, recognizing, in *Worcester v. Georgia* (1832), that Indian nations were "distinct political communities, having territorial boundaries, within which their authority is exclusive, and having a right to all the lands within those boundaries, which is not only acknowledged, but guaranteed by the United States."[2]

The concept of tribal sovereignty has survived the decades to continue to provide tribal governments with control over their internal affairs. It also has been described as the "backdrop" against which attempted regulatory intrusions by other governmental entities should be evaluated in the courtroom. The future of tribal sovereignty under the law, however, is subject to change. As stated by the Supreme Court in 1978 and again in 1983: "The sovereignty that Indian tribes retain is of a unique and limited character. *It exists only at the sufferance of Congress and is subject to complete defeasance*."[3]

This quote demonstrates that the concept of tribal sovereignty is vulnerable to congressional plenary power (explained below) over Indian law. Nonetheless, it persists and, if the policy statement issued by the Reagan administration is pursued in good faith, tribal self-determination and sovereignty can be strengthened:

> Throughout our history, despite periods of conflict and shifting national policies in Indian affairs, the government-to-government relationship between the United States and Indian tribes has endured. The Constitution, treaties, laws, and court decisions have consistently recognized a unique political relationship between Indian tribes and the United States which this Administration pledges to uphold. . . .
>
> This Administration honors the commitment made in 1970 [Nixon's announced policy of Indian self-determination] and 1975 [the Indian Self-Determination Act] to strengthen tribal governments and lessen federal control over tribal governmental affairs. This Administration is determined

> to turn these goals into reality. Our policy is to reaffirm dealing with Indian tribes on a government-to-government basis and to pursue the policy of self-government for Indian tribes. . . .
>
> This Administration intends to restore tribal governments to their rightful place among the governments of this nation and to enable tribal governments, along with state and local governments, to resume control over their own affairs.[4]

Federal Plenary Power

The United States Congress has broad authority to pass legislation affecting Indian people and their lands. Congress' plenary power is limited only by the restrictions of the Constitution, although it is tempered as well by the concept of tribal sovereignty and by the duty owed to the tribes under the federal-Indian trust relationship. Nonetheless, there are few bounds on what Congress can legislate regarding Indians; abrogation of treaties is one type of legislation that dramatically demonstrates plenary power. "Abrogation" is the word used to justify legally the breaking of solemn promises made in treaties, and it is a word that Congress has used often in legislation to take Indian lands reserved by the tribes under treaty. The Supreme Court has recognized congressional authority to abrogate treaties,[5] as well as to regulate activities on reservations.

Despite this plenary federal power, however, early court rulings were protective of tribal sovereignty by holding that statutes of general application did not apply to tribes unless such a result clearly was intended by Congress. As a consequence, the Court generally did not consider regulatory schemes to apply to tribal activities unless Congress explicitly had stated the contrary.

In 1960, however, the Supreme Court held in *Federal Power Commission v. Tuscarora Indian Nation*[6] that the standard was not actually this strict, and that federal regulation of tribal activities could occur even if Congress had not included such coverage in the statute expressly. If the statute created "a complete and comprehensive plan" of regulation, then Indian activities were assumed to be included in its coverage. Also, the Court has stated, in *Colorado River Water Conservation District v. United States* (1976), that if the purpose of a congressional act would be defeated without its application to tribal rights, then Indian activities are implicitly included.[7]

Certain limitations regarding the applicability of the *Tuscarora* rule exist. Even if a regulatory scheme is complete and comprehensive, it will not apply automatically to Indians if it somehow impacts treaty rights or other statutory obligations to the tribe. For instance, the Supreme Court found that the federal capital gains tax did not apply to timber income from Indian land that had been provided "free of all charge or incumbrance."[8] The Courts' rationale in such a case stems from the established rule that treaty rights will not be abrogated or modified absent an expressed intent by Congress to do so.

The area of federal regulation of Indian activities is indeed complex and punctuated by contradiction. The plenary power of Congress is clear, and comprehensive federal regulations generally will apply to tribal lands. As a result, the major federal legislation that impacts and regulates water use (set forth in sections 11-3 and 11-4 of this chapter) will need to be considered by tribes when selecting water use options.

But, so far, this assessment of regulatory jurisdiction has covered only two-thirds of the triangle. It is necessary to determine to what extent, if any, state laws may apply to tribal activities involving water use.

State Regulatory Interests

One hundred years ago the answer to the question of the effect of state regulation on tribal activities would have been relatively simple. One needed only to look at the 1832 *Worcester* opinion in which Chief Justice Marshall spelled out the concept of tribal sovereignty.[9] As summarized by the Supreme Court in a later case, *McClanahan v. Arizona State Tax Commission* (1973), "[i]t followed from [Marshall's] concept of Indian reservations as separate, although dependent nations, that state law could have no role to play within the reservation boundaries."[10]

Over the decades, however, the protection against the intrusion of state law lost some of its teeth. By 1962, the Supreme Court had recognized that "Congress has to a substantial degree opened the doors of reservations to state laws, in marked contrast to what prevailed in the time of Chief Justice Marshall."[11] This opening included the area of potential state jurisdiction over reservation activities; it is currently recognized, since *White Mountain Apache Tribe v. Bracker* (1980), that "any regulatory interest of the state must be given weight" in the assessment.[12]

While it is established now that state interests will be considered in assessing on-reservation regulation of activities, "there is no rigid rule by which to resolve the question whether a particular state law may be applied to an Indian reservation or to tribal members."[13] Such a determination can be influenced by a variety of factors including ownership of the land affected, whether a particular law applies to Indians as well as non-Indians within the reservation, whether the state has a constitutional "disclaimer clause" waiving jurisdiction over tribal affairs, and by a number of other considerations to be weighed by the court. Some certainty, however, has risen from this complex mixture of factors. The Supreme Court has identified

> two independent but related barriers to the assertion of state regulatory authority over tribal reservations and members. First, the exercise of such authority may be pre-empted by federal law. Second, it may unlawfully infringe 'on the right of reservation Indians to make their own laws and be ruled by them.' The two barriers are independent because either, standing alone, can be a sufficient basis for holding state law inapplicable to activity undertaken on the reservation or by tribal members.[14]

A recent case demonstrates the Supreme Court's use of this test. *Rice v. Rehner* (1983)[15] involved a situation where a tribal member sold liquor to both Indians and non-Indians from a general store on the Pala Reservation in San Diego, California. California asserted that a state liquor license was required, while the tribal member, Rehner, argued that she had followed the requirements of the tribal code permitting the sale of liquor on the reservation. In deciding the case, the Court first looked at the issue of tribal sovereignty and how it might be undermined by the assertion of state regulatory control of on-reservation liquor sales.

The Court determined that such undermining of tribal authority would occur only if the area of regulation was one historically related to the tribe's sovereign powers. The Court then concluded that "tradition simply has not recognized a sovereign immunity or inherent authority in favor of liquor regulation by Indians" and therefore, "the assumption that the States have no power to regulate the affairs of Indians on a reservation . . . would be unwarranted in the narrow context of the regulation of liquor."[16] The Court further concluded that because "the activity in which Rehner seeks to engage potentially has a substantial impact beyond the reservation, we may accord little if any weight to any asserted interest in tribal sovereignty in this case."[17] Finally, after finding no preemption of state authority by federal law, the Court ruled in favor of California.

The *Rice* case carries a disturbing message to advocates of tribal sovereignty—state interests may be considered strongly when the impacts of a tribal activity extend beyond the reservation boundaries. This lesson was demonstrated as well in a case where the Puyallup Tribe had retained treaty fishing rights "in common with all citizens of the territory." In *Puyallup Tribe v. Dept. of Game of State of Washington* (1977),[18] the Supreme Court held that the state could regulate tribal members fishing on fee land within the reservation to protect the diminishing runs of steelhead trout in the Puyallup River. "The exercise of [the tribal fishing] right was subject to reasonable regulation by the State pursuant to its power to conserve an important natural resource."[19] Without "reasonable regulation," tribal fishing could "totally frustrate the rights of non-Indian citizens of Washington" to catch steelhead from the Puyallup River.[20]

The consideration of off-reservation impacts of Indian activities could play a significant role in the analysis of state regulatory intrusions on tribal water use. For instance, state dam safety regulations arguably apply to construction of on-reservation dams in order to protect non-Indian landowners downstream of the project. A court certainly would view a state's interest as being significant in such a case. Moreover, dam safety is not an area historically associated with tribal sovereignty.

Before imposing state safety laws upon a tribal dam project, however, the court would consider whether tribal self-determination or federal preemption counsel against the application of state law. The court would look to see if the tribe itself has implemented dam safety regulations. Also, federal construction regulations incorporated within the project should preempt state safety laws. Tribal self-determination and federal preemption of state law are indeed powerful factors that courts will consider in weighing all the interests.

The broad power of the federal government to prevent state regulation on tribal lands was recognized in *State of Washington Dept. of Ecology v. U.S. Environmental Protection Agency* (1985).[21] At issue was the application of the Resource Conservation and Recovery Act (RCRA),[22] which creates a comprehensive federal program for hazardous waste management. The Act explicitly stated that disposal of wastes by Indian tribes was covered under the Act, therefore this issue was not before the court.

The controversy arose instead from the Act's provisions that allow individual states, upon petition, to assume regulatory control of hazardous waste programs within their jurisdiction. The state of Washington assumed such control and sought to regulate hazardous waste disposal on Indian reservations. The U.S. Environmental Protection Agency (EPA) refused to yield this power to the state, arguing that the federal government should remain responsible for the program in Indian Country. The tribes joined with the EPA, expressing the "fear that their reservations will become 'dumping grounds' for off-reservation hazardous wastes if the state is permitted to control the hazardous waste program on the reservations."[23]

The court ruled in favor of the EPA and tribal position and held that "EPA reasonably has interpreted RCRA not to grant state jurisdiction over the activities of Indians in Indian country." The court's holding was based not only on federal powers, but was influenced as well by the recognition that "[r]espect for the long tradition of tribal sovereignty and self-government also underlies the rule that state jurisdiction over Indians in Indian country will not be easily implied."[24]

Summary of Jurisdictional Considerations

Tribal water managers and decision-makers will face difficult assessments regarding jurisdiction as they analyze water use options. It is likely that with federal licensing and regulation dominating the water field, and tribal sovereignty providing an important backdrop in the courtroom, few state regulations will apply to tribal water use. Nonetheless, the potential application of state dam safety laws and other state regulations to specific tribal water developments needs to be assessed. More importantly, several federal requirements potentially confront tribes who wish to construct water development projects. Finally, tribal water managers also must be knowledgeable of the various regulations that impact the use of water in homes, communities, and industries.

The remainder of this chapter is devoted to providing an overview of the major federal laws that potentially affect tribal water use options. Section 11-3 summarizes the federal government's constitutional authority over water resources. Section 11-4 then presents those regulations that are likely to arise in large-scale water storage and use projects, while section 11-5 discusses the water quality standards and requirements regulated by the EPA.

11-3. FEDERAL CONSTITUTIONAL AUTHORITY OVER WATER

Federal actions in Congress, the courts, and the executive branch can affect directly the quantity and quality of water a tribe will enjoy. Indirect federal actions far away from a reservation, but in the same river basin, also can have major positive and negative effects on tribal water resources. Tribes must understand federal authority over water to obtain both direct and indirect benefits and to avoid direct and indirect harm. The source of the federal government's expansive authority over water resources arises in several provisions of the Constitution of the United States.

The commerce clause of the Constitution empowers Congress to "regulate commerce" among the several states.[25] Rivers and lakes are instruments of trade and commerce, and the authority of Congress has been interpreted by the Supreme Court to extend to tributaries that supply water to make navigation possible on larger waterways. Congress could regulate watershed development and protection extensively under the commerce clause if it so chose. Even where Congress does not regulate interstate commerce expressly, the commerce clause can prohibit states from impairing the flow of commerce. For example, state statutes in Nebraska and New Mexico that restrained the exportation of water out of state recently were ruled unconstitutional. In one of these cases, *Sporhase v. Nebraska* (1982),[26] the Supreme Court expressed the breadth of federal power over commerce: "Ground water overdraft is a national problem and Congress has the power to deal with it on that scale."[27]

The property clause of the Constitution, which empowers Congress to regulate federal public lands, is another important source of authority.[28] The exercise of authority derived from the property clause in the Desert Land Act of 1877[29] severed the nonnavigable and unappropriated water from the public domain and empowered the arid states of the West to administer water right systems. Later, at the turn of the century in *Winters*, the Supreme Court made it clear that the United States had not given away all of its rights in the beneficial use of water crossing public lands and that the creation of land reservations impliedly reserved water.[30] The property clause is also the source of the power under which Congress enacted the 1952 McCarran Amendment to give state courts jurisdiction to adjudicate federal and Indian reserved water rights.[31]

The treaty clause of the Constitution empowers the President, subject to the advice and consent of the Senate, to enter treaties with other nations and Indian tribes.[32] Examples of international water treaties that affect tribal interests in waters can be found in the U.S.-Mexico treaties of 1906 on the Rio Grande and of 1944 on the Colorado, in the subsequent accords of the 1960s and 1970s of the International Boundary and Water Commission concerning salinity control, and in the various U.S.-Canadian water treaties, including the Columbia River Treaty. Such treaties take precedence over state water rights systems.

Another important constitutional provision affecting water management is the one dealing with the "war power," which enables Congress to build water projects or regulate water in furtherance of national defense.[33] Congress also has the power generally to spend money for the "general welfare," which includes the authority to condemn the property of states and Indian tribes to fulfill a public purpose, such as a reclamation, a flood control or a pollution control project.[34] Under the Constitution's "supremacy clause" the laws of the federal government are paramount and prevail over state laws as long as Congress is acting within the specific authority given it in the Constitution. Congress frequently refrains from fully exercising its powers and commonly defers or delegates political power to the states. In more than three dozen water project statutes, for example, Congress has directed that the executive branch act in conformance with state water law.

Two other provisions of the Constitution bear on the authority of the federal government to allocate interstate water among states. Congressional consent is necessary for interstate agreements, such as the 1922 Colorado River Compact, to be effective under the compact clause.[35] Finally, the Supreme Court has original jurisdiction over lawsuits between the states.[36] In interstate suits that concern water, the Court has tended to apply notions of "equitable apportionment," considering the conditions, the practices and the laws in each state. The Court prefers to have the states resolve their water differences by compact or by congressional apportionment.

These various constitutional provisions help define the power of the United States over water. The following sections demonstrate how this power has been exercised in specific legislation.

11-4. FEDERAL REGULATION OF WATER RESOURCE PROJECTS

The list of federal laws potentially impacting tribal water use options can get very lengthy. Rather than listing every conceivable regulation potentially affecting water use, this section focuses instead on the primary licensing provisions and requirements that typically confront major water projects. When actually implementing a specific tribal water development project, however, tribes must keep in mind that other regulations may apply beyond the major requirements discussed in this chapter. Nonetheless, the following discussion provides the basic understanding needed to incorporate regulatory factors into the tribal water planning process.

In 1920, Congress enacted the Federal Power Act to be administered by the Federal Power Commission (now the Federal Energy Regulatory Commission (FERC)). Section 4(e) of the Act authorizes FERC to issue licenses for the construction, operation, and maintenance of dams and other hydroelectric facilities located on the public lands and federal reservations.[37] "Reservations" are defined under the Act to include "tribal lands embraced within Indian reservations"; therefore, dams built within the Indian reservation are subject to the FERC licensing requirements.[38] Also, projects that improve navigation or that develop or transmit power "across, along, from or in any of the streams or other bodies of water over which Congress has jurisdiction under its authority to regulate commerce" must apply for FERC licenses as well.

Section 4(e) contains the provision that licenses shall be issued "within any reservation" only after a finding by FERC that the license will not interfere or be inconsistent with the purpose for which the reservation was created. Furthermore, the license "shall be subject to and contain such conditions as the Secretary of the

Department under whose jurisdiction such reservation falls shall deem necessary for the adequate protection and utilization of such reservation." The Supreme Court has held that this provision gives the Secretary of Interior broad discretion to affix conditions to hydroelectric projects built in Indian Country.[39]

Corps of Engineers Permits

Tribes that develop water impoundment projects also must be aware of the regulatory requirements of the U.S. Army Corps of Engineers. Sections 9 and 10 of the Rivers and Harbors Act of 1899 made it unlawful to construct dams and other structures in and over the navigable waters of the United States without the consent of Congress. The Corps of Engineers currently administers this regulation, issuing permits for such structures pursuant to 33 U.S.C. §§ 401 and 403.

Broader permitting authority, however, has been provided more recently to the Corps in section 404 of the Clean Water Act.[40] Prior to dredging or depositing fill material into waters of the United States, an applicant must receive a "404 permit" from the Corps. Authority for this permitting extends not only to navigable waters, but includes the regulation of dredging and filling in all other waters such as "lakes, rivers, streams (including intermittent streams), mudflats, sandflats, wetlands, sloughs, prairie potholes, wet meadows, playa lakes, or natural ponds, the use, degradation or destruction of which could affect interstate or foreign commerce."[41]

The broad reach of the permit requirement extends not only to major impoundment projects, but also to any water development (*e.g.*, a new headgate diversion) that involves the removal or deposition of material from streams or wetlands. The Corps, however, has facilitated the process for receiving such a permit. The regulations promulgated by the Corps[42] provide that discharges of dredge or fill material into most waters is deemed permitted (under a so-called "nationwide permit") so long as the following conditions are met:

(1) That the discharge will not be located in the proximity of a public water supply intake;

(2) That the discharge will not destroy a threatened or endangered species as identified under the Endangered Species Act, or destroy or adversely modify the critical habitat of such species . . . ;

(3) That the discharge will consist of suitable material free from toxic pollutants in toxic amounts;

(4) That the fill created by the discharge will be properly maintained to prevent erosion and other non-point sources of pollution;

(5) That the discharge will not occur in a component of the National Wild and Scenic River System;

(6) That the best management practices listed in Section 330.6 of this part should be followed to the maximum extent practicable [*e.g.*, avoiding spawning grounds and critical water-fowl areas].

Under the tenets of federal Indian law, laws of general applicability normally do not apply in Indian Country. The Clean Water Act is a law of general applicability; it does not state explicitly that tribes are covered by section 404. Thus, a state delegated the authority to issue section 404 permits probably could not apply the law against a tribe for an activity in Indian Country. While the applicability of section 404 to tribes has never been interpreted by the courts, and under modern general federal Indian law principles the section would not apply, the 1960 Supreme Court decision in *Federal Power Commission v. Tuscarora Indian Nation*[43] may suggest that the Corps (as opposed to the states) might be able to require compliance with section 404. The preference for tribal authority is buttressed by the 1987 amendments to the Clean Water Act providing that tribes, similar to states, now may be delegated section 404 permitting authority.[44]

The Endangered Species Act

Subsection (2) of the Corps' requirements listed above reflects the restriction placed on federal agencies that they shall "insure that any action authorized, funded, or carried out by such agency is not likely to jeopardize the continued existence of any endangered species or threatened species or result in the destruction or adverse modification of habitat of such species."[45] This provision of the Endangered Species Act carries with it significant implications for water development projects and may inhibit a developer from gaining the necessary federal permission to proceed with a project.

Such an occurrence happened recently in Colorado in the case of *Riverside Irrigation District v. Cache la Poudre Water Users Association* (1985).[46] In *Riverside*, the applicant wanted to build a major dam on a tributary to the South Platte River. The construction, of course, involved the depositing of fill material into the riverbed so, the applicant requested a "nationwide permit" for the project. The Corps then refused to issue the permit because of the project's potential impact on whooping crane habitat in Nebraska. The Corps and environmental groups were concerned that additional depletions in the flow of the South Platte would diminish the high runoff in the springtime that is needed to prevent vegetation growth on the sandbars frequented by the cranes. The encroachment of vegetation on the habitat of the whooping crane would make the birds more vulnerable to predators. The court upheld the Corps decision to deny the applicant a "nationwide permit."

The Endangered Species Act has affected a major water project in the East as well. In the famous case of *Tennessee Valley Authority v. Hill* (1978),[47] the Supreme Court let the Endangered Species Act stop the construction of a dam that would have potentially driven a certain small fish—the snaildarter—to extinction. The Court spelled out the strength of the Act:

> One would be hard pressed to find a statutory provision whose terms were any plainer than those in Section 7 of the Endangered Species Act. Its very words affirmatively command all federal agencies "to *insure* that all actions *authorized, funded*, or *carried out* by them do not *jeopardize* the continued existence" of an endangered species or *result* in the destruction or

> modification of habitat of such species. . ." 16 U.S.C. § 1536 (1976 ed.). (Emphasis added.) This language admits of no exception. . . .
>
> Concededly, this view of the Act will produce results requiring the sacrifice of the anticipated benefits of the project and of many millions of dollars in public funds. But examination of the language, history, and structure of the legislation under review here indicates beyond doubt that Congress intended endangered species to be afforded the highest of priorities.[48]

Tribal water projects that require federal licensing or other approval will need to consider the power of the Endangered Species Act. If a project potentially impacts one of the species listed as being endangered or threatened, the necessary federal permit or license may be difficult to secure. Innovative means to prevent damage to the species and its habitat may prove essential to allow a project to proceed.

It should be noted that in a recent case, *United States v. Dion* (1986), the Supreme Court explicitly left open the question whether Congress made the Endangered Species Act applicable to Indian tribes and abrogated Indian treaty rights.[49] Thus, it is not yet resolved whether a tribal water project would meet the same fate as the Tennessee Valley Authority project that threatened the snail darter.

The National Environmental Policy Act

Federal approval and licensing of water projects also is constrained by provisions of the National Environmental Policy Act of 1969 (NEPA). NEPA requires that a comprehensive study be undertaken to assess the impact of any "major federal actions significantly affecting the quality of the human environment."[50] The courts have ruled that "major federal actions" include the licensing or permitting activities undertaken by other entities. As a consequence, an environmental impact statement (EIS) must be pursued for all major water projects that require FERC licenses, Corps permits, or any other federal approval.

The fact that a project is on Indian land does not affect the applicability of this comprehensive regulation. The Secretary of Interior's approval of Indian land leases to energy companies constitutes "major federal action." Thus, an environmental impact statement must be compiled by the federal agency (in this instance, the Bureau of Indian Affairs) prior to lease approval. This detailed statement must assess:

(1) the environmental impact of the proposed action,

(2) any adverse environmental effects that cannot be avoided should the proposal be implemented,

(3) alternatives to the proposed action,

(4) the relationship between local short-term uses of man's environment and the maintenance and enhancement of long-term productivity, and

(5) any irreversible and irretrievable commitments of resources that would be involved in the proposed action should it be implemented.[51]

The preparation of the environmental impact statement entails much time and effort in order to cover fully these NEPA requirements. Although a tribe itself will not need to do the environmental impact statement (the responsibility lies with the federal agency), many federal agencies require that the applicant (such as a tribe) provide significant technical support in the process. Consequently, in planning for a water project that includes federal involvement, a tribe must budget the time and resources that may be involved in the NEPA assessment.

11-5. WATER QUALITY REGULATION BY THE EPA

One year after the National Environmental Policy Act was enacted, Congress established the Environmental Protection Agency to administer the nation's major pollution control programs. Two such programs involve water quality regulations that need to be assessed in the course of tribal water use planning. One program controls water pollution in the environment, while the other protects drinking water from contamination.

The Clean Water Act

In 1972, Congress adopted major amendments to the Federal Water Pollution Control Act to promote clean water in the nation's streams and rivers. Known as the Clean Water Act,[52] the amendments shifted the focus from merely setting standards for quality within the streams, to implementing rigid limitations upon wastewater discharges from municipal, industrial, and other polluting sources. At the core of the Clean Water Act program is the NPDES permit (national pollution discharge elimination system permit).

The Clean Water Act mandates that "the discharge of any pollutant by any person shall be unlawful" unless it is done in compliance with the permitting process.[53] The NPDES permits incorporate limits on the extent to which pollutants may be discharged from a particular activity in accordance with a time schedule for improving overall water quality. Initially, the Act called for private polluters to implement the "best available technology economically achievable" to control their effluents by 1983; with a goal of zero discharge of pollutants by January 1, 1985. Although the Act failed to achieve its ultimate goal, the NPDES permitting system has reduced pollution in the nation's waterways.

The NPDES permitting requirements explicitly apply to activities in Indian Country. The regulations apply to "any person" that discharges effluent, and the definition section of the Act establishes that "person" includes "an Indian tribe or an authorized Indian tribal organization" as well as individuals, corporations, and all governmental entities within a state.[54] As a consequence, tribal water use activities that involve discharges to a stream must take the NPDES permit requirements into consideration.

Provisions of the Clean Water Act allow states to assume authority over the pollution control program. To activate the process,

> the governor of each State desiring to administer its own permit program for discharges into navigable waters within its jurisdiction may submit to the Administrator [of the EPA] a full and complete description of the program it proposes to establish and administer under State law. . . .[55]

The EPA administrator must approve such petition unless the state program somehow fails to incorporate adequately the standards and procedures set forth in the Act. Many states took advantage of this option and currently issue and enforce NPDES permits within their boundaries. The EPA currently retains authority over the issuance of NPDES permits on the reservations. But new opportunities for the tribes exist. The Clean Water Act was amended and reauthorized in early 1987. Under the 1987 amendments tribes may plan and operate their own regulatory programs.

The Safe Drinking Water Act

The Safe Drinking Water Act (SDWA) was enacted in 1974 to safeguard public drinking water supplies.[56] The Act directed the EPA to establish national standards for the quality of drinking water from systems that serve at least 25 people or 15 connections. The main standards are the "primary regulations" that establish the maximum level for contaminants that cause public health problems in drinking water supplies. In addition to setting quality levels, these regulations specify monitoring and reporting requirements for operators of the water supply systems.

"Secondary regulations" are also a part of the program and serve as guidelines rather than as enforceable standards. The guidelines recommend maximum concentrations of non-toxic chemicals in water that affect its taste, odor, and appearance. Finally, the SDWA authorizes the EPA to issue regulations to control the underground disposal of wastes in order to protect ground water supplies. These latter regulations mainly affect disposal of contaminants from oil, gas and mining activities.

Five categories of health-threatening contaminants are regulated in the primary drinking standards. These include: (1) inorganic contaminants such as arsenic, lead, and selenium; (2) organic contaminants, including various pesticides and herbicides; (3) microbiological contaminants that are mainly bacteria; (4) radiological contaminants including both natural and introduced sources of radiation; and (5) turbidity, which, you will recall from Chapter 7, refers to small particles suspended in the water that can carry contaminants and make treatment ineffectual. Maximum concentration levels in drinking water have been established for each contaminant, and different testing and reporting requirements also exist. For instance, turbidity is supposed to be tested each day, while inorganic chemical concentrations require testing only at one-year intervals if the drinking supply is from surface waters or at three-year intervals if the supply is from ground water.

Indian tribes are included in the definition of "municipality" in the SDWA, and water supply systems serving reservations must comply with the Act. The focus of EPA efforts on reservations, however, has been less on enforcement and more on training and education. In December 1984, the EPA entered into an interagency agreement with the Indian Health Service (IHS) to further the goals of the SDWA on reservations. Among other things, the agreement provided that

> the IHS will financially and technically assist Indians to meet the requirements of the SDWA by the following activities:
>
> a. construction and renovation of public water systems, and
>
> b. training and technical assistance to operation and maintenance organizations [*i.e.*, those who operate the tribal water supply system]. The IHS will assist the O & M organizations to establish appropriate facility operations, monitoring, and surveillance activities in keeping with good standards of practice to ensure the provision of quality of drinking water, and
>
> c. make a special effort to provide assistance to those systems identified by EPA as priority violators.[57]

The agreement also dealt with the issue of enforcement. First of all, IHS made it clear that it did not want to have any role or responsibilities in EPA enforcement activities. It then was agreed that when EPA does find a violation of the standards by a tribal water system, notification of the violation to the operator will be "designed considering the Indian culture and experiences and will refrain where appropriate from following the prepared format used for standard enforcement actions." Following the notification, the IHS and EPA "will assist the public water systems on Indian lands in any way the agencies can to achieve voluntary compliance."[58]

The Safe Drinking Water Act was amended in 1986 and now provides that the EPA administrator can delegate to tribes the enforcement authority over public water systems and underground waste disposal injection wells in Indian Country. If these functions are not delegated, the EPA will retain jurisdiction to the exclusion of the state.

Current EPA Policy

On November 8, 1984, the EPA presented the following policy:

> In carrying out our responsibilities on Indian reservations, the fundamental objective of the Environmental Protection Agency is to protect human health and the environment. The keynote of this effort will be to give special consideration to Tribal interests in making Agency policy, and to insure the close involvement of Tribal Governments in making decisions and managing environmental programs affecting reservation lands. To meet this objective, the Agency will pursue the following principles:
>
> 1. The Agency stands ready to work directly with Indian tribal governments on a one-to-one basis (the "government-to-government" relationship), rather than as subdivisions of other governments.
>
> 2. The Agency will recognize Tribal governments as the primary parties for setting standards, making environmental policy decisions and

managing programs for reservations, consistent with Agency standards and regulations.

3. The Agency will take affirmative steps to encourage and assist Tribes in assuming regulatory and program management responsibilities for reservation lands.
4. The Agency will take appropriate steps to remove existing legal and procedural impediments to working directly and effectively with Tribal governments on reservation programs.
5. The Agency, in keeping with the federal trust responsibility, will assure that Tribal concerns and interests are considered whenever EPA's actions and/or decisions may affect reservation environments.
6. The Agency will encourage cooperation between Tribal, State, and local governments to resolve environmental problems of mutual concern.
7. The Agency will work with other federal agencies which have related responsibilities on Indian reservations to enlist their interest and support in cooperative efforts to help tribes assume environmental program responsibilities for reservations.
8. The Agency will strive to assure compliance with environmental statutes and regulations on Indian reservations.
9. The Agency will incorporate these Indian policy goals into its planning and management activities, including its budget, operating guidance, legislative initiatives, management accountability system and ongoing policy and regulation development processes.

The EPA policy of deferring to tribal control is consistent with the Presidential statement of January 1983, emphasizing Indian self-governance. Likewise, recent court decisions and the changes in the water pollution control laws have focused on tribal sovereignty and the on-reservation regulatory authority of tribal governments. The time is indeed ripe for turning these statements into a solid and long-lasting framework for Indian self-regulation regarding water use and other tribal matters.

Mechanisms are needed now to assure that tribal administration of water-related programs can be effective. Effective tribal programs will justify tribal assumption of regulatory control from federal agencies. Moreover, it will encourage agreements for cooperative regulation between the tribes and the states.

A training program for tribal water managers to run reservation programs is an important mechanism to strengthen tribal control. Another important factor may prove to be the development of tribal water codes to administer both the distribution and the quality of reservation waters. To assist tribes in this latter task, Chapter 13 provides a presentation of the elements of tribal water code development and implementation. But first, it is time to examine the ways a tribe can finance water management and use.

REFERENCE NOTES

1. *United States v. Mazurie*, 419 U.S. 544, 556-57 (1975).
2. 6 U.S. (Pet.) 515, 557 (1832).
3. *Rice v. Rehner*, 463 U.S. 713 (1983) (quoting *United States v. Wheeler*, 435 U.S. 313, 323 (1978)).
4. Statement by the President, Press Release of Jan. 24, 1983.
5. *Lone Wolf v. Hitchcock*, 187 U.S. 553 (1903).
6. 362 U.S. 99 (1960).
7. 424 U.S. 800, 811 (1976) (holding that the McCarran Amendment applied to Indian reserved water rights, thereby making them subject to state court adjudication).
8. *Squire v. Capoeman*, 351 U.S. 1 (1956).
9. *See Worcester*, footnote 2, above.
10. 411 U.S. 164, 168 (1973).
11. *Organized Village of Kake v. Egan*, 369 U.S. 60, 74 (1962).
12. 448 U.S. 136, 144 (1980).
13. *Id.* at 142.
14. *Id.* at 142-43 (cites omitted).
15. 463 U.S. 713 (1983).
16. *Id.*, 463 U.S. at 723 (quoting, in part, *Williams v. Lee*, 358 U.S. 217, 220).
17. *Id.*, 463 U.S. at 725.
18. 433 U.S. 165 (1977).
19. *Id.* at 175.
20. *Id.* at 176.
21. 752 F.2d 1465 (9th Cir. 1985).
22. 42 U.S.C. § 6901 *et seq.*
23. 752 F.2d at 1470.
24. *Id.*
25. U.S. Const. art. I, § 8, cl.3.
26. 458 U.S. 941 (1982).
27. *Id.* at 458 U.S. 954.
28. U.S. Const. art. IV, § 3.
29. 43 U.S.C. §§ 321-329 (as amended).
30. *Winters v. United States*, 207 U.S. 564 (1908).
31. Codified at 43 U.S.C. § 666.
32. U.S. Const. art. II, § 2.
33. U.S. Const. art. I, § 8, cl. 11.
34. U.S. Const. art. I, § 8, cl. 1.
35. U.S. Const. art. I, § 10, cl. 3.
36. U.S. Const. art. III, § 2.
37. 16 U.S.C. § 797.
38. *Id.* section 796(2); *see Escondido Mutual Water Co. v. La Jolla Indians*, 466 U.S. 765 (1984).
39. *Escondido Mutual*, cited above.
40. 33 U.S.C. § 1344.
41. 33 C.F.R. § 323.2(a)(3).
42. *Id.* section 330.4.
43. 262 U.S. 99 (1960).

44. Water Quality Act of 1987, section 506, adding section 518 to the Clean Water Act, 33 U.S.C. § 1251 *et. seq.*
45. 16 U.S.C. § 1636(2).
46. Slip opinion (10th Cir., Mar. 26, 1985).
47. 437 U.S. 153 (1978).
48. *Id.* at 173-74.
49. ___ U.S. ___, 106 S. Ct. 2216 (1986).
50. 42 U.S.C. § 4332.
51. *Id.*
52. 33 U.S.C. §§ 1251-1376.
53. *Id.* section 1311.
54. *Id.* section 1362(4) and (5).
55. *Id.* section 1342.
56. 42 U.S.C. § 300f *et seq.*
57. EPA/IHS at 2-3.
58. *Id.* at 4.

SUGGESTED READINGS

Cohen's HANDBOOK OF FEDERAL INDIAN LAW (1982 ed.) provides the best overview available regarding regulatory jurisdiction in Indian Country. *See also* American Indian Lawyer Training Program, MANUAL OF INDIAN LAW (1982) for this topic, and American Indian Resources Institute, INDIAN TRIBES AS SOVEREIGN GOVERNMENTS (1988) for further discussions of tribal sovereignty in relationship to the jurisdictional issues. Also recommended is the National Resource Defense Council's A CITIZEN'S GUIDE ON GROUNDWATER PROTECTION.

Part IV

IMPLEMENTING AND ENFORCING TRIBAL WATER POLICIES AND PROGRAMS

CHAPTER 12

Financing Tribal Water Management and Use

12-1. INTRODUCTION

Identifying sources of funding is essential in any comprehensive tribal water management program. Financing is needed both for the development of water resources and in the regulation and control of water use. For instance, major funding must be obtained by tribes wanting to build dams, irrigation systems and other water projects designed to promote economic development on the reservation. Monies often are needed as well for constructing water and sewage treatment facilities to control the quality of the resource. Funding also is required simply to support the staff and tribal office responsible for regulating reservation water use and protection.

This chapter discusses the major options available to tribes for financing water management and development. These options include:

1. Obtaining loans from financial institutions.
2. Attracting private investment partners.
3. Issuing bonds.
4. Generating on-reservation monies through taxation and fees.
5. Securing federal grants and loans.

Each financing option, as it relates to tribal water programs, is analyzed briefly in the following sections.

12-2. OBTAINING LOANS FROM FINANCIAL INSTITUTIONS

One of the most straightforward means for securing funds for tribal water development is to obtain a loan from a bank or other lending institution. In pursuing such an avenue, a tribal goal would be to get the most favorable terms possible from the lender, including a low interest rate. A bank will offer such terms if it believes that the risk in making the loan is low—that is, that the loan is sure of being repayed, or if it is not repayed as scheduled, that the bank still can obtain adequate compensation.

Several factors intrinsic to loans for tribal projects can make them highly risky from a bank's standpoint. The perceived risks stem from the sovereignty of tribal governments and the unique protections afforded Indian lands. The following discussion addresses such tribal financial issues, including consideration of the means for overcoming the potential barriers that may otherwise block the tribe's obtainment of loans for tribal water programs.

Eliminating Tribal Immunity From Suit

Lending institutions realize that not all loans will be repayed. In such situations of default, the lender will seek to obtain compensation, often resorting to legal action. Indian tribes, like other governments, however, generally are immune from being sued. As a consequence of tribal immunity from suit, banks often are reluctant to make loans to tribes for development projects.

To resolve such a dilemma, the Indian Reorganization Act of 1934 (IRA) authorized the Secretary of Interior to issue a charter of business incorporation to tribes that want to establish separate corporate entities to conduct business. Congress included a provision that allows a tribal corporation formed under the Act to "sue and be sued."[1] This provision provides the lender with legal recourse in the event of tribal loan default, thereby reducing the risk to the lender.

Identifying Collateral

Risk to a lender also can be diminished by having the loan backed with adequate collateral. Collateral is an asset, either physical or financial, that the borrower dedicates to the lender in the event that repayment of the loan is not possible. Oftentimes, the collateral backing a bank loan is real estate owned by the borrower.

Indian tribes, however, normally cannot use their real estate as collateral for a loan. The legal framework protecting reservation lands prohibits banks and other lending institutions from assuming ownership control over the lands of a defaulting tribe. To obtain private financing, therefore, tribes must identify appropriate collateral other than tribal land.

Fortunately, tribes often have financial and physical resources other than land available that can be leveraged to secure financing for water projects. For instance, a tribe could assign to a lender the rental income from leases of real property, such as the revenue received from federal agencies that lease building space for area offices. Collateral for a loan also could come from assigning grazing fees, energy royalties, or other tribal income that is received on a regular basis. In addition, revenue generated as a result of a water development project could be used to secure the project's financing.

Another way of backing tribal loans, and thereby reducing risk to the lender, is available through the Indian Financing Act. The Act provides federal loan guarantees, of up to 90% of any particular loan, for tribes seeking funding for profit-making ventures. It also authorizes the Secretary of Interior to pay subsidies to lenders in order to reduce the interest rate on such loans to tribes.

Allowing Enforcement of Judgments

Identifying adequate collateral and eliminating tribal immunity from suit often are not sufficient to secure a bank loan for tribal water development. Lenders also are concerned about how to enforce against the collateral when a tribal borrower defaults. Even if the tribe has agreed to be sued, enforcement can be perceived by the bank as a major problem because of concerns over the adequacy of the tribal court system that would decide the matter. Consequently, many lenders require tribal borrowers to consent to suit in state courts.

Suits brought in state courts, however, can raise additional problems. Not only are some tribes legitimately concerned about consenting to state court jurisdiction, but such courts rarely have the power to enforce their judgments within Indian Country. A lender, therefore, effectively is barred from enforcing the collateral agreement, unless the tribe has agreed to place the collateral physically off the reservation.

Each of these complications to securing loans from lending institutions can now be eliminated. Care must be taken, however, to ensure that a tribe does not compromise its sovereignty through the loan agreement. Also, the complications may encourage tribes to look more closely at alternative means for financing their water management and development efforts.

12-3. ATTRACTING INVESTMENT PARTNERS

A second funding option available for tribal water projects involves private investment partners. Rather than loaning their money to a tribe, private investment partners provide direct funding for the project, with no repayment obligation on the tribe.

Two factors generally motivate private investors to provide equity in tribal projects. First, a firm may be interested in sharing in the potential profits associated with a water project. This factor is rarely compelling on its own, however, since water projects typically make little profit, especially in the early years. The tax advantage that can be obtained is the second and more attractive reason for private investment in a tribal water project.

The present federal tax system favors private investment in capital-intensive projects. Capital-intensive projects are projects, such as those found in water development, that require large cash outlays for tangible assets, *i.e.*, buildings, dams, machinery, canals, etc. To encourage investment in these projects, the Internal Revenue Service (IRS) Code provides private firms with two basic incentives.[2]

First, firms may deduct from their taxable incomes the interest and depreciation expenses associated with their investment in the project. Second, under the Accelerated Cost Recovery System, firms can write off the purchase price of assets at a quickened pace, thereby obtaining increased tax savings in the early years of a project.

Tax incentives often make equity investment in tribal water projects an attractive option for private firms. Tax advantages also play a significant role in the third alternative available for financing tribal water projects—the issuance of bonds.

12-4. ISSUING BONDS

Bonds are issued, usually by governmental entities, as a way to borrow large sums of money to finance specific projects over a period of years. Investors buy bonds and, in return, receive regular interest payments from the bond issuer. In these days of reduced federal support for water projects, bonds are receiving increasing attention as an alternative for financing water development and treatment programs.

Tax-exempt Bonds

The issuance of municipal bonds historically has been a common and effective way for local governments to raise funds for development projects. Cities, states, and public entities have met with success in marketing their bonds primarily because of the tax advantages provided to the investor—interest received by the municipal bond buyer is tax-exempt. This feature makes municipal bonds particularly attractive to those in higher income brackets and enables the issuing government to pay less interest generally on the bond than it would have to pay for a loan.

As with loans, a bond is an attractive investment only if sufficient assurance is provided that the future payments promised to the investor will be made. Consequently, the collateral and resources backing the bond are key concerns of an investor contemplating buying bonds. The more secure the bond, the less the rate of interest that needs to be paid by the issuer to attract buyers.

Many factors go into the analysis of how secure a bond is and, consequently, how high an interest rate must be offered by the issuer. The city or other bond issuer generally backs the bond in one of two ways. In offering a "general obligation bond," the issuer promises to use all its taxing powers and other methods of raising general funds to pay its obligations under the bond. A "revenue bond," in contrast, is backed only by the funds generated from the project that the bond finances. Because revenue bonds are not backed by the full faith and credit of the issuing government, they usually are considered higher risk investments and command higher interest rates.

Tribal Authority to Issue Bonds

Over the past decades, tribes generally have been left out of the municipal bond market. On December 21, 1982, however, Congress passed the Indian Tribal Governmental Tax Status Act[3] that provided tribes with important tax benefits previously accorded only to state and local governments. Most importantly, with respect to financing tribal water projects, the Act contained a provision authorizing tribes to issue tax-exempt bonds.

The Internal Revenue Service and Treasury Department have promulgated regulations defining the parameters of the Tribal Tax Status Act. In general, any governing body of a tribe, band, pueblo, community, village, or group of American Indians or Alaskan Natives is eligible to issue tax-exempt bonds. The key factor then becomes whether the project for which the bonds are being issued is related to "essential governmental functions" of the tribe. If the project is so related, then the bonds are tax-exempt and therefore are marketable at a lower interest rate.

Traditionally, projects relating to essential governmental functions were limited to such things as schools, streets, and sewer systems. The current regulations, however, are quite liberal and indicate that most tribal activities eligible for Bureau of Indian Affairs funding will be treated as "essential governmental functions" under the Act. With this broad approach, bonds issued for tribal water projects often will qualify for tax-exempt status.

Requirements of a Bond Sale

A bond sale is a complex and costly endeavor. In planning the sale, the tribe must make decisions regarding the maturity on the bonds, the dates for interest payments, the manner of payment, the interest rates, and logistical matters such as who will print the bonds. Issuers of bonds typically hire an advisor experienced in these matters to assist in the decisions. Also, bond counsel must be retained to perform two important tasks: first, to file a legal opinion regarding the eligibility of the bond as a tax-exempt issue and second, to prepare the bond itself in proper legal form.

When a bond is ready for public sale, the issuing tribe usually will require an underwriter or underwriting group. Underwriters are solicited through advertising the proposed bond sale in the Daily Bond Buyer. In responding to an advertisement and before committing to a bond issue, an underwriter will carefully examine the issuer's credit rating, the collateral behind the bond, the economics of the project being financed by the bond and other factors affecting the risk.

The underwriter's function is to purchase the entire issue from the tribe, and thereby take the risk and responsibility for selling the bonds to investors. Underwriters provide certainty to the bond issuer and stand to make significant profit if they judge correctly that they can resell the bonds at a more favorable rate. The issuing tribe's duties, however, are not over once the bond issue is purchased by the underwriter. It must keep detailed records and meet all the payments owed to the subsequent purchasers of the bonds.

12-5. GENERATING ON-RESERVATION FUNDS

A government's taxation power can generate money to repay the interest on bonds. Such taxes also can be an effective means for directly financing various aspects of tribal water management and use.

Recent court decisions have ruled that tribes have broad powers to tax individuals and entities involved in on-reservation activities. Specifically, in the 1983 case of *Merrion v. Jicarilla Apache Tribe*,[4] the United States Supreme Court confirmed broad tribal taxation powers. The power to tax was held to extend to non-Indians transacting business within the reservation, including a lessee involved in mineral extraction. The authority to tax was strengthened further in April 1985, when the Supreme Court ruled in the case of *Kerr-McGee Corporation v. Navajo Tribe*[5] that the tribe's tax ordinance did not require federal approval in order for it to be fully effective.

Another internal method of raising funds for tribal water programs can involve direct charges to those who appropriate the resource. Permit and license fees commonly have been used to generate money in order to help fund the office and personnel involved in the permitting process. However, such a charge, for example, a flat fee for processing a water use application, rarely provides significant financing. As a result, tribes must look to more innovative ways to generate revenue from those who use reservation waters.

One innovative option receiving increasing attention is a user fee imposed upon water appropriations. In other words, users are charged a certain amount of money for each acre-foot of water that they divert. Not only does this place the financial burden upon those who benefit from utilizing the resource, but it also encourages efficient use of limited water supplies.

Despite its advantages, a user charge for water can be quite controversial. Governments using such an option must consider the resentment that may be met in treating precious waters as a commodity to be bought and sold. Also, fees must be fashioned to ensure that persons with limited financial resources are not precluded from receiving necessary water supplies.

License fees and user charges can be effective in generating funds to regulate and manage reservation waters. They are limited, however, in their ability to fund large-scale water development projects. Therefore, federal funding sources, the fifth and final financing option discussed in this chapter, frequently are considered for such projects as well as for funding water management efforts.

12-6. SECURING FEDERAL GRANTS

Major federal involvement in water project financing began with congressional passage of the Reclamation Act of 1902. Since that time, billions of dollars have been appropriated by Congress for dams and irrigation networks in the West. In recent years, major federal expenditures have been focused as well on water quality issues. The Clean Water Act of 1972 initiated a program involving billions of dollars for constructing sewage treatment facilities. Water quality concerns also were reflected in the Safe Drinking Water Act of 1974, which channeled much effort and money into safeguarding the quality of public water supplies.

The Clean Water Act and the Safe Drinking Water Act now both allow tribes to start tapping traditional federal funding sources. For instance, tribes are eligible as "municipalities" to receive grants for publicly owned sewage treatment facilities under the Clean Water Act. Moreover, the newly amended Safe Drinking Water Act allows tribes to obtain grants and contracts to administer its programs, and the tribes can now apply to EPA for certain technical assistance and demonstration program grants as well.

It should be recalled, however, that the overall federal commitment to water programs, particularly major dam projects, is in doubt. The days when large reclamation reservoirs were financed primarily through federal support appear to be over. Also, the attempts to reduce the federal share in financing sewage treatment facilities should be expected to continue.

Despite some recent cutbacks and uncertainty surrounding major funding programs, several other potential sources of federal assistance exist for tribes wishing to finance water management and use. For instance, the Soil Conservation Service provides technical assistance for watershed protection, flood prevention, irrigation drainage and other programs that implement sound water management techniques. The Farmers Home Administration also supports watershed management through a subsidized loan program. For assistance in fisheries programs and habitat protection, the U.S. Fish and Wildlife Service is available for support, while the Army Corps of Engineers provides funding and direct assistance for flood control and channel rectification needs. Finally, the Environmental Protection Agency has provided funds to some tribes for controlling non-point sources of pollution (*e.g.*, irrigation runoff and drainage from mining operations) and for effluent treatment facilities.

Such programs do not constitute all potential federal sources available to tribes for financing water programs. Nor can it be expected that sources will remain the same from year to year. Funding for tribal water matters are vulnerable to the moods of Congress and to changes in policy and budgets of the Bureau of Indian Affairs and other agencies of the federal government.

Securing necessary funding, whether from federal grants or other sources, is one of the biggest challenges currently facing tribal water planners. Competition for limited grants, bond buyers, lenders, and equity investors is intense throughout the United States. Tribes will need to work hard to meet the challenge of this difficult—but essential—element in managing, utilizing and protecting valuable water resources.

REFERENCE NOTES

1. Tribes, of course, also can directly oversee water projects and can consent to suit for limited purposes and with respect to certain assets without chartering a corporation under section 17 of the IRA.

2. Tax advantages can (and do) change periodically, depending on congressional action.
3. The Act was amended in 1984. Specifically, the initial sunset provision was removed, and several tax benefits added.
4. 455 U.S. 130 (1982).
5. 471 U.S. 195 (1985).

CHAPTER 13

Tribal Water Code Development

13-1. INTRODUCTION

A tribal water code can serve as the cornerstone of a tribal water management program. It is the embodiment of tribal goals, philosophies and priorities regarding reservation water resources. It also provides the administrative and regulatory framework necessary to achieve management objectives. In this day and age it would be difficult, if not impossible, for any government to develop and operate a water management system without a comprehensive water code. This chapter focuses upon the development of a water code as an integral and key part of a tribal water management system.

Preliminarily, a word of caution is in order. In the code development process drafters often tend to look for an expeditious way to develop a code and present it to the governing body for consideration and passage. The "model code" concept is utilized frequently, as is referral to existing codes from other tribes or jurisdictions and, in some instances, this is acceptable and proper. As is often said, "There is no need to reinvent the wheel." However, tribal water codes pose a much more complex situation than do most other subjects covered by tribal laws. The differences among the respective reservations must be taken into account. Factors such as the amount of ground and surface water, present tribal needs, projected needs, the local economic base and competing users need to be identified and evaluated. These factors likely will shape the philosophy and content of the tribal water code.

13-2. PRELIMINARY CONSIDERATIONS

Data Collection

Unlike laws regarding crimes, domestic relations, wills and a host of other areas, a water code deals with a tangible natural resource. Wise management of the resource, to protect the quality and quantity of water available now and in the future, must be based upon sound knowledge. Consequently, a critical first step in water code development involves the collection and development of that basic information.

This requires research into all potential sources of existing information about reservation water resources. It may require delineation by geographic description of boundaries or by watershed area. A determination also should be made as to whether information about water resources outside reservation boundaries may be relevant. This may be true in situations where the headwaters of a stream that flows through the reservation are situated outside the reservation. Recall the discussion in Chapter 6 concerning the importance of the concept of a watershed to effective water resource management.

The sources for existing information are varied, and imaginative detective work frequently yields valuable results. The United States Geological Survey, state water resources office or state engineer's office, National Weather Bureau, local water master's office and state colleges and universities are such potential sources of the information. The information gathered should be reviewed, catalogued and stored in a manner that makes it available for ready reference and that can be expanded in the future.

Once all sources of existing information have been exhausted, a professional review of the information gathered should be done to determine whether a firm, factual description of reservation water is provided. That is, from the information can it be determined how much water flows into, falls on or arises under the reservation; how much flows off and where the difference goes?

In most cases that information is not in hand after the initial literature survey, and this means that some efforts will be needed to identify and perform additional studies or projects to complete the data base picture. This may mean the construction of precipitation gauging stations, stream gauging stations or other devices discussed in Chapter 6. This type of project should be commenced early in the process since long-term records are required before useful trends and projections can be identified.

The next logical step is a calculation of future water needs. As noted in Chapter 9, this type of study commonly is done in planning for municipalities and involves a mathematical projection of water needs for specific years in the future based upon population, present use, and tribal plans and goals that impact the water resource. At this point the tribe would begin to determine the extent of its practicably irrigable acreage.

With the steps described thus far, some fundamental facts can be utilized for the direction and philosophy of the water code. If the total amount of water on the reservation is known, along with the present level of use and the projected future uses, it will be clear whether all available water is presently in use and if so, the code should address conservation and regulation of existing allocations. On the other hand, the analysis may indicate that there is a significant quantity of unallocated water which can be the subject of further plans for tribal water projects.

Key Staff

The development of any law immediately brings the need for attorneys to mind. Although some may view this as an evil necessity, it is a necessity nonetheless. Not only must laws be written in precise language so that the intent behind them is clear, some, like tribal water codes, must be written with the potential for challenges by outside entities in mind. Consequently, legal principles such as jurisdiction and due process must be addressed correctly within the code.

While most attorneys can manage the legal complexities readily, most do not have the technical background needed to develop a water code. This lack of technical expertise necessitates obtaining the services of a hydrological engineer, a person who is schooled and, hopefully, experienced in the dynamics of water and the various systems and devices used to pump, divert, transport and store it. An engineer who has experience working with municipal or irrigation water systems can not only provide invaluable advice into the technical and practical aspects of the water code but is also the obvious person to undertake the review of data gathered in the literature survey and to conduct the studies designed to expand the data base. Once the decision is made by a tribe to begin a water management system, a hydrological engineer ideally should be added to the staff or retained as a consultant.

One of the measures for selecting a person for this position, whether as a staff member or a consultant, is to consider how a court would view the person as an expert witness. Education, experience and credibility are required, and the more, the better. It is also desirable to insure that the engineer has no conflict of interest by virtue of having worked for another water user or jurisdiction that is a competitor with the tribe for water.

Basic Legal Requirements

Before pen is ever put to paper on a water code, there are some basic legal points that should be examined.

First, the extent of tribal water rights should be determined, if not by litigation or other conclusive legal means, at least by estimation within the tribal system. In many instances, the actual amount of water to which a tribe is entitled under the *Winters* doctrine will not have been the subject of any court order. It is important that the tribe calculate some estimate of the amount of water it could put to beneficial use. This, along with the calculations described earlier, is a key to the planning process and provides direction for the code. In the event tribal water rights are challenged or become the subject of litigation, the availability of such information is essential. Note, however, that the tribal water code may be designed to regulate all water allocations within the reservation boundaries, not just tribal water use.

Second, the development and enactment of the tribal water code must follow the legislative process established for the promulgation of any tribal law. These steps, usually set out in tribal constitutions, must be followed precisely to insure that the code is duly enacted and not invalid because of procedural defects.

Third, and most problematical at this point, is the Secretary of the Interior's self-imposed moratorium on the approval of tribal water codes. This means that since January 15, 1975, when the moratorium was imposed, the Secretary has not approved water codes for tribes that have constitutional provisions requiring secretarial approval of tribal laws. A tribe without a secretarial approval restriction in its constitution presumably can adopt a water code and a court should uphold the code as a proper exercise of inherent tribal sovereignty.[1]

At the time the moratorium was imposed, the Interior Department planned to develop regulations governing the approval of tribal water codes. There was a fear, shortly after the moratorium was imposed, that the regulations would be a device by which tribal water rights would be limited or subject to mandatory quantification contrary to the principles of the *Winters* doctrine. Regulations that provide the criteria for the Secretary to approve water codes were proposed twice by the Carter administration, but were never finally promulgated.[2] If rules are ever proposed again tribes should review them and make their comments known. If and when the rules are finally adopted, tribes will need to review them carefully to ensure their water codes will be able to pass secretarial muster. The tribal need for independent water management systems in the face of increasing competing uses may give rise to sufficient political pressure from Indian Country to force the revocation of the moratorium.

Administrative Considerations

The decision to develop a tribal water code should be done only after careful consideration of some administrative facts of life. Water rights and water regulation are major components of tribal rights and sovereign powers, not to mention, in some instances, the key to economic development. Yet, water rights and regulation involve costs.

Water code development contemplates administrative, regulatory and enforcement activities. This means personnel, travel, office space, support staff and overhead costs. Even though a water management system includes some income in the form of permit fees and licenses, it should be clear at the outset that such a system rarely can be self-supporting and will require the infusion of additional monies to operate. Clearly, the commitment to the identification and protection of tribal water rights must be deep to initiate this process.

Time can be another limiting factor. If there is an immediate need for a water management program it is probably too late to develop the program in a reasoned, orderly manner. The literature review and completion of additionally needed studies alone may take years. Moreover, after a comprehensive water code is developed, the implementation of that code will take considerable time. One detailed study that took into account the search for qualified staff, the hiring process, the procurement of office space, the forming of tribal committees and a host of other details required for implementation estimated the time involved to be in excess of 576 days.

13-3. THE TRIBAL WATER CODE

At the end of this chapter is an outline of tribal water code provisions (Supplement A). The outline attempts to demonstrate a potential format as well as the possible content for a tribal water code. Each of the major headings contained in the outline (headings which represent the code chapters) is discussed in this chapter.

Water Code Chapter I: General Provisions

Chapter I of the water code contains provisions that are a basic statement of tribal water rights and the basis for enactment of the code. These provisions, in particular, should be shaped with the potential for legal challenges to tribal water rights and the code itself in mind. The statements made here may be pivotal in a later determination of these issues.

The use of a section setting out findings is a device seen increasingly in legislation, even federal statutes. The importance of water to tribal existence would be an appropriate topic here as would the delineation of problems experienced under state administration of water rights, if such has occurred, as partial justification for the assertion of tribal jurisdiction over water. A final finding might include a statement to the effect that under a dual regulatory system of two governmental entities, the effective regulation of reservation water resources cannot be achieved because of conflicting goals, objectives and philosophies. In some situations, however, tribes may find it advantageous to administer certain aspects of the water code jointly with states.

The declaration of rights should be a statement of the tribe's water rights under the *Winters* doctrine either as established by litigation or as perceived by the tribe based upon a comprehensive review of the technical literature and legal precedent. The declaration of rights might extend beyond the right to water and include the right to manage, develop and preserve all water resources on the reservation, irrespective of ownership.

The nature of the tribe's ownership of water can include a general statement of the reserved rights theory as contained in the *Winters* doctrine and subsequent cases as well as specific reference to any treaty, executive order or legislation that further defines tribal rights.

The application of the water code can be an important statement of territorial, personal and subject matter jurisdiction that obviously must be based upon sound legal principles. This section should also establish the date upon which the provisions of the code become effective.

Finally, the definition section should provide clear definitions for all legal and technical terms, the names of tribal bodies and personnel and other terms frequently encountered throughout the code.

Water Code Chapter II: Miscellaneous Provisions

Chapter II of the code contains those sections that do not fall logically within any of the other major headings established under this format. In addition to providing rules for the interpretation of the water code, it establishes the groundwork for the promulgation of rules and regulations, which, as is seen later, is an integral part of the management system, and for the establishment of fees to be charged for certain functions under the code.

Of particular significance is the inclusion of a section establishing procedures for review of the code. In any code development process, code provisions need to be evaluated continually and amended periodically. The "final" draft of the code may well appear to be totally adequate. However, the operation of a system under the code inevitably will reveal certain deficiencies. A mandatory, periodic review will insure that the code and the management system are maintained at the highest level of effectiveness and efficiency.

Water Code Chapter III: Notice of Enactment and Effect

Chapter III of the water code anticipates a situation where the tribal water code is newly developed and water rights were previously regulated under state law. The transition from the state system to a tribal system on a specific date is a critical step. Fair, timely and effective notice to those persons who have water rights under state law is essential and is the primary topic of this chapter. Various types of notice may be employed including posting, publication, public hearings and personal notice. This chapter also should address the question of how permits previously issued under the state system will be handled under the tribal system.

Water Code Chapter IV: Water Committee

Chapter IV of the code is the first to deal with the establishment of the internal management framework. Within most tribal structures, the tribal governing body does not have the time to become involved in all aspects of government that normally would require its attention. The common solution to such a dilemma has been the delegation of authority to committees established for particular purposes. An appropriate committee, or the mechanism to create a new committee, already may exist within most tribal structures. This approach is useful, not only because it spreads the workload, but also because it allows broad involvement of tribal members who are not members of the governing body and allows the participation of persons with expertise, interest or experience in a particular subject.

The most important aspect, then, of this code chapter is the delegation of power to a water committee. The nature and extent of authority delegated is within the discretion of the governing body. It should be kept in mind that the operation of a water management system involves an extensive amount of activity that is beyond the purely administrative and that would have to be done by the governing body if not delegated. Within the structure outlined here, the holding of hearings and the promulgation of regulations are among the most significant activities delegated to the committee.

Water Code Chapter V: Water Regulations

Laws, tribal or otherwise, are difficult to change once enacted, because the legislative process must be repeated for any amendment. It, therefore, has become a common practice to limit legislation to broader topics and to allow the actual implementation of the law through rules and regulations adopted by administrative bodies. This is especially true for situations where the subject of the regulations is such that periodic changes may be necessary and the changes need to be made in a manner less cumbersome and time consuming than changes in the law itself. Highly technical details often are implemented best by regulations. The Code of Federal Regulations (C.F.R.) is the system utilized by the federal government to implement federal laws. The law underlying any regulations should state that, once the authority is delegated, the duly enacted regulations have the force and effect of law and violations of them will be subject to appropriate sanctions.

That system of regulating is proposed under this format. This chapter of the water code, therefore, would provide specific authority to the water committee acting as an extension of the tribal governing body. The chapter would list subjects for which the committee is to prepare, enact and administer regulations. Any particular concerns or direction for the regulation of any such subject needs to be set forth in the appropriate code section.

In actual practice, such an approach is likely to result in a set of regulations that is longer and more extensive than the water code itself. If this is a concern, some of the subjects listed to be adopted as regulations can be included instead in the code itself as independent chapters. Again, these should be subjects that will not require frequent amendments or modifications.

The drafting of such regulations clearly indicates the need for a multiparty effort, including an attorney for the legal aspects, the hydrological engineer for the technical aspects and the water committee for policy input and decisions.

Water Code Chapter VI: Water Administrator

While the water committee is envisioned as a body that meets from time to time to deal with those matters within its jurisdiction, sufficient staff also are needed to do the daily work required under the water code. The office of the water administrator should be established to provide that function, which includes: information, enforcement, advising and administration.

Ideally, the position of water administrator is the place for the hydrological engineer, who has the education and expertise to perform the required work. The additional staffing may include technicians and other support personnel.

Generally the water administrator is charged with the administration of the water code and its implementing regulations. This responsibility includes an information function involving the collection and maintenance of data pertaining to water resources and the conducting of studies to develop additional data. The enforcement function requires inspections, detections of violations, and the initiation of appropriate actions to remedy, cease or sanction these violations. The administrator serves as an advisor to the governing body and the water committee on subjects within his jurisdiction and expertise and thus provides the technical input into the policymaking process. As the head of a tribal department or office, the administrator also is responsible for the administration of his office, staff, budget and other internal matters.

Water Code Chapter VII: Guidelines for Administration

The chapter on guidelines for administration provides the place for the direct inclusion of tribal policy regarding its water resources within tribal law. Throughout the operation of the water management system, the water committee and the office of the water administrator will be placed in positions where they will have to make interpretations of the water code when faced with a particular fact situation. They also will need to articulate tribal policy or views in their dealings with individuals and other governmental entities. This chapter of the code should be the source of those policy guidelines.

The type of policy statements made here typically include a basic priority for water use to further the purpose for which the reservation was created, which is usually as a homeland for the tribe and its members. This follows the *Winters* doctrine and sets the stage for more specific guidelines.

A list of priorities for water use might be established to guide action in situations where there are competing uses for limited water. It is common to find domestic water use as the highest priority, with others, such as agriculture, fish and wildlife, industry, recreation, and power, prioritized based upon local interests and economics. Nonconsumptive uses and protective action also might be prescribed in order to preserve cultural, historic, spiritual and environmental values held by the tribe.

The administration of the water code also may result in situations where a decision or action will produce an economic hardship on persons or entities, and it is possible and desirable to provide some guidance in those instances. The evaluation of the impact of such a decision on water use and income as well as on the investment made and on other uses, should be required in such cases.

In areas of limited supply or extensive use, guidelines also might be set out directing that the most effective use of available resources be made. Included here might be statements regarding wasting of water, maximizing efficiency of diversion, withdrawal and application systems, storage, pollution, obstruction of flows and other factors.

Again, this portion of the code is important in that it directly provides the philosophy to be utilized in the administration and interpretation of the rest of the code.

Water Code Chapter VIII: Applications for Permits

In this code chapter, the mechanism for applying for a permit needs to be established. A permit application process is not unique to the water setting; similar processes may be found in a number of other codes that require permits, such as zoning or building codes. Basically, a step-by-step process should include: application forms and the specification of the information that will be required; the application fee; a provision for internal review of the application; a provision for notice to the public that an application has been submitted and is under review; the receipt of comments and objections; and the decision whether to grant or deny the application. The final decision should be subject to appeal under other provisions of the code.

Water Code Chapter IX: Water Permits

Once the decision has been made to grant a permit, it is necessary to describe how that is done and what it means.

The first step involves the development of a permit form. Next, the code must provide flexibility to impose conditions upon a permit. The code also should authorize entry upon the land involved by tribal personnel for inspection and enforcement purposes. The issuance of special permits for unusual situations and the modification of permits subsequent to their issuance under certain circumstances also should be provided for in the code.

Perhaps the most significant provision under this chapter is the section describing the effect of a permit. Under most state systems a person is given a right, in the nature of a property right, to use water under a permit. Consideration might be given here to providing that a tribal permit constitutes tribal permission to use water subject to any conditions imposed and does not convey any ownership of the reservation's water.

Water Code Chapter X: Determination of Availability and Need

In areas where the water supply is limited and demands are high, the process provided in this chapter would be extremely valuable in resolving disputes as well as in insuring the use of sound management principles. The primary application of this chapter occurs when a water supply common to a particular area is or will be used beyond its capacity. The purposes of the proceedings provided for here are to evaluate present and future needs, to determine the characteristics of the water supply involved, to explore methods of increasing the supply, to assist in land use planning and to provide information to the tribe and the public about the water in question.

Once the issue of possible overuse is raised, the system calls for an investigation of the water supply and its uses by the water administrator. The information gathered is put into report form and notice of a hearing is served on the affected parties and published. At the hearing the report is reviewed and other information or input is received from oral or written statements. Based upon the information received, a determination of both availability and need is made. Based upon that determination, permits are granted, revoked, denied or modified as necessary. This is a prime example of a situation where the policy guidelines might come into play.

Any determination made or action taken under this chapter should be subject to appeal by an aggrieved party.

Water Code Chapter XI: Transfer and Loss of Rights

Once a water management system is in place, it is important to be able to "keep tabs" on water use. In many systems, once a water right is granted and recorded, it continues to exist even if it is not actually used for an extended period of time—unless some individual challenges the validity of the right. This code chapter represents an effort to facilitate the process of tracking rights granted under permits so that a more accurate picture of water use is portrayed by the resulting statistics. That result cannot, of course, be achieved solely by the code, and having personnel available for inspections and enforcement will be essential.

The process of transferring or exchanging water rights can be provided for and calls for the creation of a new set of forms and criteria defining when such acts will be allowed. The voluntary relinquishment of rights back to the tribe also can be authorized.

The loss of rights granted under a permit typically will occur by virtue of nonuse, abandonment or unauthorized change in use. Based upon the facts involved, the loss of rights may be total or partial. The loss of rights by other legal principles—adverse possession, prescription, estoppel, acquiescence—or by outside proceedings may, or may not, be authorized.

Any person who faces a modification or loss of rights under this section is entitled to timely notice and a hearing. Provision also should be made for an appeal from that hearing.

Water Code Chapter XII: General Hearing Provisions

The Indian Civil Rights Act and many tribal constitutions require that tribal governments provide all persons affected by their actions with basic legal rights such as due process and equal protection of their laws. While the hearing itself is part of the due process requirement, how the hearing is called and conducted also is subject to the due process test. This code chapter is outlined to cover all of the elements that are required to provide the parties involved with basic fairness as required under the concept of due process. Any hearing held under the code would be conducted in accordance with this chapter.

The first step is to provide for notice of the hearing to the affected parties. The notice must be served in a timely manner to allow adequate time for preparation. In terms of content it must include information about the right to a hearing and the issues and code sections involved, as well as the date, time and place of the hearing. Where the parties are known, service of the notice should be by personal delivery or by certified mail with return receipt requested. The use of publication or posting should be limited to instances where the parties are unknown or where the hearing is of general interest.

In addition to what might be considered "routine" procedural rules, code provisions should state what will constitute the record for purposes of any subsequent appeals and a rule regarding what types of evidence will be admissible at a hearing.

A tribe is not bound by the standards used in state and federal judicial or administrative proceedings in those areas. The basic requirement is that the rules established be fair so as to withstand a challenge alleging violations of due process.

Once a hearing is held and a decision is reached, the parties involved must be given notice of that decision.

Water Code Chapter XIII: Appeals and Judicial Review

The appeal process, like the initial hearing, also must provide the proper measure of due process to the parties involved.

In most tribal structures, the appeal from an administrative decision is to the tribal court. The provisions of this code chapter should specify what can be appealed, who can appeal, how the appeal is initiated and what time limits exist for the filing of the appeal. This process generates a whole new set of forms that will need to be prepared. Notice to the affected parties, again, must be discussed.

The format of the appeal must be considered. The process outlined here envisions the transmittal of the record from the hearing, which consists of testimony, evidence, stipulations, any pleadings, motions, offers of proof, objections and rulings and the final decision, to the tribal court. On appeal, that record is reviewed and the parties are allowed to submit written arguments on the issues. The scope and standards for review are specified and courses of action available to the court are set forth. Careful consideration should be given to the latter point since there may be a need to order that certain steps be taken or not taken by the parties, either as an interim protective step or in addition to reversing, affirming or modifying the decision made at the initial hearing.

The fact that the decision of the tribal court in the appeal is final and binding on the parties should be set out in a final section.

Water Code Chapter XIV: Prohibited Acts and Penalties

Throughout the rest of the code, provisions require or prohibit certain actions. As one aspect of this chapter it should be specified that any violation of the code is subject to the penalties set forth.

Any actions that are prohibited but have not been addressed previously should be included here, such as wasting of water, obstruction of tribal officials charged with administering the code, overstatement of use and the like.

Finally, the potential penalties should be specified. Here, jurisdictional issues again come into play and most codes likely will be limited to civil penalties in order to be applicable to Indians and non-Indians within the tribe's territorial jurisdiction. Civil fines will be the most common sanction. Major and minor violations may be defined to facilitate application of the penalty sections. In addition to civil fines, other sanctions may be provided to be used where appropriate, such as revoking a permit or requiring payment of damages to an injured party.

13-4. CONCLUSION

A tribal water code is much more than "just" a tribal law. It is a statement of rights to, and an exercise of inherent sovereign powers over, a natural resource that is critical to tribal survival. It cannot be developed and implemented properly without the careful deliberation and thought due such a weighty subject. The code will move the tribe closer to the goals of effective management and protection of tribal rights and interests. The technical, legal and policy input must be shaped into a system that reflects sound principles of water management if those goals are to be achieved.

REFERENCE NOTES

1. *See Kerr-McGee Corp. v. Navajo Tribe of Indians*, 471 U.S. 195 (1985).
2. *See* 42 Fed. Reg. 15885 (Mar. 17, 1977) and 46 Fed. Reg. 944 (Jan. 5, 1981).

SUPPLEMENT A: OUTLINE OF TRIBAL WATER CODE PROVISIONS

I. GENERAL PROVISIONS

A. Findings
B. Declaration of Rights
C. Nature of Ownership
D. Application of Code
E. Definitions

II. MISCELLANEOUS PROVISIONS

A. Severability
B. Construction
C. Rules and Regulations
D. Review of Code
E. Optional Charge
F. Extension of Time Limit
G. Representation
H. Amendments

III. NOTICE OF ENACTMENT AND EFFECT

A. Notice Required
B. Contents of Notice of Enactment
C. Preparation of Public Notice of Requirements and Effects
D. Public Notice of Requirements and Effects
E. Notice—How Given
F. Interim Permits
G. Forfeiture of Consideration of Claims to Preexisting Rights

IV. WATER COMMITTEE

A. Water Committee—Creation, Membership, Terms
B. Disqualification of Members
C. Resignation of Members
D. Dismissal on Grounds of Non-Attendance of Meetings
E. Water Committee—General Powers
F. Water Committee—Power to Promulgate Regulations
G. Water Committee—Power to Preserve Water
H. Water Committee—Power to Assess Water
I. Water Committee—Power to Designate Local Management Areas

V. WATER REGULATIONS

A. Authority and Power of Water Committee to Promulgate
B. Force and Effect of Regulations
C. Procedure Required
D. Fee Schedule
E. Critical Ground Water Areas

F. Streamzone Alterations
G. Construction in and Adjacent to Waterways
H. Riparian Habitat
I. Recreation Areas
J. Public, Community Water Systems
K. Surface Water Utilization
L. Well Construction
M. Dam Safety
N. Water Storage Facilities
O. Hydraulic Power Generation
P. Irrigation Systems
Q. Well Drillers, Licenses
R. Emergency Powers

VI. WATER ADMINISTRATOR

A. Water Administrator—Appointment
B. Water Administrator—Staff
C. Water Administrator—Information Function
D. Water Administrator—Enforcement Function
E. Water Administrator—Advisory Function
F. Water Administrator—Administrative Function

VII. GUIDELINES FOR ADMINISTRATION

A. General Policy Provisions
B. Guidelines for Making Most Effective Use of Available Resources
C. Additional Policy Guidelines

VIII. APPLICATIONS FOR PERMITS

A. Description of Use and Application for Permit—Required
B. Description of Use and Application for Permit—Contents
C. Permit Fee
D. Public Notice of Descriptions of Use and Application for Permits
E. Objections Affecting Descriptions of Use and Application for Permits
F. Form and Contents of Objections
G. Reply to Objections by Applicant
H. Hearing Regarding Issuance of Permits
I. Public Comment
J. Investigation and Review of Permit Issuance
K. Issuance or Denial of Permits

IX. WATER PERMITS

A. Form of Permits
B. Conditions of Permits
C. Entry on Land as a Condition of Permit
D. Effect
E. Revocability
F. Special Permits

G. Modification of Water Permits
H. Appeal to the Issuance of a Water Permit

X. DETERMINATION OF AVAILABILITY AND NEED

A. Initiation of Proceedings for a Determination of Availability and Need
B. Purposes
C. Order to Water Administrator
D. Water Administrator—Information Gathering
E. Water Administrator's Report
F. Proposed Determination of Availability and Need
G. Notice of Proposed Determination of Availability and Need
H. Notice of Hearing on Proposed Determination of Availability and Need
I. Hearing on Proposed Determination of Availability and Need
J. Final Determination of Availability and Need
K. Subsequent Actions
L. Appeal

XI. TRANSFER AND LOSS OF RIGHTS

A. Transfer and Assignment of Water Rights
B. Exchange of Claims and Permits Under This Code
C. Voluntary Relinquishment of Claims or Rights
D. Loss by Nonuse or Abandonment
E. Permit Review for Evidence of Abandonment or Nonuse
F. Loss by Change in Use
G. Loss by Adverse Possession, Prescription, Estoppel or Acquiescence
H. Loss by Outside Proceedings

XII. GENERAL HEARING PROVISIONS

A. Applicability of This Part
B. Right to Hearing—Notice
C. Notice Content
D. Informal Disposition
E. Time and Place of Hearing
F. Continuances—Hearing
G. Hearing Officer
H. Hearing Record
I. Forms of Evidence
J. Consolidation of Hearings
K. Recording
L. Decisions

XIII. APPEALS AND JUDICIAL REVIEW

A. Right to Appeal
B. Who May Appeal
C. Time for Appeal
D. Notice of Appellate Proceeding
E. Transmittal of Record

F. Continuances
G. Briefs
H. Scope of Review
I. Additional Powers

XIV. PROHIBITED ACTS AND PENALTIES

A. Waste of Water Prohibited
B. Obstruction of Tribal Officers
C. Overstatement of Use
D. Contamination, Pollution of Water Sources
E. Violation of Regulations
F. Major Violations Defined
G. Minor Violations Defined
H. Civil Fines
I. Standard for Imposing Fines
J. Corrective or Remedial Work
K. Damages to Injured Party
L. Revocation or Conditioning of Permit
M. Suspension of Penalties
N. Other Relief

GLOSSARY

Abandonment—With regard to water rights, the loss of a water right from nonuse with intent to abandon. (*Compare with* "forfeiture," defined below.)

Abrogation—The legal term used to describe the breaking of solemn promises made in treaties.

Adsorption—The surface retention of solid, liquid or gas molecules by a solid.

Advection—The process by which solutes are transported by the bulk motion of the flowing fluid in a ground water system.

Aggradation—The gradual buildup of a streambed as a result of extensive soil erosion in a watershed that increases the stream's sediment load.

Allotments—Land held by individual Indians that was transferred from tribal ownership.

Alternative Cost—A technique used to estimate a project's benefits when the product being evaluated could be produced by some method other than that involved in the proposed project.

Anaerobic—Devoid of oxygen.

Appurtenancy Rule—A common law rule that restricts changes in the use or diversion of water by tying a water right to the land on which it is used.

Aquifer—The area of the subsurface that contains ground water. Confined aquifers are bounded above and below with impermeable layers. Unconfined aquifers have the water table as the uppermost boundary and are generally recharged directly from the ground by surface water.

Artesian Aquifer—A confined aquifer where the water level in the aquifer well rises above the aquifer to the earth's surface.

Benefit-Cost Analysis—An evaluation procedure used to compare the benefits and costs of a particular project in a situation where an economic market does not function or does not function completely.

Biological Oxygen Demand—The quantity of oxygen required or consumed by microorganisms in the biological decomposition of organic matter in water.

Call—The process employed in times of water shortages whereby a water master notifies holders of junior water rights that they must curtail water consumption.

Cash Income Calculation—The economic benefit anticipated based on the assumed crop yield from an irrigation project and the income derived from selling the crops in the marketplace.

Chemical Oxygen Demand—The quantity of oxygen required to oxidize industrial waste in water.

Cone of Depression—The term used to describe the slope of the water table in the vicinity of a well when the well is pumping water from the aquifer.

Darcy's Law—A mathematical equation that describes water flow through an aquifer. Darcy's Law states that the rate of flow of ground water through rocks depends on the type of rock and its ability to transmit water, the length of the flow path and the pressure change driving the flow.

Discounting—A procedure used to compare costs and benefits in order to obtain the present value (or present worth). In discounting, costs and benefits that occur earlier are weighed heavier those that occur later.

Dispersion—A natural process that affects pollution movement and is caused either by mechanical mixing or molecular diffusion. Mechanical mixing occurs as a result of microscopic variations in ground water velocity within the pore spaces of an aquifer. The inherent random motion of solute particles and the concentration of gradient existing between the ambient ground water and the contaminated water causes molecular diffusion.

Dissolution—The dissolving of a mineral by water.

Economic Feasibility—The net direct benefit of a project.

Epidemiological—Disease-related.

Equilibrium Price—The price level that would tend to prevail in a marketplace if supply and demand remained constant.

Evaporites—Sedimentary rocks that form as water evaporates and leaves behind salts.

Evaporation—The process by which heat energy changes water from a liquid to vapor.

Evapotranspiration—The term used to describe the evaporation and transpiration processes collectively.

Family Living Increase—Represents the economic benefits that accrue to families who settle on newly irrigated land but that are not reflected in the income received from growing crops.

Field Capacity—The volume of water that a freely drained soil can hold for long periods of time.

Financial Feasibility—The payment capacity or ability to pay for a project.

Forfeiture—With regard to water rights, the loss of a water right as a result of nonuse. Unlike abandonment, intent is not a necessary element.

Frontal Precipitation—The lifting process that occurs when, and at the point where, circulation brings air masses that have different temperatures and moisture contents together.

Geology—The earth science that studies the rocks of the earth.

Gross Direct Benefit—The sum of the family living increase and the cash income calculation (both defined above).

Hydraulic Conductivity—The speed at which water moves through an aquifer during a particular time period, usually expressed in feet per day.

Hydrogeology—The science that focuses specifically on the characteristics and properties of aquifers.

Hydrologic Cycle—The name for the complete description of the ways in which water circulates through the environment.

Hydrology—The science that relates to water in the environment.

Hydrolysis—The decomposition or alteration of a chemical substance by water.

Igneous Rocks—Rocks formed when hot, mobile rock material called magma solidifies.

Infiltration—Water movement into the soil.

Infiltration Capacity—The maximum rate at which a soil can receive moisture.

Instream Flow—Water in streams or rivers that is used for nonconsumptive purposes such as the preservation and enhancement of fish, wildlife, recreation and water quality.

Interception—The process describing precipitation that comes in contact with the vegetation canopy (leaves, twigs. stems, branches and fruit of trees and plants) and evaporates before reaching the soil surface. Interception values reported are based on a specific time period such as an individual storm event or annual interception.

McCarran Amendment—The 1952 federal statute that waived the federal government's sovereign immunity in state general stream adjudications and all other suits involving federal reserved water rights.

Metamorphic Rocks—Rocks formed when preexisting rocks are subjected to extreme changes in temperature, pressure and shearing stress forces within the earth.

Microbiological Activity—The change in the chemical composition of water by the activities of microorganisms.

Opportunity Costs—Uses made impossible by the choice of other uses.

Orographic Lifting—The lifting that occurs when air masses are forced up the windward side of slopes, hills and mountain ranges.

Overdrafted—A term describing the condition of a aquifer when the rate of ground water withdrawal exceeds the rate of natural recharge. Also referred to as "mined."

Overland Flow—Water that runs off the land to rivers or streams when the soil's infiltration capacity is reached. Also called "runoff," this flow is measured in cubic feet per second.

Oxidation-Reduction—The process that changes the electrical charge of an ion and alters its propensity to form chemical bonds with other substances.

Percolation—Water movement through the soil.

Practicably Irrigable Acreage (PIA)—A term used to describe the amount of arable land that it is economically feasible to irrigate on a reservation; in water rights quantification proceedings the PIA standard is used to determine the quantity of water a reservation may be entitled to for agricultural purposes.

Plant Available Water—The amount of water that is available to plants and that represents the difference between the field capacity and the wilting point.

Porosity—A measure of the extent of pores in a particular kind of rock that gives an indication of the total amount of water an aquifer can hold.

Precipitation—A deposit of water on the earth in the form of rain, snow, sleet or hail.

Present Value—The dollar value of a cost or benefit after discounting, *i.e.*, adjusting the dollar value to account for the rate of interest or inflation. Also referred to as the "present worth".

Prior Appropriation Doctrine—The primary water rights doctrine in the West that is based on the equity phrase "first in time, first in right." To establish a prior appropriation right a person must show an intent to appropriate water and divert it to a beneficial use.

Radioactive Substances—Elements that change spontaneously into other elements by the emission of charged particles from the nuclei of their structures.

Residence Time (of Water)—The amount of time that water is stored in a particular component of the hydrologic cycle.

Res Judicata—A legal principle that establishes that once an issue is determined by a court, it is determined conclusively (that is, it cannot be reexamined and redetermined). Thus, the principle of *res judicata* establishes the finality of legal decisions.

Riparian Doctrine—The water rights doctrine based on the principle that landowners adjacent to a natural stream have a right to use the flow to the extent that such use does not interfere with the concurrent rights of downstream users.

Riverine—When ground water is an integral part of the surface flow of streams and rivers.

Sedimentary Rocks—Rocks formed from the erosion and transport of other rocks.

Sediment Load—The amount and size of sediment a stream can carry naturally based on the stream's energy level.

Solutes—Dissolved chemical constituents in water.

Sovereign Immunity—The legal concept that provides that a government cannot be sued without its express consent.

Specific Capacity—A measure of a well's productivity that is determined by dividing a well's discharge by its drawdown. The larger the specific capacity, the better the productivity.

Specific Yield—A measure of the volume of water an aquifer will release upon pumping. In an unconfined aquifer, specific yield is the equivalent of the storage coefficient (defined below).

Stemflow—Precipitation that follows the stem of plants to the soil surface.

Storage Coefficient—An indicator of how much water is available in an aquifer for stream flow or well discharge. In an unconfined aquifer, the storage coefficient is the same as the specific yield (defined above).

Stratigraphic Relations—The arrangement of the various layers of the rocks in the earth's subsurface.

Stream Adjudication—Litigation to quantify water rights. Often referred to as a general stream adjudication; usually occurs on the state court level.

Thermal Convection—The uplifting process that occurs when air close to the earth's surface becomes warmer than the air above.

Throughfall—Precipitation that falls through the vegetation canopy cover to the soil surface.

Transpiration—The process by which water vapor returns to the atmosphere through plants.

Turbidity—The extent to which sediments in water interfere with how well the water lets through light. Turbidity causes light to be scattered through and absorbed by water.

Water Balance—A tool for water management planning that establishes the amount of water in a watershed.

Watershed—Area of land drained by a stream or river or by a system of streams and rivers.

Wilting Point—The point at which plants can no longer take water from the soil. *i.e.*, no more water is available in the soil to be taken from it.

***Winters* Doctrine**—Established in 1908 U.S. Supreme Court decision (*Winters v. United States*), the doctrine provides that Indian tribes have reserved water rights.

INDEX

Table of Cases

ABOUT THE CONTRIBUTORS

Ann E. Amundson is a lawyer in Boulder, Colorado, and served as a senior editor for the 1982 revision of the Indian law treatise, Felix S. Cohen's A HANDBOOK OF FEDERAL INDIAN LAW.

F. Lee Brown, Jr. is a professor of economics at the University of New Mexico and co-director of the Natural Resources Center, an interdisciplinary component of the University of New Mexico School of Law. He is the coauthor of WATER AND POVERTY IN THE SOUTHWEST: CONFLICT, OPPORTUNITY AND CHALLENGE (1987).

Lloyd Burton is an assistant professor in the Graduate School of Public Affairs at the University of Colorado, Denver campus, and is also co-chairman of the University of Colorado Conflict Resolution Consortium. His graduate school dissertation, entitled *The American Indian Water Rights Dilemma: Historical Perspective and Dispute Settling Policy Recommendations*, was published by the U.C.L.A. LAW REVIEW (Spring 1988).

Shaul Ben-David is a professor of economics at the University of New Mexico, whose areas of expertise include water and energy resources, in which he has conducted extensive research and published numerous articles of international scope.

Allen V. Kneese is a resource economist and senior fellow with Resources for the Future, which is based in the Washington, D.C.. His publications include MEASURING THE BENEFIT OF CLEAN AIR AND WATER (coeditor, 1984) and THE SOUTHWEST UNDER STRESS: NATIONAL RESOURCE DEVELOPMENT ISSUES IN A REGIONAL SETTING (coauthor, 1981).

Douglas R. Nash, a member of the Nez Perce Tribe in Idaho, is an attorney in private practice in Pendleton, Oregon, and has worked extensively with the Confederated Tribes of the Umatilla Indian Reservation on water issues.

Steven J. Shupe is an attorney and water resource consultant based in Santa Fe, New Mexico; coeditor of the monthly WATER MARKET UPDATE; and author of *Water in Indian Country: From Paper Rights to a Managed Resource*, 57 U. COLO. L. REV. 561 (1986).

Catherine Vandemoer is director of Watershed Management Systems, a small consulting firm specializing in water resource investigations and water resources planning and management. From 1985-1987, she was the associate director of the American Indian Resources Institute's Water Resources Program. Born in Mexico, Ms. Vandemoer holds a Ph.D in watershed management from the University of Arizona, where her dissertation research involved the evaluation of ground water recharge strategies utilizing Central Arizona Project water and the hydrogeochemical effects of such strategies.

Gary D. Weatherford, an attorney with the San Diego, California law firm of Ferris, Brennan & Britton, has written extensively on water issues, including coauthorship of THE SALTY COLORADO (1986) and coediting of both WATER AND AGRICULTURE IN THE WESTERN U.S. (1982) and NEW COURSE FOR THE COLORADO RIVER (1986).

Charles F. Wilkinson is a professor of law at the University of Colorado School of Law. In addition to having written numerous articles on Indian and natural resources law, Professor Wilkinson is coauthor of two standard law texts, FEDERAL INDIAN LAW (2d ed. 1986) and FEDERAL PUBLIC LAND AND RESOURCES LAW (2d ed. 1987); was the managing editor of the 1982 revision of the Cohen treatise, HANDBOOK OF FEDERAL INDIAN LAW; and has recently published AMERICAN INDIANS, TIME, AND THE LAW (1987).